Big Brother Watch

BIG BROTHER WATCH

The State of Civil Liberties in Modern Britain

Edited by Alex Deane

First published in Great Britain in 2010 by
Biteback Publishing Ltd
Westminster Tower
3 Albert Embankment
London
SE1 7SP

ISBN 978-1-84954-044-5

10 9 8 7 6 5 4 3 2 1

A CIP catalogue record for this book is available from the British Library.

Set in Constantia
Printed and bound in Great Britain by CPI Cox & Wyman, Reading RG1 8EX

Contents

About Big Brother Watch

Big Brother Watch is a campaign from the founders of the TaxPayers' Alliance, fighting intrusions on privacy and protecting liberties.

Big Brother Watch produces regular investigative research papers on the erosion of civil liberties in the United Kingdom, naming and shaming the individuals and authorities most prone to authoritarian abuse.

We hope that Big Brother Watch will become the gadfly of the ruling class, a champion for civil liberties and personal freedom, and a force to help a future government roll back a decade of state interference in our lives.

The British state has accumulated unprecedented power and the instinct of politicians and bureaucrats is to expand their power base even further into areas unknown in peace time.

Big Brother Watch campaigns to re-establish the balance of power between the state and individuals and families.

We look to expose the sly, slow seizure of control by the state – of power, of information and of our lives – and we advocate the return of our liberties and freedoms.

Big Brother Watch is on your side.

Alex Deane gratefully acknowledges Richard Smith and Lord Vinson for their ongoing support, and Big Brother Watch founder Matthew Elliott for his ongoing leadership.

Contributor Biographies

Josie Appleton is Director of the Manifesto Club, which campaigns against the hyper-regulation of everyday life. The club leads campaigns against vetting, photo-bans, speech codes, the overregulation of alcohol and other forms of state intervention into civil life. She was educated at St Catherine's College, Oxford and has written on freedom issues for publications including *The Times*, the *Daily Telegraph* and *The Guardian*.
http://www.manifestoclub.com

Tony Benn has served as Chairman of the Labour Party and Secretary of State for Trade and Industry. He was Member of Parliament for Bristol South East 1950–1960, Bristol South East 1963–1983 and Chesterfield from 1984 until his retirement from the House of Commons in 2001.
http://www.tonybenn.com

Luca Bolognini is Chair and founder of the Italian Institute for Privacy and a board member and founder of the European Privacy Association. He is a graduate in Law from the Alma Mater Studiorum University of Bologna and a regular media commentator on privacy policy and e-commerce. He was the editor and author, with Diego Fulco, of the first Italian commentary on 'Privacy Code for lawyers and private investigators'.
http://www.lucabolognini.it

Stephen Booth is a research analyst at Open Europe, a think-tank which calls for new thinking about reform of the European Union. He holds an undergraduate degree in Political Science and was

awarded the Jean Monnet Prize for his Masters in European Studies from the University of Sussex.
http://www.openeurope.org.uk

Simon Davies is the Director of Privacy International. A past visiting fellow in law at the University of Greenwich and the University of Essex, he is a visiting senior fellow within the Department of Management of the London School of Economics. He is also co-director of the LSE's Policy Engagement Network.
http://www.privacyinternational.org

David Davis is Conservative MP for Haltemprice and Howden. A former senior executive with Tate and Lyle, he has twice been a candidate for the leadership of the Conservative Party and has served as Conservative Party Chairman and shadow Deputy Prime Minister. For five years he was the shadow Home Secretary, resigning as an MP in 2008 to force a by-election (which he won) and provoke wider public debate about the erosion of civil liberties.
http://www.daviddavisforfreedom.com

Alex Deane is a barrister and the Director of Big Brother Watch. He read English Literature at Trinity College, Cambridge, is a World Universities Debating Champion and the author of two previous books, including The Great Abdication. He was David Cameron's first chief of staff. A previous version of his introduction appeared online at Critical Reaction.
http://www.bigbrotherwatch.org.uk

Terri Dowty is the Director of Action on Rights for Children, an organisation that focuses on the effects of new technologies on children's privacy, freedom, consent and data protection rights. She is also on the advisory council of the Foundation for Information Policy Research, where she co-authored a major report for the

Information Commissioner on children's databases, and the 2009 'Database State' report for the Joseph Rowntree Reform Trust.
http://www.archrights.org.uk

Damian Green is Conservative MP for Ashford and minister for immigration at the Home Office. He was educated at Balliol College, Oxford and was President of the Oxford Union. A former financial journalist, he worked in the Prime Minister's Policy Unit 1992–94. Prior to the 2010 election, he held the shadow immigration minister portfolio from December 2005, with responsibility for borders and immigration, the National Identity Scheme and the e-borders programme.
http://www.damiangreenmp.org.uk/

David Green is the Director of Civitas, the Institute for the Study of Civil Society. Amongst other books, he is the author of *Individualists Who Co-operate*, *Prosperity with Principles* and *We're (Nearly) All Victims Now: how political correctness is undermining our liberal culture* and is the editor of *Sharia Law Or One Law for All?* He has written for many newspapers and has appeared on *Newsnight*, the *Moral Maze* and the *Today* programme.
http://www.civitas.org.uk

Daniel Hamilton is campaign director at Big Brother Watch. A graduate in Politics and International Relations from Royal Holloway University of London, prior to joining Big Brother Watch he was Head of European Insight at a leading polling and political research consultancy. He is a regular commentator on frozen conflict zones and the politics of the United States, Brazil and Serbia.
http://www.bigbrotherwatch.org.uk

Michael Harris is public affairs manager of Index on Censorship,

founded as a magazine in 1972 by writers, journalists and artists to defend free expression in the Soviet Union and Warsaw Pact countries; now, alongside the magazine, it is the free speech campaigning organisation. He is vice-chair of Lewisham Council and an uneasy civil libertarian in the Labour Party. He has written for *The Independent*, *The Guardian* and has been involved in undercover investigations for the *Sunday Times*, the *Daily Telegraph* and the BBC's *Panorama*.
http://www.indexoncensorship.org

Guy Herbert is the General Secretary of NO2ID and has worked for twenty-five years in publishing, from retail bookselling to literary agency. He is now a business affairs consultant covering computer games as well as conventional literary and film properties. He has presented evidence for NO2ID in a number of parliamentary enquiries.
http://www.no2id.net

Francis Hoar is a barrister. Educated at the University of Bristol and a member of Clarendon Chambers, he practises in criminal, civil and human rights law. He contributes to the Criminal Bar Association's responses to government consultations on law reform and his writing on witness anonymity was cited in the House of Commons research paper on the Coroners and Justice Bill in 2009.
http://www.clarendonchambers.com

Martin Howe is a Queen's Counsel specialising in EU law, intellectual property and public law. Formerly a member of the Conservative Party's Commission for a British Bill of Rights, he is the author of *A Modern Bill -of Rights*, *Tackling Terrorism and the European Human Rights Convention* and *Liberty under the Law*.
http://www.martinhoweqc.com

Julian Huppert is Liberal Democrat MP for Cambridge. Previously on Liberty's National Council, a county councillor and Liberal Democrat group leader, he was also a research scientist, working on the structure and function of DNA at the University of Cambridge. He is a member of the Home Affairs Select Committee and the Joint Committee on Human Rights.
http://www.julianhuppert.org.uk

Philip Johnston has worked for the *Daily Telegraph* for twenty years, previously as chief political correspondent and later as home affairs editor. He is currently assistant editor and leader writer and writes a weekly column. His recent book *Bad Laws* was published in the spring by Constable.
http://www.telegraph.co.uk

Dominique Lazanski is a Big Brother Watch columnist and technology policy analyst at the TaxPayers' Alliance. She spent over ten years in the internet industry, many of them in Silicon Valley, and has a long-held interest in public policy and participatory government. She has written and spoken on digital issues over the years from a free market and entrepreneurial perspective and holds degrees from Cornell University and the London School of Economics.
http://www.bigbrotherwatch.org.uk

Mark Littlewood is the director general of the Institute of Economic Affairs. He was previously head of media for the Liberal Democrats and was the founder and national co-ordinator of NO2ID. He also served as campaigns director for Liberty. He is a regular commentator on national radio and television over a wide range of issues.
http://www.iea.org.uk

Leo Mckinstry is a columnist for the *Daily Express* and also writes regularly for the *Daily Mail*. The author of nine books, including a biography of Lord Rosebery which won the 2006 Channel Four political book of the year, he has more recently written a trilogy of books about the RAF in wartime. Before becoming a writer in 1995, he worked for the Labour Party at Westminster and served as a Labour councillor in Islington.
http://www.express.co.uk

Stefano Mele is a fellow of the Italian Institute for Privacy. He is a lawyer specialising in information and communication technology law and holds a Ph.D. in Italian administrative and private law, common and comparative law.
http://www.italylegalfocus.com/Stefano_Mele.asp

Brian Monteith is an international communications consultant and writer. He was a Conservative Member of the Scottish Parliament, where he was Convener of the Public Audit Committee for four years. He voted against the Scottish ban on smoking and regards himself as a libertarian. He is the author of *The Bully State – The End of Tolerance*.
http://www.thinkscotland.org/provoke-scotland/articles.html

Jesse Norman is Conservative MP for Hereford and South Herefordshire, senior fellow at Policy Exchange and honorary fellow in Philosophy at University College, London. His books include *Compassionate Conservatism* (2006), *Compassionate Economics* (2008) and *Churchill's Legacy: the Conservative Case for the Human Rights Act* (2009).
http://jesse4hereford.com

Pietro Paganini is a professor in business administration at John Cabot University. He is a board member and founder of both the

Italian Institute for Privacy and the European Privacy Association. He is also co-founder and partner at Competere Geopolitical Management, a transatlantic consulting firm based in Milan, Rome and Washington, DC. http://www.pietropaganini.it

Dominic Raab is the Conservative MP for Esher and Walton. He previously worked as an international lawyer at Linklaters in the City and at the Foreign and Commonwealth Office, before serving as chief of staff for respective shadow Home and Justice Secretaries, David Davis and Dominic Grieve. He is the author of *The Assault on Liberty – What Went Wrong with Rights*.
http://www.dominicraab.com

Simon Richards is Director of The Freedom Association, a cross-party organisation campaigning for freedom of expression, free trade, free enterprise and national independence. The Association organises The Freedom Zone and puts the case for individual liberty through its Freedom Societies at universities around the UK.
http://www.tfa.net

Jason Smith is Convenor of www.birminghamsalon.org, a public forum for debate where ideas are vigorously scrutinised and no topic is off-limits. A freelance journalist contributing to Sp!ked and Culture Wars websites among others, he is a member of the Battle of Ideas Festival organising committee and for many years worked in the licensing trade, opening bars and restaurants in London and throughout the UK.
http://www.jasonsmith17.blogspot.com

Harry Snook is a barrister. He previously worked in the European Parliament, producing a paper on the effectiveness of the EU's structural and cohesion policies. He is the author of *Crossing the*

Threshold – 266 Ways the State Can Enter Your Home, published by the Centre for Policy Studies in 2007.
http://www.stalbanschambers.co.uk/members/harry_snook

Toby Stevens is the Director of the Enterprise Privacy Group. He has spent the past twenty years working across government and major companies in the fields of information security, privacy and identity, and authored the Information Commissioner's 'Privacy by Design' strategy.
http://www.privacygroup.org

Foreword

Civil liberties are the foundation of freedom, and democracy depends upon our defending them vigorously.

This book chronicles the growing threat to those liberties, now made easier by the new technologies which are available.

The cause we are taking up should appeal to people across the whole political spectrum and we need to support each other.

The price of liberty is eternal vigilance and solidarity with all those who attempt it.

I hope this book is widely read and studied.

It is a book for our time.

Tony Benn

Introduction

Alex Deane

It was surprising and disappointing to watch as the Labour government – which gave us the Freedom of Information Act – became the most authoritarian British regime in modern times. As Big Brother Watch set out in our manifesto before the 2010 election, the arrival of a new government offered an opportunity to undo some of that work – and indeed, both parties in the coalition pledged before the election to reverse the rise of our surveillance state, and reaffirmed that intention in the Coalition Agreement. That promise is very far from being fulfilled.

Here is a whirlwind tour of the live issues in the liberty and privacy spheres.

What has already been done by the coalition

The **ContactPoint database** has been scrapped. A database designed to hold the details of all the children in England, accessible to hundreds of thousands of people, was a dreadful and disproportionate intrusion into private life, the very apex of both our peculiar national obsession with paedophilia and the modern mania for surveillance. It undermined childhood and threatened our proud tradition of volunteerism and its abolition is tremendous, both in what it achieved and the direction and purpose it gave to this area of our national life.

Identity cards for UK nationals have been scrapped. Much more importantly, so has the database behind them – meant to be an alarmingly comprehensive 'single source of truth' held by the state about the citizen (with swingeing penalties for failure to notify the authorities about changes promptly). The end of the scheme represents the apotheosis of perhaps the most successful public campaign in modern times

On the other hand, foreign nationals are still required to have them; whilst the possibility of cards for British citizens has been ended for the time being, the relevant structure still remains for foreigners. In fact, it has been accelerated and made obligatory for them. The implementation of the required structure for cards – the equipment, the cards, the chips, the readers, the staff training and so forth – is the important thing. The question of who is to be entered into such a database and carry those cards is just a practicality. The potential future implementation of a wider scheme is rendered much, much easier by the existence of cards for foreigners.

Furthermore, cards are not needed for foreign nationals in the first place – if they are here legally, they have passports or similarly verifiable and satisfactory identification documents. If they're here illegally, how likely are they to comply with the ID card scheme?

Reviews that are being/going to be held by the coalition

The removal of **DNA profiles** of innocent people from the national DNA database is perhaps the issue on which the need for reform is most clear-cut. When the European Court gave judgment in the case of Marper in 2008, the practice in England and Wales of retaining (and uploading to the database) DNA samples acquired by the police from those later acquitted of offences was decried by the highest possible authority. The practice has remained ever since, without redress. That failure to act made a perverse kind of sense under the last government, which believed that it was right for the state to keep DNA profiles, however acquired. But both parties in the new government pledged to change the situation in light of the vast swathes of innocent people on the database today (remember 'reclaim my DNA'?). So, it is therefore surprising and disappointing that nothing has been done.

The police have (probably rightly) continued in their indiscriminate DNA-snatching practice unabated, on the basis that they follow the guidelines given to them by the Home Office until they are changed. So the guidance should be changed *tout de suite*. James Brokenshire regularly receives enquiries from his parliamentary colleagues about when action is to be forthcoming; each MP has a number of concerned constituents affected by this issue – and holding answers can only hold for so long, especially in light of such specific, clear pledges. Not only did the Conservative Party run their 'reclaim My DNA' campaign, they also gave a smaller but very specific pledge in the 2010 manifesto, to the effect that those wrongly accused of minor crimes would have an automatic right to have their profile withdrawn from the database. But, as I say, nothing has been done, and chief constables continue merrily to add thousands such samples to the database.

Covert surveillance by local councils (under the Regulation of Investigatory Powers Act or otherwise). Many are surprised to discover that the power to conduct covert surveillance rests with local councils, who can authorise themselves to mount surveillance of their residents – and do so, regularly. Big Brother Watch identified over 8,500 separate operations in the past two years. It's not for the serious crimes or terrorism people thought the legislation was for – it's for putting your bins out at the wrong time, for dog fouling, for spying on council employees, for breaking the smoking ban, for littering, for noise nuisance. If true, the things being investigated are wrong, but they don't justify covert surveillance – it's entirely out of proportion. The cure is worse than the disease.

Such issues can be solved without such excessive powers: since 2007, Bradford Council has disowned these intrusive tools. Instead, they write to people saying, we're going to investigate (for example) a noise nuisance complaint in your area (I suppose this is 'overt surveillance'). Unsurprisingly, compliance goes up – so, even without reference to privacy, just in terms of success, these powers are unnecessary. Surveillance powers should be removed from local authorities altogether: if an offence is serious enough to warrant covert surveillance, it shouldn't be in the hands of councils – it should be with the police. If not, then innocent victims of it should have a right to know that they were watched, a right you currently don't have (so it's not scaremongering, but simply stating the obvious, to say, 'it could have happened to you'). It would change the whole culture of surveillance if those conducting it knew that their actions would have to be justified to their victims. There should be a requirement for a councillor to sign off on the surveillance, so that there is at least an element of democratic accountability in the process. Furthermore, councils should be required to obtain a warrant before conducting such surveillance. A promise on the last point was specifically made in the Conservative Party's manifesto – nothing has yet been done.

Reform of the **Independent Safeguarding Authority**. Established in 2006, the ISA was created after the murder of Holly Wells and Jessica Chapman by Ian Huntley. Those working with vulnerable groups, such as children and adults with learning difficulties, face enhanced criminal vetting procedures before taking up their posts. Whilst of course professionals working in these environments should have background checks, volunteer groups rightly complain that the scheme is overly draconian and intrusive in nature and is actually harming those it seeks to protect by making people less likely to be willing to help in future. Theresa May has announced that the ISA would be 'fundamentally re-modelled' in order to reflect a 'common sense' approach to vetting those working with children and vulnerable adults, and halted the previous government's plans to force all volunteers to register with the ISA from July 2010. The Home Office has calculated that the 'scaling back' of the project will save taxpayers around £100 million per year. The manner of this reform has yet to be clarified and those who are kind enough to give their time in the fields concerned remain uncertain about the future of their work (especially in light of the ongoing, often intrusive, often problematic 'enhanced' Criminal Records Bureau checks which hold up the appointment of thousands of perfectly normal people to perfectly normal jobs). Big Brother Watch would scrap the ISA altogether but in the absence of such a decision the reforms must at least be announced post-haste.

CCTV regulation: our report into CCTV showed that the number of council-run CCTV cameras has trebled in the last ten years. That's working off a high base: a decade ago, people were already alarmed by the extent to which we were being watched. Our report doesn't reflect the large number of cameras held by others: by Transport for London, by government ministries, or in private hands. So the true figure is really very high.

It matters because CCTV cameras are not good in and of themselves. To be worth paying for, they have to help to prevent or help to detect crime. If they don't do either, then they are worse than useless – people feel a false sense of security because of them, policing techniques are increasingly reliant on them, they cost a lot and they intrude on privacy.

Cameras are often not working or turned off (as happened in an unpleasant beating in Somerset) or pointing in the wrong direction – all are much worse than them simply not being there, as law enforcement becomes dependent on an unreliable resource. When they're working and turned on and pointing the right way, footage is often scrubbed before law enforcement officials collect it. When they're working, turned on, pointing in the right direction and not scrubbed, the quality of footage is often such that courts cannot use it. They let people down all the time.

There have been forty-four proper studies of CCTV: taken together, they show that crime is not driven down by CCTV (with the exception of a marginal benefit to safety in car parks). That was confirmed by a recent Metropolitan Police report, which stated that one crime per year was 'solved' per thousand cameras. I'm not a Luddite. Technology has a role to play in law enforcement. There are specific cases you can point to where CCTV has helped – but against those must be weighed the millions of man-hours and millions of pounds that get pumped fruitlessly into cameras, and the harm done to society by the presumption of guilt implied by monitoring everyone all the time.

The public purse offers finite resources, and money spent in this way is money that cannot be spent on other forms of policing, such as officers on the street. It's a question of balance. We're the only country that's gone so far down this path. The Shetland Islands have more CCTV cameras than the San Francisco Police Department.

Even putting aside the occasional cases of outright abuse of the network, there are obvious privacy issues raised by CCTV which usually go ignored, but shouldn't. People are increasingly concerned by the capture and retention of the images of innocent people without their consent. Part of society is unambiguously private, like bedrooms (sometimes intruded into by those who run CCTV, but in principle private). Part of society is unambiguously public and needs to be monitored, for example customs areas at airports. There is an argument taking place about what happens in the rest. Some think it's OK in principle to record the rest, all the time, just in case. I don't. That goes too far.

One of course has to rebut the facile 'nothing to hide, nothing to fear' – the reverse should apply in a free society. If you have done nothing wrong, why should the state record your whereabouts and what you're doing? If you think that if you have 'nothing to hide, nothing to fear', that privacy has no place in the discussion of CCTV, then you will note that the largest proportion of violent crime in this country is domestic violence in one form or another – and you won't mind having a camera in your house. If you're not doing anything antisocial, you won't mind having an ASBO. If you're not doing anything criminal, you won't mind a curfew. If you have nothing to hide, why do you have curtains? Anonymity is not a crime.

CCTV is being used in this country to monitor and identify peaceful protesters. Surveillance is being conducted on a routine basis of those exercising democratic rights of protest – freedom of assembly, speech, movement.

We are also building up a data set of personal information which is valuable and open to future abuse (especially given the rapid development of facial mapping). Only a fool would presume that all people in all future governments and all those in power in future times will be benign.

The advocates of CCTV often claim that 'people like it'. Certainly, asked something like 'do you approve of the use of CCTV to fight crime?', most people will answer yes. But in the absence of choice between CCTV and another method of law enforcement, is that *really* an endorsement of CCTV so much as a desire to see crime solved?

There should be a requirement for a public consultation process before cameras are installed. Tests I'd suggest should be applied to CCTV:

- Necessity – is a camera really needed in location X? If so, is it still needed? Once it's gone in, it should periodically be reviewed. Councils install cameras and then good ones, like Havant, strip out cameras that do nothing (in Havant's case, thirty cameras); bad councils just leave them.

- Privacy considerations should be applied to already-installed cameras – even if a camera is required in location X, should it be able to pivot to this or that angle, showing a view of private property, into that bedroom etc?
- The decision-making process should be public – because nobody knows the problems and crime in your area better than you do.

Automatic Number Plate Recognition (ANPR) regulation: ANPR is currently being used to take up to 14 million photographs of vehicles and their occupants each day. In London, cameras that were installed to police the congestion charge are now also accessed by the police for number plate recognition. There is a balance to be struck between surveillance, security and crime prevention, and an unacceptable level of intrusion into people's lives. The coalition claims to be determined to ensure that measures which impinge on civil liberties, like this one, are proportionate and properly controlled.

The Freedom Bill will apparently regulate CCTV and ANPR to ensure that their use is 'proportionate and retains public confidence'. We therefore await it with great interest.

The **Counter-Terrorism agenda**, including:

Random stop and search. Again, Britain has lost on this issue in the European Court – twice. Hundreds of thousands of people have been stopped under these powers, and of course no terrorist has been caught. Rather than a genuine counter-terrorism tool, in practice it has often constituted a way of bullying and hassling the increasingly abject population. We have to decide what kind of society we want to live in. Random stop and search allows the state to confront the individual in the street, without cause, and demand your papers. It's wrong.

28-day detention continues under the coalition. Five people have been detained to the 28-day limit. Three were entirely innocent, being released quite without charge – each case constituting a shocking abuse of freedom. The remaining two were charged, but in both cases the Metropolitan Police have confirmed that the relevant evidence relied upon to charge them was obtained within four and twelve days of arrest respectively. The Liberal Democrats explicitly pledged to bring the limit down to fourteen days. In light of the examples we have seen, the case for that seems irresistible. At the height of Northern Ireland's 'Troubles' in 1984, the members of the British Cabinet were targeted by an IRA bomber at Brighton. Norman Tebbit was pulled from the rubble of the Grand Hotel several hours after the explosion: both he and his wife were seriously injured. Margaret Thatcher and her husband Denis both narrowly avoided injury themselves. Five people were killed. The government itself was attacked in the most physical, personal and literal sense. Yet even then, government did not infringe upon liberties as the last government did with the extension of detention without trial, or with...

Control Orders: there are now nine people on Control Orders in the United Kingdom. There have been forty-five to date (of whom seven have absconded!). It is a standing affront to the rule of law that anyone's liberty is curtailed not only without charge, but without even knowing the nature of the allegations against them. Each time a case actually goes to court, the government loses and another such order falls. Control Orders should be abandoned immediately, rather than defeated on an ad hoc basis as the government loses case after case. After all, it is unjust enough to limit the liberty of a person in this way – but to continue to do so, knowing that the case will be decided against the government when it wends its way to court, but keeping them so 'controlled' until then, is morally bankrupt. It entails further months of unjustifiable action in each case, simply on the basis of which gets to see the inside of a courtroom first. The Liberal Democrats explicitly pledged to scrap them. They should have their way.

Issues on which action is needed – but about which no action has been taken, no review conducted and no announcement made

Trial by jury – the defence of trial by jury was a specific Liberal Democrat pre-election manifesto pledge and a position with which I venture to suggest most Conservatives would agree. There is no reason for the coalition to neglect defence of this basic fundamental principle, which – after the introduction of multiple reasons to admit hearsay and bad character evidence into proceedings, the erosion of the right to silence, and closed proceedings – is once again under renewed threat as trials without juries are initiated.

The **right to protest** is a basic element of both freedom of expression and freedom of assembly. Maya Evans, a 25-year-old chef, was arrested at the Cenotaph for quietly reading out the names of ninety-seven British soldiers killed in Iraq. She was convicted under section 132 of the Serious Organised Crime and Police Act, which requires protesters to obtain police permission before demonstrating within one kilometre of Parliament. Her conviction is perhaps the clearest possible demonstration of the abuse of free speech and the constraints applied to the right to protest peacefully. She cannot possibly be said to have offered any threat to anyone, and her cause – whilst you might agree or disagree with her – was plainly sincere, and is an aspect of a debate of public importance. If the state can stop such 'protest', what *can't* it stop?

Reform of the **Civil Contingencies Act of 2004,** perhaps the most authoritarian piece of legislation passed in peace time. It vastly extends the arbitrary powers of ministers, while making them less answerable to Parliament. The Act allows a minister to declare a state of emergency in which assets can be seized without compensation, courts may be set up, assemblies may be banned, and people may be moved from, or held in, particular areas, all on the belief that an emergency might be about to occur. Only after seven days does Parliament get the chance to assess the situation. If the minister is wrong, or has acted in bad faith, he cannot be punished.

Reform of the **Information Commissioner's Office** (ICO): in the middle of a Metropolitan Police investigation, the ICO white-washed Google's capture of private information being transmitted via wi-fi with their Street View cars – I talk about this issue later in this book, so suffice it to say that it's plain that this is one of the most important privacy issues of our time and that action from the Office supposedly in place to protect us has been lacking. The Conservative Party pledged to strengthen the ICO's powers. This has not been done; either the ICO should be stronger, or perhaps it should not exist at all.

Reform of the **Office of the Surveillance Commissioner**: after four years of operation, the Commissioner reported that the amount of unlawful surveillance conducted in this country has *increased* during his reign. The report disclosed (as if this was a good thing) that a 'considerable proportion' of the errors were due to the incorrect transposition of telephone numbers. That is to say that people were snooped on for no good reason due to administrative incompetence by the snoopers, and they have no right to know that their conversations were listened to, or who did it, or for how long, or what they heard. These unauthorised operations were not only intrusive, but also often extensive – the longest lasted for twenty-four days. That's over three weeks of illegal surveillance by the state of people against whom nothing at all has been proven, and who subsequently have not even been charged, without any apparent repercussions for those who did it. Because the Commissioner refuses to release any details of these unlawful operations, the victims of this outrageous intrusion will never know that they and their families were watched. When the Commissioner's report was discussed by our national broadcaster, in a moment of delicious but apparently unappreciated irony the OSC – responsible for bringing accountability and transparency to this opaque and sometimes frightening field – refused to discuss the matter in public.

Children should not be **fingerprinted in school** for registration purposes or in order to get school dinners or library books – certainly not without parental permission (again, this was a specific Liberal Democrat pledge). Equally they should not be the subject of facial recognition technology. Both of these practices are in place in schools in the United Kingdom – fingerprinting is actually quite common.

Powers of entry to private property: our research showed that some 20,000 local council bureaucrats are empowered by over 1,000 different laws and regulations to enter private property without a warrant and without notice. This proliferation has spurred many of the most absurd laws of modern times, and like others in this list changes the nature of the relationship between the individual and the state. When so many 'faults' exist it's almost as if normal life is unlawful – in the end, with so many technical infractions (energy regulations on your refrigerator, for example) they'll catch you for something. Specific promises to address this by requiring a warrant to effect entry were made by Dominic Grieve at a Big Brother Watch/Centre for Policy Studies event before the election (the footage is available on our YouTube channel) and were included in the manifesto. These promises should be carried out.

Chip and bin: our research revealed that 2.6 million households in this country had had microchips installed in their dustbins (and none of them had been told about it). Plainly it was going to lead to 'pay as you throw' schemes. That was explicitly banned for the present by Eric Pickles but chips continue to be installed 'to encourage recycling' – it's the same technology and can be switched to other uses, and it is equally intrusive.

The **European Arrest Warrant** and accompanying European Investigation Order let ill-trained police from any European Union country arrest British people for 'crimes' that aren't even offences in the UK or the United States. Patrick Reece-Edwards, from Dartford, spent several weeks in jail after Polish prosecutors sought his extradition on charges of possessing a forged motor insurance certificate. Dimitrinka Atanasova, a Bulgarian legal secretary, fled to Britain after threatening to expose her boss (the chief prosecutor) for misconduct. The chief prosecutor then personally requested her extradition from Britain on what a British judge agreed were 'bad-faith' (trumped-up) charges. Crucially, her case predated Bulgaria's EU membership and adoption of the EAW. She was freed, but only after several months in Holloway Prison. Edmond Arapi, a Staffordshire waiter, was seized under an EAW issued by Italy after being sentenced to sixteen years in absentia for a murder in Genoa in 2004. Yet he never left Britain in 2004. He spent time in Wandsworth prison before the Italians finally admitted it was a case of mistaken identity. Why have we allowed this to happen in our country? Britain has an opt-out – it should be used. Furthermore, the Lisbon Treaty created an ill-defined Public Prosecutor for Europe. The sooner the existence of this post is challenged the easier it will be to stop it.

A new privacy law/libel reform: two different schemes are currently mooted on this front (one by Lord Lester, one by Lord

McNally); neither seems to possess any strong-willed governmental support. A requirement that Privacy Impact Assessments be conducted in relation to any initiative which involved data collection or sharing was proposed in the Conservative manifesto. There has been no action or hint of future action on this.

The Census: before the election, the Conservative Party's position on the forthcoming Census (with which Big Brother Watch entirely agreed) was that it is 'increasingly invasive and intrusive... [and] will erode public support, cost more and result in a less accurate survey. Just because the government has the legal powers to ask these questions does not give the state the licence to ask anything they want.'

So said Nick Hurd, then shadow Cabinet Office spokesman. That is a very different position to that taken by our new Cabinet Office minister... Nick Hurd. The man responsible for administering the census, Glen Watson, confirms that coalition plans for the forthcoming census are... entirely unchanged. Mr Hurd's urgings about scaling back the census seem to have fallen on his own deaf ears. Francis Maude says that 'the expenses already committed to the census mean any changes are difficult.' The 2011 Census Mr Hurd so decried, and will now enforce, is thirty-two pages long (frequently duplicating data already held by the authorities on databases such as the electoral register, school records, tax returns and GP information). It requires the disclosure of your proficiency in English, your health, when you last worked, disclosure of the identity of your overnight visitor(s), the kind of central heating you have, and makes the entirely hollow but nevertheless bullying threat of fines of £1,000 for non-compliance. Last time (in 2001), 390,000 people declared themselves Jedi and 3 million people refused to comply, and as there were fewer than 100 prosecutions, non-compliance comes pretty much entirely without repercussions.

Body Scanners: I discuss the worrying and unreviewed spread of body scanners in Chapter 23.

A commitment to introduce **no new large state databases** and greater checks on data-sharing within government. The recipient of public services should be at the centre of IT design not, as currently, viewed as a passive end-user.

The **transfer of police powers to private security firms and council wardens** should simply be stopped. Private security firms and members of the public empowered through the Community Safety Accreditation Scheme do not have the vetting or public trust accorded to professional police officers.

Worse than Labour

There are three grounds on which the coalition has ventured even beyond Labour's dismal record:

The **Summary Care Record** (SCR) – the massive NHS database of all our medical records was controversial enough for Labour to suspend before the election. It is unnecessary and intrusive, as well as wildly expensive. The Conservatives said that 'a Conservative government would "dismantle" central NHS IT infrastructure, halt and renegotiate NPfIT local service provider contracts and introduce interoperable local systems' and the Liberal Democrat health spokesman said that 'the government needs to end its obsession with massive central databases. The NHS IT scheme has been a disastrous waste of money and the national programme should be abandoned.' Nevertheless, some three weeks into government by those two parties, a disgraceful U-turn was performed. Doctors (most of whom say they wouldn't go on to the database themselves, or allow their families on to it) have managed without it until now.

For the second year running the NHS topped the Information Commissioner's Office list of data breaches in UK organisations: 3,000 breaches were found (how many others weren't?). How can we have faith in the new online programme, when the NHS can't keep our private data safe now? Those abuses are bad, and took place when files were restricted to individual hospitals and the people who worked in them. How bad will abuse be when files can be accessed *nationally*? Do you trust everyone who has an NHS pass, including temps? The SCR will give over half a million people access to our medical records. Our research has shown how vulnerable the NHS is to breaches of privacy – this will make things much worse. I say that this is worse than Labour because at least Labour were honest about their intentions.

Empowering **credit rating agencies to chase benefit fraudsters**: the move to commission agencies like Experian to act, in effect, as bounty hunters to catch people committing benefit fraud is a very bad idea. Nobody approves of benefit cheats, and of course when receiving benefits one has to sacrifice a certain amount of privacy in return for the certainty that one's receiving that benefit legitimately. But mining private data on a routine basis on the off-chance of catching people out is a disproportionate invasion of privacy. There continues to be a presumption of innocence in this country, and trawling credit data and treating everyone in that broad category of people as suspects brings that presumption into question.

Furthermore, there is or should be a clear delineation between the state and the private sector. Taking powers of legal investigation and enforcement which ought to sit with the state, and granting them to private organisations, blurs that line. Worse still, if profit-making companies are rewarded by the number of people they catch they will have a perverse incentive to sling accusations in any even marginally plausible case – because they'll have nothing to lose and potentially something to gain in the smearing. There's a reason we don't pay the police per arrest – we'd all wind up getting nicked all the time.

The **Intercept Modernisation Programme** (IMP) – perhaps the worst example of all. The IMP will allow the security services and the police to spy on the activities of everyone using a phone or the internet. Every communications provider will be obliged to store details of your communications for at least a year and obliged in due course to surrender them up to the authorities. The authorities will be able to track every phone call, email, text message and website visit made by the public on the absurd pretext that it will help to tackle crime or terrorism.

Announced in 2008, the IMP was so controversial that even Labour suspended it. The Conservative Party's manifesto for the 2010 general election featured a commitment to 'review relevant national databases and systems to develop a clear statement of purpose for each in line with the principles of proportionality and necessity' – including the IMP – and the Coalition Agreement promised to 'end the storage of internet and email records without good reason'.

Buried in the Strategic Defence and Security Review, the government plans to continue with its introduction – despite the Conservative Party's recent pledge to reverse the rise of the surveillance state, a commitment now fairly and squarely broken.

Couple this with the U-turn on the Summary Care Record discussed above, which continues despite similarly clear and concrete promises to the contrary from both parties of government, and a troubling picture emerges; it is fascinating and dreadful to see the speed of bureaucratic capture and reversion to bureaucratic authoritarianism on show.

Finally, and perversely, the thumpingly expensive IMP is being re-established at a time when public finances are stretched to breaking point and many aspects of less controversial state provision are being cut.

The scheme should be abandoned, like ContactPoint – not continued and extended.

Conclusion

In addition to all of the above, it should be noted that a wider review of the nature of the relationship of citizen and state is now effectively impossible. The British Bill of Rights (and responsibilities) proposed by the Conservative Party before the last election is plainly not going to happen. The Liberal Democrats are dead-set against it and whatever the merits of the case for a post-Human Rights Act delineation of rights and responsibilities, it is not to be for as long as the coalition is with us.

It will not have escaped your attention that most issues covered in this introduction fall under the 'review' heading. It's crazy that this area is languishing like this. It's one of the few fields on which the two governing parties wholeheartedly agree. Furthermore, as we all know all too well, the government is broke. This is an obvious policy area in which progress can be made whilst making savings. Complex databases, snooping surveillance operations and high-tech devices used to conduct them, the jobsworth bureaucrats who run all of it – the apparatus of the bully state costs a great deal of money. That expenditure is avoided when these leviathans are cut. We can be freer *and* save money all at the same time.

One cannot and must not write off the government's intentions on freedom, privacy and liberty until those processes are complete. But one might wonder why such reviews are necessary in the first place. The fundamentals of these issues have not changed since the coalition came to power. This matters because right now is likely the high point in the government's interest in freedom. The longer action is delayed, the more likely it is that bureaucrats get their claws into hitherto (more) principled politicians. The pressures of everyday events, of headlines, of terrorism, of the need to be seen to be doing something, will bite. Rather than being good news, the plethora of reviews and consultations may be disastrous.

Human rights and the law

Jesse Norman MP

Human rights today are more often the subject of argument than thought – both among politicians and the general public. This is far from disastrous when there is a settled public understanding of what British human rights are and have been, how they came into being and what they do.

But that understanding does not exist today. On the contrary, human rights have become highly contested ground. Red-top and other newspapers regularly denounce certain rights, while claiming others for themselves. And politicians are only too happy to cater to a growing public mythology in which our basic human rights are an EU imposition, or a charter for socialism and state interference, or a hindrance to the fight against terrorism.

In an age of easy categorisation and sloppy thinking, even language itself is often taken as a guide to political positioning. On this view lefties speak of 'human rights', righties of 'personal freedoms' and those in the middle of 'civil liberties'. Or is it the other way round?

What makes the problem worse is that important political issues now more than ever turn on public debate about these rights and freedoms. These include not merely high-profile matters such as the detention and extradition of terrorism suspects, but the more mundane ones that affect every person in this country, and that are discussed at length in this book. For example: is CCTV an unwarrantable intrusion or a vital means of public security and reassurance? Under what circumstances, if any, should the state be allowed to enter your home, tap your phone or monitor your email without your knowledge?

To address these issues in a balanced way, we need to rebuild the public understanding of the nature, importance and origin of human rights. And to do that, we need to move away from abstract argument and take a fresh look at some of the relevant history.

Edmund Burke and human rights

Scepticism about human rights is not a new phenomenon. The argument has often been made over the centuries that such rights do not exist but are merely a philosopher's fancy; that they are contrary to the traditions and spirit of the common law; and that politically they infringe the principle of parliamentary sovereignty.

After all, was it not Burke himself who denounced the 'rights of man' as harbingers of revolution in his *Reflections on the Revolution in France* (1790), saying 'Against these ... rights of men let no government look for security in the length of its continuance, or in the justice and lenity of its administration'?

In fact, however, this objection is the opposite of the truth. In the first place, Burke was not opposed to rights as such, only to 'abstract' or 'metaphysical' rights. These are rights which have been divorced from a context of legal custom and tradition, rights which mankind is somehow deemed to have enjoyed in an original state of nature. They are uncertain in their full meaning, and potentially revolutionary in their effects.

In sharp contrast to these abstract rights, however, Burke praises 'recorded' rights, that is, rights which have been elaborated through the common law. In a crucial but often neglected passage from the *Reflections*, he says:

> Far am I from denying in theory; full as far is my heart from with-
> holding in practice ... the *real* rights of men ... If civil society be made
> for the advantage of man, all the advantages for which it is made

become his right ... Whatever each man can separately do, without
trespassing upon others, he has a right to do for himself; and he has
a right to a fair portion of all which society, with all its combinations
of skill and force, can do in his favour.

The last two sentences are a masterly statement of Burke's 'Old
Whig' or 'compassionate' conservatism.

So, then, what distinguishes recorded from abstract rights? Simply
this: recorded rights are, in effect, summaries of human experience.
They are established, they are well-understood, and they have
been filtered, elaborated, nuanced and defined in a huge range of
different contexts through countless legal judgments. It is in their
status as the product of the common law, of the judge-made law of
the land, that Burke sees their legitimacy; and in their protection
against the tyranny of the majority that he sees their value. From
time to time these rights or freedoms may be codified or recorded
in statute, and for Burke this is to be welcomed when such a statute
operates, in his words, on the principles of the common law.

Thus it is crucial to note that Burke is not opposed to change as
such. Far from it: for him acceptance of change is the indispensable
corollary of commitment to the established order. As he famously
put it, 'a state without some means of change is without the means
of its conservation'. Thus, far from reviling the 'glorious revolution'
of 1688, Burke celebrated it as the necessary and limited change
required to preserve the constitution. For him, then, the continuing substance in the body politic – the framework within which any
change must occur – is the British constitution, and in particular
the common law.

Blackstone, Dicey and the Legal Tradition

Burke would not have considered this line of thought as in any sense
innovative, and indeed would have been appalled at the idea. On
the contrary, he regarded himself as writing from within the very

heart of British legal, constitutional and specifically parliamentary traditions.

He was correct. For the greatest British legal authorities have always recognised that some basic rights are an essential part of the rule of law. Article 39 of Magna Carta 1215, for example, contains the prohibition 'No freemen shall be taken or imprisoned or disseised [*expropriated*] or exiled or in any way destroyed, nor will we go upon him nor send upon him, except by the lawful judgment of his peers or by the law of the land' – the basis of Articles 5 and 6 of the Human Rights Act today.

Burke's readers would not have needed to look as far back as the thirteenth century for confirmation of this point, however. For the wider argument had in fact been made very forcefully decades before the *Reflections*, with the publication of the magisterial *Commentaries on the Laws of England* (1765–9) of Sir William Blackstone.

Blackstone's was the first full-scale presentation of English law, and specifically the common law, for over 200 years. It had three huge merits: it was systematic, presenting the law in a coherent way from first principles; it was written in English, not Latin; and it was aimed not merely at lawyers but at squires, merchants and other educated laymen. It went through eight editions in eleven years, and was vigorously circulated not merely in Britain but in the American colonies. It has had an inestimable influence on the development and spread of the rule of law in the English-speaking world.

For Blackstone, rights are not merely an accretion to the rule of law: they are intrinsic to it. In his words, 'the principal aim of society is to protect individuals in the enjoyment of those absolute rights, which were invested in them by the immutable laws of nature ... Hence it follows, that the primary end of human laws is to maintain and regulate these *absolute* rights of individuals.' At the end of the *Commentaries* Blackstone gives a rather Whiggish account of the origins of these rights and liberties, encompassing Magna Carta, the

Petition of Right, the Habeas Corpus Act, the Bill of Rights, and the Act of Settlement. He thus links both Parliament's constitutional function and its own history to the growth of individual freedoms and restraint on the Crown.

In Blackstone's analysis, there are three 'absolute' rights: the right to personal security, the right to personal liberty and the right to private property. These are rights of individuals, not groups, and they are specifically chosen in opposition to different forms of tyranny and oppression. Moreover, they are to be read widely. Thus the right to personal security includes 'a person's legal and uninterrupted enjoyment of his life, his limbs, his body, his health and his reputation', while the right to personal liberty includes 'the power of removing one's person to whatsoever place one's inclination may direct without imprisonment or restraint, except by due process of law'. And Blackstone notably argued that these primary rights were in turn supported and protected by a range of subordinate rights, such as the right of subjects to access to the courts and the right of petition. These protections are the forerunner of the modern idea that the law should provide effective remedies.

This broad line of thought was taken up, developed and given a characteristic twist by the great constitutional theorist A. V. Dicey towards the end of the nineteenth century. As with Blackstone, Dicey's *Introduction to the Study of the Law of the Constitution* (1885) has been massively influential ever since first publication.

For Dicey the British constitution rested on two foundations: parliamentary sovereignty and the rule of law. Parliament had unfettered power as the supreme law-making institution. But it was itself held to certain unchanging principles that constituted the rule of law, and these guaranteed the rights and liberties of the individual. These principles were that no one could be punished except by court order with due process and for a distinct breach of the law; that everyone was subject to law and to the jurisdiction of the courts; and that the general principles of the constitution were derived from judicial decisions in court, which is from judge-made law.

Dicey also picks out three particular rights: the rights to personal freedom, to freedom of discussion and to public meeting or freedom of association. The latter two are not those of Blackstone, but Blackstone's other rights, to personal security and private property, are clearly assumed elsewhere in Dicey. Where the two theorists differ is that for Dicey these rights, indeed rights as such, have no special status. There are no 'absolute' or foundational rights. Rights may be well-established, but ultimately they remain the products of judge-made law, of the normal processes of courtroom adjudication. As such they can change: slowly as legal practice evolves, or rapidly through an Act of Parliament. For this reason, perhaps, Dicey is generally rather dismissive of formal statements, charters or guarantees of rights; his thought seems to be that if the rights in question are not sufficiently embedded in the law, customs and manners of a nation, then formal guarantees are likely to be of little value.

But Dicey's position is slightly less clear than it might be, for two reasons. The first is the obvious point that formal guarantees may themselves be a way to strengthen the customs and manners of a nation, by recording a public and social commitment to certain basic values.

The second point is more subtle: it is that regardless of Dicey's official position there clearly are some rights that he takes to be, if not entrenched, then very well-established indeed – these are the rights assumed in his conception of the rule of law itself, such as the right to due process. A more fully-fledged conception of the rule of law might identify other such rights, and point to them as being wholly or partly constitutive of the rule of law. Parliament would preserve its own unfettered sovereignty, but there would be something self-defeating about the exercise of that sovereignty in the abolition of those basic rights.

What rights are not

Unsurprisingly, then, Burke, Blackstone and Dicey share a broadly consistent view of English law and the importance of certain established rights and liberties within it. Not only that: they see it as a primary purpose of government and of the rule of law to protect the liberties of the individual. Good government is maintained by constitutional arrangements that are deliberately slow-moving and yet flexible.

Human rights are sometimes considered to be the product of left-wing ideology. But in Britain this line of thought suggests the contrary. To see why, consider what these rights are not. They are not natural, pre-ordained or the products of God's law. They belong to individuals, not to groups or classes. They are not, by and large, economic or social in character. They are not divorced from, but are the products of, legal tradition and social custom. They are not conceived of in the abstract or grounded in a-priori reflection, but based on experience. They are not independent of specific legal remedies, but backed by them. They are not entrenched against Parliament as superior law, but explicitly acknowledge the sovereignty of Parliament.

By contrast, there is a liberal or radical conception in which human rights are all or many of these things. The French Revolution was founded on such a conception, and Burke's genius was to predict in advance that, and how, such a revolution would end in disaster. But the American Revolution is arguably a more interesting case, because it allied radical rhetoric in the style of Paine with radical innovation in its entrenched and written constitution – and specifically the Bill of Rights – and then grafted the whole on to English legal traditions directly and recently inspired by Blackstone himself. From this rich and heady mixture came, in the course of a century, not merely the extraordinary energy of American statecraft, but a powerful and distinct conception of national identity, of what it was to be American at all.

Human rights today

This historical background casts a long shadow forwards. It allows a different perspective on the two documents that dominate discussion of human rights in the UK today: the European Convention on Human Rights 1951 (ECHR) and the Human Rights Act 1998, which reproduces the Convention's rights within British law.

It is a matter of historical fact that the European Convention was in large measure the creation of two Conservative British politicians: David Maxwell Fyfe, later Lord Kilmuir, and Sir Winston Churchill. The need for such an instrument and for its accompanying institutions assumed special urgency during the Second World War. As early as 1942, Churchill as Prime Minister had looked ahead to consider the political landscape of continental Europe. With Germany defeated, he believed the only realistic way to hold a dominant USSR at bay would be through what he termed a 'Council of Europe', led by Britain. This, he believed, would be a bulwark against any new totalitarianism.

After his landslide defeat in the 1945 general election, Churchill remained true to this idea, leading the public argument for European solidarity. He became Chairman of the new United Europe Movement. He commissioned his son-in-law Duncan Sandys to organise a major international congress in May 1948 in The Hague, in the face of opposition from Attlee's Labour government. And in a rousing opening speech at the Hague conference he specifically advocated a Charter of Human Rights, 'guarded by freedom and sustained by law'.

Churchill believed that British victory in the recent war was above all the victory of certain basic values – values that were the cornerstone not merely of Western civilisation, but of civilisation as such. The purpose of the Charter was to protect and extend those values. This approach was later made explicit in the formal motion proposing the new Convention, which stated that it 'would maintain intact the human rights and fundamental freedoms actually existing in the respective countries at the date of signature'.

Churchill's bold proposal was adopted. The British lawyer and politician David Maxwell Fyfe then became the chairman of the new Council's legal and administrative council in August 1949, as well as serving as rapporteur on the committee drafting the European Convention on Human Rights A former minister in Churchill's government and then deputy Chief Prosecutor at Nuremburg, Maxwell Fyfe was well qualified for the arduous task of negotiating the language of the Convention rights, and then shepherding them through the various national governments, including that of the UK, which was in fact the first nation to sign.

The European Convention thus marks a vital codification of the common law, not its repudiation. It was framed by British jurists, working within a common law legal tradition stretching back past the US Bill of Rights 1791 to encompass our own Bill of Rights 1689, and the Petition of Right 1628. So it is not surprising that its essential principles – including the right to a fair trial, the right not to be held without charge, and the right not to be subject to cruel and unusual punishment – are limited, well-grounded and proportionate. After all, they are manifestations of the English common law as it took shape during a centuries-long jostling for power between the different estates of the realm. The same is true by extension for the Human Rights Act.

The necessity of British human rights

Where does this brief summary leave us? I would suggest there are several lessons to be drawn.

The first is that the British human rights tradition is something of which we should be utterly proud. It guarantees our personal freedoms and civil liberties, and underwrites the rule of law. Its rights are not abstract but, as Burke says, 'recorded' – written down first in common law judgments going back 800 years, and more recently codified in statute. It has spread out across the continents. It is a great gift from this country to the world. We should rejoice, for example, in the fact that Britain was not merely the first country to prohibit torture, in 1640, but that this prohibition has now spread around the world, and is enshrined in international statute.

The second lesson is that our human rights tradition has always been intrinsically conservative. As judge-made law it has proceeded by degrees. As statute in the Human Rights Act it respects the sovereignty of Parliament. Big-C Conservatives can and should themselves feel some pride in the leading parts played by Maxwell Fyfe and Churchill in the creation of the European Convention, and so in the Human Rights Act. But as the product of a slowly building consensus, the broader tradition has long transcended party politics.

The third point is to note what this tradition rules out. It is rightly sceptical about the status and value of abstract, 'metaphysical' rights. It runs contrary to the standard pat claims about the importance of a 'written constitution', both because British human rights, and indeed much of the constitution, are already written down, and because most advocates of a 'written constitution' actually seek to entrench the courts constitutionally, which would politicise the judiciary. And this tradition cuts against the introduction of new socio-economic and other rights, which generally have little if any grounding in our law or practice.

And finally, we should acknowledge and support the Human Rights Act itself. This is not to say, of course, that public concern about rights inflation is misplaced, or that all is perfectly well in the public administration of human rights in this country, or in its relation to the European Court.

But the Human Rights Act is the wrong target. It is not an instrument of the European Union. It creates no new rights, and has not itself been a cause of rights inflation. It has not materially hindered the fight against terrorism. It does not impose huge new costs on business. And it has already shown its worth in protecting the rights, liberties and freedoms for which this country has always been celebrated.

Most of all, of course, the Human Rights Act is a crucial tool with which the individual can fight the increasing tendency to authoritarianism and surveillance in our society. And that is surely justification enough.

They've got your number: the silent boom in mass surveillance

Guy Herbert

When were you last a criminal suspect? Most people might indignantly say, 'never!' But if you are a UK resident (or tourist) it would be when you last took a plane, ferry or Eurostar. Unless, that is, you have ever worked for local government as an employee or a contractor, are a council tenant, council-tax payer, or voter. Then it could be more recently.

The National Fraud Initiative[1]

Under the National Fraud Initiative (NFI), local authorities are required to provide to the Audit Commission specific details[2] of everyone who is on their payroll, who receives a pension, of trade creditors (including payment history), tenants (and their national insurance numbers) and residential leaseholders, the council tax and electoral registers, insurance claimants, care home residents, bus-pass and disabled parking badge holders, and all licensed market traders, taxi drivers and individuals licensed to sell alcohol.

This mountain of personal data is subjected to computerised cross-referencing in a number of different ways. It is further combined with information from other organisations including government departments, and private sector organisations. 1300 now take part.[3]

The Audit Commission is actively recruiting more participants, and is looking to suck up information from financial institutions, central government departments and agencies, housing associations, private pension funds, recruitment agencies, retailers and the voluntary sector [4] to add to the mix. The information would be exempted from normal data protections by the Serious Crime Act 2007,[5] and the Commission would like the new participants to be *forced* to participate, as that Act permits ministers to order. Called for government purposes 'data matching', in the private sector this is known by a less anodyne term: 'data-mining'.

Some of these exercises strike me, and may strike you, as legitimate – with big gains to be made from almost no intrusion. There is no obvious problem with checking whether anyone on a list of pensioners has died. It is a single, simple fact, without any moral significance and relatively easy to check. I do not know of any case where someone, while still alive, has had his or her pension stopped by the NFI on the grounds that they are officially dead.[6]

But the broader principle being promoted by the Audit Commission and the National Fraud Initiative is that 'zero tolerance of fraud' justifies the collection, sharing and mining of all sorts of data about millions of people – where they live and with whom, and the details of their work and finances. '...The right tone from the top in an organisation is vital, as is a zero-tolerance approach towards fraud,'[7] it sententiously declares. This is, at the very least, questionable.

Zero tolerance sounds good as rhetoric. But in the real world there is always ambiguity and error. A determination to drive out some evil *at all costs* means those costs will rise indefinitely high. Practically speaking, 'zero tolerance' of something as elusive as fraud is an insane goal.

We can from the Audit Commission's 2008/9 NFI report[8] make a rough estimate of how many innocent people were investigated, and how many more have a black mark against their name. Even without the dominion over private-sector data it wants to build, page 12 of the report says the Commission found 3.5 *million* 'data matches' in the last exercise – presumably meaning *significant* data matches, the black mark – of which 5 per cent were rated urgent, requiring investigation. That means there were as many as 175,000 investigations. Figures for outcomes are scattered, but adding up all the claimed successes on page 20 (which may also have some over-lap) results in 46,995 individual 'wins' for the Audit Commission, a third of them cancelled blue badges. That implies over 125,000 unsuccessful investigations.

The costs of the National Fraud Initiative could certainly be measured in money; and so could the results. But they aren't. For an audit body the exact accounting is strangely absent.

The cost to the Audit Commission is said to be £2 million for 2008/9, and to have yielded £215 million in savings. That would be impressive. However, one can look in vain for any comprehensive estimate of costs, which would surely include the costs to bodies of providing that data, the costs of all investigations and prosecutions, and recruitment costs to replace staff dismissed. As for benefits, the putative savings appear to include *all* detected fraud, whether or not sums are recovered, and some strange formulae for calculating potential future costs. For example, the largest category of saving in money terms is pensions paid to dead people, which is reckoned on the basis that they would have gone on undetected until the notional pensioner was ninety. The largest in number of cases, and third in size of 'savings', is blue badges and bus passes surviving their legitimate owners. There are tens of thousands of these, each arbitrarily counted as £500 saved, whether it was being actively exploited, or left forgotten in a drawer after granny died.

In real taxpayers' money – which is what should interest people not infected with the inquisitorial mission of the Audit Commission – the costs and gains almost certainly do not look as impressive as a £215 million return on £2 million. And, as I pointed out above, some of the simplest, least objectionable processes are the most productive. 'Deceased matching' alone, clearly not a large part of the £2 million, brings in (in the Commission's terms) almost £99 million.

But I'd suggest not only should such schemes be checked against their *actual* financial results, They should also be measured in privacy and dignity, and personal security, which are a loss to every person under secret examination. Do we really want to live in a country where every detail of every person's life is held on official files and cross-checked behind their back in the hope of catching them out? Our justice system and our free society is founded on another principle, one that makes openness part of fairness and accepts that the guilty may sometimes go free to avoid the persecution of the innocent.

We should also try to take account of the huge number of false positives (albeit they represent a small fraction of the whole). These inevitably result in mistakes, unsubstantiated allegations and unjust penalties. The logic of zero tolerance is that any quantity of injustice to the innocent becomes tolerable in pursuing it.

As the process continues, the greater the number of false positives, in the real world of misspellings and coincidences, it will generate. The more matching there is the more people will be presumed guilty of fraud, and will have to prove their innocence. You may not be *prosecuted* without proof against you, but note that in 2008/9, there were 269 successful prosecutions[9] against (from the same sum as before) as many as 46,276 individuals sanctioned in some way. We have no idea how many of the 125,000 unsanctioned had to fight hard to keep their financial rights, and clear their names; we cannot tell how many of those punished without prosecution just did not feel able to fight.

E-Borders

After that you may feel you are better off out of the country. But don't think that will take you away from surveillance. It brings you within the remit of e-Borders.

What's that? A scheme 'to help secure the border', says the Home Office agency in charge,[10] which the casual reader would assume means it has something to do with immigration controls. Securing the border must surely, logically, mean determining who or what crosses it, and checking they are supposed to be doing so? Few people would object to that in principle.

But it seems to be a bit more ambitious than that. For a start you have to provide – or rather your travel agent or carrier has to provide – copious information about you and your journey even if you are a British citizen leaving the country. Apart from details of your travel document and the flight or ferry or train, this is described as 'non-mandatory'. But if the carrier has the information they *must* provide it. It is worth quoting in full:[11]

SCHEDULE 2 Information specified to extent known by carrier: immigration
1. The passenger and service information is the following details in respect of a passenger –
(a) name as it appears on the reservation;
(b) place of birth;
(c) issue date of travel document;
(d) address;
(e) sex;
(f) any contact telephone number;
(g) e-mail address;
(h) travel status of passenger, which indicates whether reservation is confirmed or provisional and whether the passenger has checked in;
(i) the number of pieces and description of any baggage carried;
(j) any documentation provided to the passenger in respect of his baggage;
(k) date of intended travel;
(l) ticket number;
(m) date and place of ticket issue;
(n) seat number allocated;
(o) seat number requested;
(p) check-in time, regardless of method;
(q) date on which reservation was made;
(r) identity of any person who made the reservation;
(s) any travel agent used;
(t) any other name that appears on the passenger's reservation;
(u) number of passengers on the same reservation;
(v) complete travel itinerary for passengers on the same reservation;
(w) the fact that a reservation in respect of more than one passenger has been divided due to a change in itinerary for one or more but not all of the passengers;
(x) Code Share Details [the name of any other carrier who will carry the passenger];

(y) method of payment used to purchase ticket or make a reservation;
(z) details of the method of payment used, including the number of any credit, debit or other card used;
(aa) billing address;
(bb) booking reference number, Passenger Name Record Locator and other data locator used by the carrier to locate the passenger within its information system;
(cc) the class of transport reserved;
(dd) the fact that the reservation is in respect of a one-way journey;
(ee) all historical changes to the reservation;
(ff) General Remarks;
(gg) Other Service Information (OSI);
(hh) System Service Information (SSI) and System Service Request information (SSR);
(ii) identity of the individual who checked the passenger in for the voyage or flight or international service;
(jj) Outbound Indicator, which identifies where a passenger is to travel on to from the United Kingdom;
(kk) Inbound Connection Indicator, which identifies where a passenger started his journey before he travels onto the United Kingdom;
(ll) the fact that the passenger is travelling as part of a group;
(mm) the expiry date of any entry clearance held in respect of the United Kingdom;
(nn) card number and type of any frequent flyer or similar scheme used;
(oo) Automated Ticket Fare Quote (ATFQ), which indicates the fare quoted and charged;
(pp) the fact that the passenger is under the age of eighteen and unaccompanied; and
(qq) where the passenger is a person under the age of eighteen and unaccompanied –
(i) age;
(ii) languages spoken;
(iii) any special instructions provided;
(iv) the name of any departure agent who will receive instructions regarding the care of the passenger;
(v) the name of any transit agent who will receive instructions regarding the care of the passenger;
(vi) the name of any arrival agent who will receive instructions regarding the care of the passenger;
(vii) the following details in respect of the guardian on departure –
(aa) name;
(bb) address;
(cc) any contact telephone number; and
(dd) relationship to passenger; and
(viii) the following details in respect of the guardian on arrival –
(aa) name;
(bb) address;
(cc) any contact telephone number; and
(dd) relationship to passenger.

This information will be stored and may be freely passed between immigration authorities, police and intelligence services and HM Revenue & Customs. (It is also demanded by many countries as a condition of your being allowed to land or enter their airspace.) A joint Home Office/FCO paper of March 2007[12] implies some sharing of travel information with and between some forty entities, government and commercial, British and overseas. The e-Borders Operations Centre at Wythenshawe near Manchester has been collecting such passenger information since 2008.[13] The culmination of the £1.2 billion plus[14] Home Office programme is supposed to have it holding all details of ALL passenger movements in and out of the UK for ten years.

Unsurprisingly, something quite so ambitious is not yet (June 2010) working perfectly.[15] You can scarcely guarantee your movements are *not* being watched in some detail, however. The UK Borders Agency seems unfazed by the suggestion by the European Commission[16] that it is in breach of EU law by violating the privacy rights of citizens of other EU countries travelling to Britain under their native laws (frequently far stronger than Britain's). Perhaps that is because, according to the Board of Airline Representatives in the UK,[17] airline systems are not able to provide passenger data according to individual passenger wishes. It is all or none. That is, all.

A further hint that this is not to be limited to what an ordinary person might deem part of securing the borders comes in the revelation that it is intended to cross-reference all this data and scan people's patterns of movements. This is a feature, not a bug. The original Regulatory Impact Assessment[18] said:

> The value of passenger information is not confined to a single journey. In this respect, it is essential that law enforcement and intelligence agencies can retain passenger information for a sufficient period of time to achieve the aim of maintaining an effective border security capability. In the national security context, experience has taught that during the investigation following a terrorist incident the ability to historically track the movements of the suspected perpetrators or indeed attempt to identify them by reference to their travel is a vital investigative tool. As the terrorists may have entered the country a considerable time before the incident the retention of the data for a reasonable time is therefore necessary. In addition, for immigration control purposes the ability to refer to an audit trail

of movements is key to risk assessing passengers. An audit trail of movements which illustrates a passenger's compliance will weigh in that passenger's favour while evidence of non-compliance will clearly attract closer examination by an immigration officer. We see these as fundamental building blocks for enhancing border security.

The familiar rhetoric is about (tiny numbers of) terrorists justifying mass monitoring. Now that has less weight, the story is trapping suspected smugglers from their movement patterns.[19] Collect data on everyone and you can decide later of what they might be guilty.

There really is no objection from civil libertarians (at least the ones I talk to) to holding a database of wanted people, fugitives from the police, known suspects, those barred from entry or exit by court orders etc. There's no objection to checking travel documents electronically at borders so that such people can be stopped, or (with an appropriate warrant) tracking the movements of those who are the subjects of an ongoing lawful investigation.

What is fundamentally different is the Borders Agency scheme to track everyone around the globe in order to be able to confect suspicions by a data-mining mechanism – and then share those suspicions with other agencies, perhaps even less scrupulous about privacy and the presumption of innocence.

Information sharing sickness

You might be surprised I didn't discuss CRB checking, or the proliferation of demands for 'ID' in everyday life. But the two schemes of mass surveillance I have described above are much less known, have grown up in near-silence, and both illustrate a propensity for bureaucratic expansion. I could have picked dozens of other examples.[20]

There is a fashion – or a sickness – in government for seeking to solve particular problems through this sort of general surveillance. 'Information sharing' has come to be seen almost as a good in itself in the higher reaches of bureaucracy, and certainly only as a tool for good. It is a bone at which the Blair administration worried for years.

The attitude was made explicit in a document published by the Department of Constitutional Affairs (now the Ministry of Justice) in 2006: the 'Information sharing: vision statement',[21] carried through in the terms of reference of the Thomas-Walport inquiry and almost slipped into law as 'Information Sharing Orders' under the Coroners and Justice Bill.

According to the vision statement:

> Information sharing is key to the government's goal of better public services – delivering better outcomes for citizens, for businesses and for society as a whole. The Data Protection Act provides the framework that ensures the sharing can take place in a way that respects individuals' rights to privacy and keeps their personal information secure from abuse.

Even before that, the Cabinet Office had identified[22] four barriers to information sharing: 1) human rights law, especially the constructive privacy protections under Article 8 of the Convention, 2) the Data Protection Acts, 3) common law confidentiality, and 4) the fundamental rule of administrative law, the doctrine of *ultra vires*, which says official bodies may not do things that the law does not empower them to do.

In practice, the Data Protection Acts are readily side-stepped. The Information Commissioner is bound to do whatever it is that modified regulations tell him to do; and the law can be amended expressly to permit whatever is required, which can then comfortingly be said to be conducted subject to data protection rules. We saw this with the Audit Commission's stealthily expanding role.

Sometimes that is not enough, and barriers are swept away peremptorily. The Children's Act 2004, in a single section, simply set aside all common law and statute rules that would stop information being used for what was to become ContactPoint.[23]

But the developing philosophy of government by information

management that I named 'the database state' in 2004 has become
Whitehall orthodoxy without any systematic public debate or
engagement with critics. The underlying conception is of managing
the citizen centrally as a single file, rather than permitting separate
relationships with separate organs of state. There is a technocratic
impatience with mediating institutions such as Parliament and the
rule of law. In this view, information sharing is seen as one-sidedly
good for everyone, as set out very clearly in the long series of official
documents on 'Transformational Government'.[24]

After the HMRC child benefit discs scandal of 2007,[25] information sharing was temporarily discredited. At least in public. So
came about the Thomas-Walport Review,[26] set up by the Ministry
of Justice in order to represent the idea of information sharing in a
friendly light. Its terms of reference required it to:

> ... seek to take account of technological advances and strike a balance
> that ensures appropriate privacy and other safeguards for individu-
> als and society, while enabling sharing information to protect the
> public, increasing transparency, enhancing public service delivery
> as well as the need to minimise the burden on business.

And so it did, giving the Ministry an opportunity to make proposals for general information-sharing powers to be given to ministers,[27]
something that did not in the end get through Parliament.

NO2ID set out its views on the principles of information sharing
in its evidence to the Thomas-Walport Review. Repudiating the
implicit bias of that review, we said:[28]

> There are no intrinsic benefits of data-sharing (which is a name for
> a wide class of processes or acts, not a coherent thing), and we do
> not accept the implied trade-off between individual privacy and any
> generalised social benefit. While all social relationships depend on
> some form of communication of personal information, data-sharing
> is purely ancillary to the relationships and individual or collective
> enterprises it facilitates ... NO2ID regards privacy and personal
> control of personal information as primary goods, interfering with
> which requires specific justification in each case.

The Home Affairs Committee, in its 2008 report, 'A Surveillance Society?' (Fifth Report of Session 2007–08)[29] said much the same thing in more diplomatic language:

> The Government should give an explicit undertaking to adhere to a principle of data minimisation and should resist a tendency to collect more personal information and establish larger databases. Any decision to create a major new database, to share information on databases, or to implement proposals for increased surveillance, should be based on a proven need.

We say that the 'barriers' are not random obstacles. They are principles that have evolved in the courts and been captured in statute precisely because they protect things in human life that are worth protecting. Nothing has changed by the emergence of modern networks and databases to devalue that. Quite the contrary. We need such protections more than ever.

What now?

Meanwhile, though there is a change of government, administration is eternal. 'Transformational Government' has vanished from current official websites. The talk is now of 'Smarter Government'. Yet poke beneath the surface and many of the old centralising tendencies remain. Many of the advocates of broader data-sharing about citizens now talk as if it is a natural concomitant of public information being made available to private individuals that individuals' information should be shared across government.[30] This is an utter non sequitur, a barefaced rhetorical trick.

But the corporate imperative to use personal information willy-nilly for bureaucratic goals has not wavered, and under the shifting jargon, the conception of government as benign guardian of all there is to know about citizens remains.

And not just in Whitehall, in Westminster, too:

Early Day Motion 215: Public Value of the Edited Electoral Register
14.06.2010[31]

That this House believes that the edited electoral register provides very significant social and economic benefits for the UK as a
whole; notes that the edited electoral re[g]ister does this by helping charities to fundraise, helping reunite lost friends and family
(including the 3,000 people found by the Salvation Army), locating
and connecting organ and bone marrow donors, enabling adoption
organisations to find biological parents of adoptive children, and as-
sisting businesses to provide age verification, to reduce credit card
fraud, minimise identity theft, pursue bad debts, repatriate dormant
financial assets to their rightful owners, and support probate; and
opposes all steps which might further significantly restrict access to
or abolish the edited electoral register.

This is hopelessly naive. 'Helping charities to fundraise' means
enabling all sorts of direct mail for good or bad. Missing persons may
have very good reasons for not wishing to be found, as the Salvation
Army itself recognises. Details of your address are so useful to fraudsters (rather than against them), that the financial services industry
devotes a week a year to telling us to shred documents containing
personal details. Spreading any personal information around has
costs as well as benefits, but the cheerleaders for the database state
purblindly insist on focusing only on the rosiest picture of benefits.

It is also true of the public: one of the objections I have grown
used to hearing as a campaigner against the collection and collation
of information under the ID scheme was 'but they already know
everything about you'. No 'they' don't. Or 'they' wouldn't be so
obsessed with knowing more.

I fear a lot of people still think of government as a benign person,
the kindly Big Brother that Winston Smith ended up loving in *1984*.

But, generally speaking, organisations only know about you what
they need to know in order to perform their functions. It is not generally applicable knowledge, as something in your mind is. It lies in

the files, applies to the specific relationship, and is activated only when procedure requires it. That is as it should be.

Those legal 'barriers to information sharing' do inhibit 'them' from using that information for other purposes, or passing it on to third parties who might want to, even if 'they' are abstractly aware of its existence. That, too, is as it should be.

'They' in general *don't* know everything about you. Some of them would like to know more, and are starting to do so. That is not as it should be.

Information is power. It is often said, but it is not quite right. Information is power to the extent that you can use it to exercise power.

The ID scheme is going, for now, but more cumbersome means of compiling ever more indexes to your life are still being pursued. Whitehall is still building the sinews of the database state.

Freedom is a one nation issue

Damian Green MP

Civil liberties used to be a minority interest, largely associated with the left of the political spectrum. It is a sign of how the world has turned that a new centre-right coalition government has made one of its early priorities the restoration of civil liberties we used to take for granted, against the opposition of a Labour Party which seems mysteriously to have forgotten everything it used to know about the importance of freedom in allowing citizens to live a fulfilled life.

Over the last decade we have steadily and unwittingly turned into a surveillance society. Britain used to pride itself on the individual's ability to control his own life, but today our population is more spied upon and controlled than most other democracies. Some of the underlying freedoms which underpin parliamentary democracy were being seriously eroded by the previous government. A functioning National Identity Register would have been the biggest intrusion into the privacy of the British people ever devised, and the first Act of this government will be to make sure it is dismantled.

The Identity Documents Bill marks a significant turning point. It is a clear symbol of the move away from the ideology underpinning Labour's overreaching state control – that government knows best.[32] The ID Cards Scheme was just one example of this. By contrast, the Coalition Agreement between the Conservatives and Liberal Democrats states that 'We share a conviction that the days of big government are over; that centralisation and top-down control have proved a failure ... In short, it is our ambition to distribute power and opportunity to people rather than hoarding authority within government'.[33]

I do not impugn the motives of previous ministers. I believe rather that they misjudged their reaction to the rise of Islamist terrorism and chose the relatively easy route of clamping down on the entire population instead of concentrating on the tiny number who actively wish us harm. The unintended consequence of this was a surveillance state, as the habit of assembling databases and sharing information across government departments became entrenched. The state wanted to provide more security, better public services and a secure personal identity. Instead it made us all potential suspects who cannot be trusted with control of our own identity. We must change this mindset. We may need a smaller state. We certainly need larger citizens, who have more control over their own lives, and more control over the state.

In this essay, I want to explore one reason why it is so vital that we start to rebalance the relationship between the citizen and the state. As a One Nation Conservative, I believe we have a duty to help those who need help, and that such help is the mark of a civilised society. Therefore while we start to reform our society, rolling back the state and enhancing individual liberties, we must ensure that this group of the most disadvantaged also sees the benefits. An essential part of the help we need to give the disadvantaged is the personal space and ability to control their own lives, and freedom from the dictates of a nannying state – adding up to what we call 'civil liberties.' This is counter-intuitive for those who believe that civil liberties are an effete middle-class obsession (see any of David Blunkett's tabloid columns). In fact the most likely victims of the surveillance state are the respectable poor, who will have been spied on throughout their daily lives, and who are not held fit to bring up their own children.

Freedom for all

That there needs to be an alternative to Labour's top-down approach in order to help the most disadvantaged in our society is clear. After years of more and more centralised control, ever more intrusive policing and increased public spending, the result is an underclass dependent on the state yet distanced from their communities. The policy that has been practised in recent years is failing, resulting in today's broken society. One reason for this is that the so-called tough and intrusive measures that the last government introduced often disproportionately affected lower socio-economic groups.

There were an extraordinary number of initiatives targeted on the poor, which were meant to make them more secure. Too many of them failed in that laudable objective, while constricting the freedoms of those they were designed to help.

These included an initiative designed to keep young people out of the court system through pre-court disposal orders, over two hundred thousand of which were issued to young people for first- or second-time minor offences in 2007–08.[34] The Antisocial Behaviour Act 2003 gave police new powers to disperse groups of two or more young people in authorised areas. Home Office records show that in 2006, when Labour's authoritarian tendencies were at their peak, there were over 1,000 designated dispersal zones in England and Wales.[35]

Another controversial measure is stop and search. There were over a million stop and searches of people in 2007–08, with the Metropolitan Police accounting for more than forty per cent of all stop and searches recorded in England and Wales.[36] Some of these were under section 44 for terrorism purposes, which the government's own Independent Reviewer of Terrorism has criticised for being used inappropriately, saying that 'examples of poor or unnecessary use of section 44 abound'.[37]

Britain leads the world in the use of CCTV, with one estimate suggesting there are up to four million cameras in the UK.[38] Almost sixty thousand of these are controlled by local authorities, which equates to one council-owned CCTV camera for every 1000 people in the country. Walking down the street in England a person can be captured on CCTV up to three hundred times in one day.[39]

And our children are on more and more government databases. The largest of those started by Labour, ContactPoint, was set up under the Children's Act 2004 and was designed to hold basic information on all children under eighteen in England. As of last March there were 12.4 million records on ContactPoint with a further 445,000 records in the archive.[40] The coalition government will scrap this database.

An area of concern for me personally is the national DNA database, which holds profiles of almost a million innocent people.[41] In November 2009, the Human Genetics Commission published a report suggesting that police are arresting people just to get their DNA and increase the size of the national DNA database.[42]

And, as is often the case across law enforcement policies, certain groups are especially vulnerable to big-net tactics. More than 400,000 profiles belong to children aged under fifteen.[43] As of November 2008 about 30 per cent of the black population over the age of ten had their DNA retained, and the Home Affairs Select Committee's recent report into this issue concluded that 'it appears that we are moving unwittingly towards a situation where the majority of the black population will have their data stored on the DNA database.'[44]

In its influential judgment on *Marper* v. *United Kingdom*, the European Court of Human Rights expressed concern that 'the policies applied have led to the over-representation in the database of young persons and ethnic minorities, who have not been convicted of any crime.'[45]

The results of this so-called toughness have been widespread failure.

There has been a substantial rise in youth crime, with over a fifth of under-sixteen-year-olds admitting that they committed a crime in the last twelve months, and 30 per cent saying they carried a knife or gun in the same period.[46]

Almost seventy thousand under-eighteens were prosecuted for indictable offences in 2007, accounting for 16.5 per cent of all indictable offence prosecutions. Fifty thousand of these were convicted of an indictable offence, a figure which has been rising since 2003.[47]

There were almost a million violent crimes in the last year for which we have figures, and almost a million people were believed to be the victims of alcohol-related attacks.[48]

And while there may be one surveillance camera for every fourteen people in the UK, figures released by the Metropolitan Police found that prosecutions due to CCTV evidence fell by more than half in the last five years, partly as many images they produce are judged inadmissible in court due to their poor quality.[49]

The effects are also seen in our education system. In the last academic year for which we have figures there were 8,130 permanent exclusions from all schools – a significant number.[50] But look at the figure for fixed period exclusions from state-funded secondary schools – 324,180.[51] Children who are eligible for free school meals are around three times more likely to receive either a permanent or fixed period exclusion than children who are not eligible for free school meals.[52]

We have become a 'walk-on by' society, with Labour's top-down approach to fighting crime tying up the police in red tape and performance targets. A recent report concluded that one result of this is the creation of a nation of 'passive bystanders', with six out of ten people unwilling, for example, to intervene to stop a group of 14-year-old youths vandalising a bus shelter.[53]

Protecting the poor

We have been failing the poor even in the terms preferred by the authoritarians: those who argue that the only freedom that matters is a safer street and neighbourhood. We have not made the poorer neighbourhoods safer, however much we have intruded in the lives of their inhabitants.

We need to be brave and imaginative enough to 'trust the people', if I may resort to an old Tory phrase in these multi-party times. This is an entirely practical attitude. We have all seen how difficult it is for the police to operate effectively when whole communities clam up against them, regarding them instinctively as the enemy. What struck me after my own arrest, and my successful campaign to have my DNA taken off the database after I was cleared, was the anger in the letters that came in from those in a similar position. Former army officers, magistrates, grandmothers in small towns who had never dreamed of offending, were all united in their distrust of the police and the authorities more generally. These are the people we have always thought of as the backbone of respectable society. Alienating them from the law enforcement authorities would be a disaster.

Of course we need to treat the non-criminal majority with the same respect whatever their socio-economic background. One Nation should mean one set of rules for all, and one set of rights for all. Extraordinarily we reached a point under the previous government where this was a controversial view. The argument against this, which is never quite put explicitly, is that this level of freedom and control is impossible for the poor. It is regarded as too risky. If we respond to the breakdown in society that has happened in some parts of the country with a reduction in state control, surely the result will be that the criminal will simply prey ever more easily on the respectable? I think we must challenge this outlook, not just because it is patronising and insulting, but also because it is a

counsel of despair. If we start from the presumption that a significant percentage of our fellow citizens are permanently incapable of
exercising full civic rights, then we will never live in a stable and
relaxed country.

This means we need to restore trust between people themselves,
as well as between individuals and the state. The difficult part of
this – the part that runs counter to conventional wisdom – is that
they cannot demonstrate this trust unless they themselves have
the freedom to express it. If you need CCTV to protect you from
your neighbour or her children, then the CCTV may give you some
short-term relief, except when it's smashed or no one is monitoring
it, but it will not provide long-term confidence that your streets
or your tower block are safe. That only comes when, to use an
old-fashioned working class phrase, everyone is looking out for
everyone else.

The citizen and the state

If we are to start treating people as full citizens, with the full range
of civil liberties, including the right not to be spied on, not to be put
on a database on the off-chance, not to be constantly supervised by
the state's enforcement mechanisms, we, and they, need a bonding
framework. Successful communities have this, as do successful societies. It derives from a sense of mutual responsibility which can only
be exercised as a matter of free choice. You can penalise someone
for dropping litter, if you are prepared to pay for a warden on every
street corner twenty-four hours a day, but you cannot force them to
think, when they leave their front door, what they can do to improve
this area.

Since only truly free people can exercise these responsibilities, we
should ask which freedoms particularly contribute to this instill-
ing of civic responsibility. I believe it is the freedom to make some

decisions about the vital local services which are at the heart of any community.

David Cameron has said that 'where Labour think that an individual's identity consists in being recognised, registered and assisted by the state, Conservatives think that identity is derived through membership in society. Labour thinks that social justice means equality, achieved and guaranteed by government. We think it means community, built and maintained by people themselves.'

For example, the ability to exercise some control over your local school, or at the very least the chance to choose whether it is suitable for your child, is key. Michael Gove's proposals to open up the school network to new entrants are therefore not just an educational step forward, but a contribution to freedom and civic responsibility.

Similarly, we should give more power to local communities to decide on the buildings that surround them. Not just the number of houses but the design priorities of the estate. The rat runs that we used to build on council estates were never popular with the people that lived there. Nor was the idea of parking cars out of sight. The people who live in an area should be trusted to run their own children's leisure facilities. They really care about them. They should be enabled to have a much greater input into the local policing priorities.

On top of that proposition I argue the need for personal and community empowerment. What we need is to help the formation of self-run bodies by independent people. Self-policing is the best and most effective policing. Problems like vandalism and graffiti which so enrage people are most likely to be minimised if the buildings, the flower beds, the very streets feel as though they belong to the whole local community. If your children have planted the bulbs or painted the community centre, they are less likely to damage them in a fit of bored rebellion.

The database state

Away from the streets, the previous government was also assiduous in narrowing the extent of individual freedom. In particular it wanted as much information as it could assemble on databases. Worse, it wanted the right to use that information as it saw fit, without any agreement from the citizen affected.

A sensible regime would insist on a test of consent which would ensure that you have explicitly approved of what is being done with your private information. The notion of 'implied consent' (such as is being used in NHS databases) which means that unless you explicitly withdraw from a system it is assumed that you agree to your information being available to all is a dangerous nonsense. Private companies have to make you agree explicitly to them using your information. It is if anything more important that the state should have to go through similar hurdles before using it.

Above all we must change our mindset. Just because technology has transformed the way government can use personal information does not mean that a sensible government will take that choice. In all eras of technology, the principle that the state should serve the citizen and not vice versa is a good one. The bigger the capacity to collect and share information, the greater danger there is to privacy, and therefore to freedom. Instead of gun-toting revolutionaries, modern freedom fighters are likely to be wholly peaceful and respectable. Some may even be a little geeky, as the geeks know what goes on behind the screens that now control so much of our daily lives. It is time for the freedom fighters of the world to fight back against the controlling state.

Free the people

None of this is politically easy or obvious. It is much easier to make the intellectually lazy argument that if you have nothing to hide you have nothing to fear. This argument rests on two fallacies. The first is that the state is generally benevolent and competent, and can be trusted more than voluntary or commercial organisations. Nothing in the history of big government argues that this is the case. The second is that secrecy and privacy are the same thing. It is perfectly reasonable to want to keep aspects of your life private even if there is no guilty secret you are trying to hide.

Nevertheless there will always be a market for those who want to talk tough and argue that diminishing the freedom of the individual, especially the disadvantaged individual who may well be inarticulate and inexperienced in the ways of the state, is a price worth paying for safer streets. I would argue instead that it does not make the streets safer in the long term, and the destruction of individual freedom and control leads to a weaker society, diminished communities and constricted lives. We need to have the courage to set people free.

Powers of entry to private property

Harry Snook

> *The poorest man may in his cottage bid defiance to all the forces of the Crown. It may be frail, its roof may shake; the wind may blow through it; the storm may enter, the rain may enter – but the King of England cannot enter; all his force dares not cross the threshold of the ruined tenement. – William Pitt the Elder (1708–1778)*

The state of the law surrounding forcible entry to private domestic premises is about as close to an uncontroversial topic as one can find within the broader subject of state–citizen relations. The lack of debate is occasioned not by any merit in the current position, but rather by the fact that the eclectic collection of powers involved constitutes such an unmitigated mess that almost nobody believes it can be left alone without reform. The necessity for the law of entry to be clear, concise and comprehensible is universally acknowledged and does not require subscription to any particular philosophy of government or civil liberties: just as one need not be a statist to appreciate that the executive may sometimes need urgent access to the private domain, equally one need not be a libertarian in order to insist that the rules be clear and that the regime make sense.

In the course of this chapter we shall briefly describe three respects in which the current law is unsatisfactory: firstly the great prevalence of these powers both in number and in the frequency of their exercise, secondly their lack of a single legal underpinning and consequent bewildering diversity in form, and finally the alarmingly broad and sweeping nature of some of the provisions in question.

We shall also scan the present and peer into the future for any signs of hope of reform, and touch upon what form this might take.

First though we must define what we mean by a 'power of entry' in the context of a private dwelling. At its simplest, the phrase refers to a provision of statute law that gives to a class of persons the power to enter the dwelling when they would not otherwise be allowed to do so. Usually, though not in all cases, the persons in question will be employees of a public body, most likely a local authority. In other cases they may be employed by a private company fulfilling a public function, for example gas or electricity engineers. Finally, they may be agents seeking to take control of goods in satisfaction of unpaid debts.

By entering without permission, we mean that the entry can be carried out by force – to be blunt, kicking down the door – if the owner or occupier fails to allow access. Sometimes this may legitimately be an act of first rather than last resort, particularly if the object of the entry would be defeated by the seeking of permission.

Little explanation is required of how significant such powers are in turning what would otherwise be an actionable trespass into the execution of a lawful right. Where they apply, they abrogate the distinction between the private and the public space, subordinating the right of the citizen to privacy in his home to some greater public end. Whilst any rational person would recognise that such setting-aside of the usual boundaries is sometimes appropriate – indeed, on occasion, vital – it must nonetheless be acknowledged that the civic cost of the act must make it all the more important that the relevant law be properly configured. It also follows that we should be concerned to monitor the number of such powers in force, and the frequency of their exercise.

In April 2007, while researching a paper for the Centre for Policy Studies,[54] I identified a total of 266 separate statutory powers permitting entry into a private home, having their source in both primary and secondary legislation. It is a function of the absence of any underlying legal framework for powers of entry that the figure arrived at is somewhat subjective. It does not, for example, include those powers which are theoretically exercisable over private dwellings but which would require such an unlikely concatenation of circumstances that one can confidently expect them never to be so used. It does not include those powers that are exercisable over 'private premises' only where these are *not* used as a dwelling. Where a power is created by Act of Parliament, it counts only this one act of creation, and not the numerous regulations or ministerial orders that authorise the use of the already-created power by particular bodies in particular circumstances. By adjusting any of these criteria, in particular the last, one could easily arrive at totals far in excess of 266, although at some cost in terms of conceptual precision.

In any event, the conservative figure of 266 is already far in excess of that which most people would give if asked to estimate how many different exceptions have been created to the general rule that their home is private. By the time one has mentally counted off the police, fire brigade, customs, child protection officers, and three sorts of utilities companies, one is still only in double figures, even allowing for each to benefit from multiple separate powers. It is no surprise therefore that amongst the spreading panoply of statutory entry provisions falling outside these predictable categories, contributing both to their number and to their bewildering diversity, one finds not only the obscure but also the humorous, and occasionally the downright bizarre. In 1952 for example, Parliament saw fit to confer upon the police a power to enter private premises – including the home – in pursuance of their duty to prevent and investigate improper acts of hypnotism. Forced entry to effect the cleansing of 'verminous persons' is authorised by a 74-year-old law still in force. And in 1998, Parliament provided for searches of private dwellings to locate evidence of a nuclear device being constructed or detonated. al-Qaeda agents planning to obstruct any such entry should be warned: a fine of up to £5,000 could follow.

A brief foray through the scores of other such laws still in force reveals powers related to endangered seals, landmines, television licences, 'foreign bees', drink-driving a tube train, violent comic books, illicit milk, bingo, porn, fireplaces, bedroom sizes, archaeology, hosepipes, high hedges, shopping trolleys, overgrown trees and trading with Libya.

It is tempting to assume from the obscurity of some of the purposes for which entry powers are provided that they amount to little more than museum pieces, serving only to broaden the spines of legal textbooks and having little to do with the average citizen's experience of privacy in his own home. However, a Freedom of Information Act request to the Department of Environment, Food and Rural Affairs revealed that the power under the Bees Act 1980 was used 3,190 times in England alone during 2006. One can dismiss the notion that the 266 powers identified in 2007 represent two dozen realities and two hundred curiosities. The greater the number of powers on the statute books, the greater the number of occasions on which the public/private boundary is crossed.

But how did the law of entry come to be in this state? Like so many aspects of British law surrounding the state and its citizens, it is an accident borne out of a failure to adapt eighteenth-century principles (highly advanced for their time) to the realities of subsequent eras. Specifically, the root cause is the operation of the principle that the state has no general power to enter a private dwelling, but can employ only those which the law specifically provides in the circumstances in which it provides them. At the time when the key statements of this principle were made – the seminal case of *Entick* v. *Carrington* in 1765, the words of William Pitt that began this chapter – this was cutting-edge civil rights theory. In an era that has been described as the Age of Absolutism in reference to the autocratic monarchies of continental Europe, the notion that the state was so constrained to what the law specifically permitted was both radical and reliable, affording the citizen a very clear yardstick against which to measure the propriety of any proposed entry into his home.

However, the efficacy of this model was largely dependent on the fact that an eighteenth-century state had very few reasons why it would wish to enter the private homes of its citizens, or why it would be expected to. The state might collect taxes, it might billet troops, and it might seek out and arrest those who were its enemies, but it did very little else that might bring it across the threshold. It did not monitor pollution. It did not survey endangered species. It did not – unfortunately for some – enforce workplace safety.

Beginning in the late nineteenth century and accelerating dramatically in the middle decades of the twentieth, the state's role expanded dramatically to encompass responsibilities that the jurists of the *Entick* v. *Carrington* era could never have contemplated, from public and individual health to education, environment, housing, social security and all manner of other duties that were laid at its door. It is scarcely surprising, given the vastly increased breadth and depth of the interaction between state and citizen over the past century, that the number of circumstances in which an exception to the general rule of privacy must be made has also multiplied. If a dozen powers were all that were needed to discharge the responsibilities attributed to the state in the 1760s, then the number of current provisions begins to seem almost modest when one considers the increased workload that it has taken on since that date.

A further source of increase has been the insertion into English law of entry powers whose origins lie not in the deliberations of Parliament but in the decisions of the European Union or the United Nations. Two particular pieces of UK legislation, the United Nations Act 1946 and the European Communities Act 1972, function as 'gateways' through which these external, supranational bodies can give domestic legal effect to their resolutions. The medium through which this integration of laws is effected is secondary legislation – i.e. orders and regulations – issued by either the Queen in Council under the United Nations Act or the Secretary of State under the European Communities Act. Such statutory instruments can and do contain powers of entry to private dwellings. This 'gateway' situation is distinct from that where a minister makes an order under a conventional British statute: in the latter case, the secondary legislation merely *applies* a power already approved by Parliament in the primary legislation itself, while in the former, it *creates* a new right of entry of which there is no mention or reflection in the Act of Parliament under which the regulations are made.

The number of dwelling-entry powers brought into British law through these gateways is relatively small: twelve under the European Communities Act and ten under the United Nations Act when counted in 2007. But they are significant not only in the contribution that they make to the overall total but also in that they have come in 'under the radar', compromising the protective effect of a system where Parliament individually scrutinised and approved each proposed statutory entry power.

The early jurists' insistence on specificity, on the absence of a general power of entry and the gradual addition of exceptions to the presumption on a case-by-case basis, was the eighteenth-century citizen's gain and his twentieth-century descendant's loss. Where once it provided certainty by establishing a general rule of privacy, now it prevents certainty by making each of the now-numerous exceptions to that rule individual and unpredictable. Since they are separately provided in many different Acts of Parliament drafted by many different hands, they vary wildly in their terms.

Some statutory entry powers require that an officer seeking to enter a dwelling give notice to the occupier, but whether the period of notice is twenty-four hours, seven days, 28 days or whatever other period Parliament happened to alight on varies erratically from Act to Act. Others require no notice to be given at all, or provide for notice to be withheld in appropriate circumstances. Some powers cannot be exercised with force unless a magistrate (or sometimes a judge) has issued the appropriate warrant, while others authorise force without this safeguard. Still others omit to mention the use of force at all, leaving it to the courts to find it authorised by implication. Some powers require the officer exercising them to identify himself to the occupier, others do not. Some, though not all, provide that it is a criminal offence to obstruct a person exercising them, but what is the penalty for such a transgression? A fine of two hundred pounds? Five hundred? Five thousand? Six months in jail or two years? Each provision is different.

The critical problem with this diversity is that it leaves the citizen at a loss to understand what the rules are regarding how, when and by whom his home can be entered, and what he can do to stop it. Whilst the officers exercising the power can be expected to know its terms, those on the receiving end would have to engage in an exercise of legal research to arrive at the same understanding. A citizen cannot possibly hope to understand whether the state is breaking the law if he does not know what the law is. And for those experiencing the intrusion of the state into their private space, it is simple, clear and universal rules, rather than hundreds of separate provisions, that will afford the greatest assistance in understanding and reacting to the situation.

It is fair to say that within this diversity there is a rough correlation between the 'severity' of an entry power, that is to say the extent to which it might have severe consequences for the householder, and the restrictions imposed upon its exercise by the Act of Parliament that creates it. Generally speaking, the more serious the misconduct that the officers are hoping to discover, or the more intrusive the search is likely to be, the more rigorous the safeguards in terms of the need for a warrant, the seniority of the judge granting it, and, where appropriate, the period of notice given. Unfortunately this correlation is imperfect and there are some worrying 'outliers'.

Chief amongst the anomalous powers is the 'Writ of Assistance', a powerful sort of long-term search warrant held by certain officers of HM Revenue & Customs. The Writ allows its holder to bypass the normal safeguards on the behaviour of customs officials, who are otherwise required to obtain a warrant from a Justice of the Peace (JP) before effecting a forcible entry to a dwelling. A Writ of Assistance is not limited to a specific investigation or purpose, but can be used whenever it is considered necessary by HMRC managers. It is not time-limited, but is valid for the entirety of the reign of the monarch in which it is issued, potentially a period of many decades. An officer holding such a writ can break into a private house in order to seize any goods which he believes are liable to be forfeited to Her Majesty's Revenue & Customs (HMRC), without justifying this action to any independent judicial authority beforehand.

Such is the potential for arbitrary and oppressive use of this astonishingly broad power that the newly-independent United States of America prohibited Writs of Assistance in their Constitution. Some two and a quarter centuries later, the British Parliament also decided it was time the issue was dealt with. It made only a gesture in the Finance Act 2000 however, providing that an officer with a Writ of Assistance should normally still obtain a JP's warrant, unless the goods to be seized are likely to be removed, destroyed or lost before this can be done. However, the decision on whether this 'danger' is so great that entry should be forced without the permission of a JP is left to the officer holding the writ. The so-called restriction therefore amounts to little more than an admonition that such an officer should ask first, if he thinks he can spare the time.

Perhaps the most troubling aspect of the Writ of Assistance is how poorly its exercise is documented. Whilst DEFRA is meticulous in logging its inspection of beehives, HMRC only carries out a 'statistical exercise' once every twenty-five years or so. The last time it was conducted, in 2004–05, 102 uses of the Writs were recorded.

A second example of an overblown entry power – and a telling case of authority making life easy for itself when nobody is paying attention – is that contained in the Transmissible Spongiform Encephalopathies Regulations 2006. This secondary legislation, made under the European Communities Act 1972, aims to detect and prevent the spread of BSE, or 'mad cow disease', and achieved some notoriety when it was used with ridiculous disproportion against a family's pet cow kept well out of the food chain.[55] The power is exercisable by force, without a warrant, by an unlimited number of officers and an optional accompanying European Union official, at any time they deem reasonable. It is applicable to domestic premises. It is a criminal offence to obstruct the exercise of the power, punishable by a £5,000 fine and up to two years in prison. On the other hand, the officers themselves benefit from a blanket legal immunity in respect of anything they do in the exercise – or, amazingly, even the *purported* exercise – of their powers.

The existence of powers of this nature demonstrates clearly that reform is well overdue: there is no point in trusting Parliament to craft limited, specific exceptions to the general principle of privacy if the result is as described. As I argued in 2007, the time has surely come to put *all* existing and future powers of entry on a single footing, providing a simple and consistent underlying framework to regulate notice periods, warrants, numbers of officers involved and the sanctions for obstruction. This would not in any way create a general power at large for government to enter the home, and nor, for the same reason, would it reduce the overall numbers of entry powers on the statute books. It would, however, deal with their incomprehensible diversity and eradicate the excesses of those that are currently drafted too broadly and generously to officialdom, including the freakish Writ of Assistance.

In September 2007, shortly after the issue of entry powers had attained some prominence in the media, the then Prime Minister Gordon Brown gave a speech at the University of Westminster in which he undertook to lead the writing of a 'new chapter in the story of British liberties'. He referred explicitly to entry powers, acknowledging that there were 'at least 250' of them and promising that there would be efforts to harmonise police powers and offer 'guidance' on the exercise of others.

Regrettably, no significant steps were taken in this regard, and the sole quantifiable development in the law of entry was the addition of a modest contingent of further powers to the existing total.

There is, however, real hope for the institution of a single code of conduct for the exercise of entry powers. The Conservative peer, Lord Selsdon, has for some years been pressing the issue with a determination and tenacity matched only by his courtesy and good humour. His Powers of Entry Etc. Bill, which would regulate not only those powers exercisable over dwellings but those relating to all private premises, passed its third reading in the House of Lords on 6 April 2010. It proposes an eminently sensible and workable set of rules, easily understood and remembered, which would do nothing to detract from the efficacy of local government or the availability of immediate entry in emergencies, but which would constitute an enormous improvement in the consistency and clarity of the law. It would give every citizen a more than even chance of being aware at least of the basic rules involved when an officer claims to be entitled to enter, regardless of the obscurity or novelty of the statutory provision under which he is acting.

The general election of May 2010 interposed before the Bill could reach the Commons, but it has already come further and gained more support than in any of its previous incarnations. If the new government chooses to facilitate its passage into law, it will not only begin to acquire for itself a reputation as a reforming administration, but will earn the gratitude of all householders – not just the verminous and the hypnotic – for a simple but meaningful improvement to their sense of freedom.

Is the bully state on the run?

Brian Monteith

The Nanny State is long dead in Britain and much of the Western World. Not because we are now free of it, but because it has been replaced by the Bully State – a more insidious, more sinister and more dangerous deviant of patriarchal state compassion.

In October 2009 my book *The Bully State – The End of Tolerance* attempted to capture, chronicle and explain the growth of the Nanny State and how it had metamorphosed into the Bully State – not just in Britain but across the developed world.

I charted the growth of well-meaning public health campaigns, and how they had turned from preventing communicable diseases towards controlling people's lifestyles through what they eat, drink or inhale. I described how concern for health and safety protection – driven by politicians addicted to intervening on our behalf and a growing political correctness that demonised opponents of people who 'knew what was good for us' – had seen the Nanny State inexorably grow.

The difference between nanny and bully is simply demonstrated by the change from the voluntary use of seat belts to their enforcement by law, punishable with a fine and points on your driving licence. Gone are the adverts telling you to use seat belts for your own good but leaving you to ultimately decide – replaced by the criminalisation of the potential victim.

Once the results from the laws proved disappointing, as they usually did, so greater enforcement was justified and adopted, more rules were dreamt up until what had started as the gentle guidance, the mild remonstration of Nanny, became the full force of law that would criminalise people for previously normal behaviour.

Thus compulsory seat belt laws that made no measureable difference to total fatalities or injuries were extended to the back seats of cars; smoking bans were expanded until they covered not just public spaces but private spaces too, such as people's own cars if they used them to work; terrorism laws were used to police householders disposing of their rubbish without separating it for recycling, and foods were banned, such as Marmite in school breakfast clubs, to fight the epidemic of obesity that was a creation of junk science in the first place.

Since 2009 a great many laws, regulations and powers have been passed (but few repealed) and many politicians have come and gone. The most significant development in the United Kingdom has been the May general election of 2010 that has seen the Labour governments of Tony Blair and Gordon Brown finally removed from office and a new coalition government formed by the Conservatives of David Cameron and the Liberal Democrats of Nick Clegg.

Does this change mean that the Bully State is dead, that the bullies have been removed from the playground and we might be free to do as we wish – or at least have Nanny back telling us where we are going wrong?

The message so far is mixed, with some good and some disappointing announcements. Before one becomes too optimistic it is necessary to remember that both the Conservatives and the Liberal Democrats have their own policies that lead to nannying or bullying the public – maybe the bully has simply changed the colour of the school tie but kept the jackboots?

It was the Conservatives who, after all, invented the phrase 'nanny state' when Ian McLeod MP wrote about it in *The Spectator* in 1965; and it was the Conservatives who introduced under Edward Heath the compulsory use of crash helmets and under Margaret Thatcher confirmed the seat belt law that Labour had introduced.

Within a month of coming to power David Cameron announced that he was appointing Lord Young of Graffham, one of Margaret Thatcher's favourite ministers, to hold a government-wide review of health and safety laws with particular emphasis on reducing the compensation culture. Speaking to the BBC after the announcement, Lord Young had his own legislative intervention to offer – the banning of advertisements for personal injury compensation claims by lawyers.

So, rather than tackle the cause (the health and safety regulations) Lord Young chose to tackle the symptom (the compensation culture), suggesting a further regulation that would be a restriction to trade from what is meant to be a business-friendly government fighting a deep recession.

Lord Young has apparently been working on such a review for the Conservative Party since December 2009 and presumably he must have been taking soundings from business. His first comments were to say he wanted to restore 'common sense' and that he was looking at the regulation of office working environments, commenting, 'I don't think offices are dangerous places.' (*Daily Telegraph*, 15 June). Speaking to the BBC Lord Young said health and safety was very important but had been made a 'joke' because it had been extended into areas that 'frankly are not dangerous', citing restaurants that had banned toothpicks on safety grounds and contestants in a pancake race who had been told to walk, not run, because of rain.

As could be expected, the British media went to town trawling up entertaining examples of conkers being banned in school playgrounds unless children wear goggles and the like, but it remains to be seen whether Lord Young will stop any of these ridiculous bans whilst restricting lawyers from seeking perfectly normal business.

In advance of the election the Conservatives had responded to our growing grumpiness at being pushed around with their offer to create a Big Society where we are invited to take more of a responsibility in the community. Fair enough if it means we have a say in what is imposed upon us, but it appears completely at odds with another proposal to rename the health ministry the Department of Public Health, which may seem a mere trifle but is Orwellian in conception – and revealing.

It suggests that David Cameron has swallowed the conceit that our bodies belong to society and that in the name of prevention his Big Society can tell the English (but not the rest of the UK) what to eat, drink, smoke and drive. If Cameron's big society and Brown's big government have one thing in common it is that they are both big!

The Conservative promise to abolish the NHS Summary Care Database – a policy also of the Liberal Democrats – was abandoned within weeks of taking power and announced through a written answer. It was as if the old sly bullying government had not changed.

Other Conservative proposals such as subsidising all families (as opposed to helping those that are poor) and helping all people who chose to be married are in their own way just another form of nannying by using the coercive power of the state to redistribute wealth from one group to another. And not necessarily from rich to poor but from, say, poor single mums who work and pay taxes or poor unmarried couples with children towards wealthy married couples who may have no children. Subsidising marriage for its own sake by the power of law is Tory bullying.

There is no doubt in my mind that the defeat of Labour was good news, for the coalition can now deliver on their mutual commitment to end the UK's adoption of an identity card and all the database systems that would operate with it. We cannot, however, relax in the assumption that the argument has been won – would one serious terrorist incident with the loss of lives in Britain bring about a change of heart from Cameron or Clegg?

While the defence of civil liberties has always been a prominent refrain from the Liberal Democrats, the party has in the past advocated just as intrusive public health interventions as Labour, revealing to all of us Nick Clegg's confusion over personal rights. Thus we have an incoherent Conservative Party embracing an even more incoherent Liberal Democrat Party – is it possible to expect anything other than an incoherent coalition government?

Another plan that appears to have crashed and burned following Labour's defeat was its hope of changing the restriction on alcohol levels for drink driving from 80 mg in 100 ml of blood to 50 mg. Labour Transport Secretary Lord Adonis had commissioned a report by academic Sir Peter North, who produced fifty-one recommendations after the election was held. Needless to say those behind the change to 50 mg, including Sir Peter, actually want 20 mg as the eventual limit (effectively zero as the law has to allow for natural levels of alcohol that may occur without alcohol consumption).

North argued that 50 mg would still allow people to have a pint of beer, but has clearly forgotten that beers come in different strengths. The likelihood is that to avoid doubt punters just won't drink to avoid breaking the law (achieving the real agenda), putting further pressure on precarious pubs. Meanwhile the evidence shows that those breaking the law are usually well over the limit and the difference between 50 mg and 80 mg would not deter them. In other words it would be a lot more effort for police, great inconvenience for moderate drinkers and economically costly, without achieving the desired effect.

More insidiously the report also backed random breath tests – a policy unofficially and illegally adopted by many British police forces. The random stopping of motorists removes the presumption of innocence that all Britons are entitled to, but why let an age-old right get in the way of trying to improve conviction rates – even though it actually makes policing far less efficient as countless innocent drivers are held up and tested? Fortunately the Conservative Transport Secretary, Phillip Hammond, was quick to make it known he would not necessarily take up North's recommendations.

(*Scottish Daily Express & Scottish Daily Mail*, 17 June 2010). We shall have to wait and see.

Another chink of bright light was the fact that disgraced Labour MP Nigel Griffiths (the *News of the World* revealed how he had entertained a prostitute in his Commons office) decided not to seek re-election. This was the same Nigel Griffiths who tried to ban any adverts of foods using cartoon characters or celebrities such as Tony the Tiger or the Honey Monster on the grounds that it encouraged obesity. Good riddance to a politician willing to meddle with our Sugar Puffs. On the downside the defeat of Lembit Opik meant the loss of a defender of individual rights – it remains to be seen if his Conservative replacement will be as robust in supporting an individual's right to smoke.

On balance individual politicians come and go, however, and of greater concern should be the willingness of the government of the day to take matters in hand and begin to reverse the growth of state intervention in our social activities.

Although in this post-devolution age Cameron's and Clegg's policies in areas such as health and policing are designed essentially for England they should not be dismissed as irrelevant to others. In public health and behavioural engineering what is introduced in one country is usually gazumped by a neighbouring one. Such is the competition between politicians for fame and glory that there is no idea too bad or too destructive that it cannot be advocated in a yet more malign and malicious form in another jurisdiction – the Bully State has discovered globalisation.

In Europe the first comprehensive smoking ban in public places started in Ireland, where the politicians seized the opportunity for their nation to take the credit for having the most restrictive policy. Having seen that it could be delivered in Ireland – despite its famed pub culture – Scottish politicians scrambled to adopt it with greater force, using the new powers bestowed upon their devolved parliament. Soon the policy travelled south to England and Wales despite the then Labour government's manifesto saying that any restrictions would be limited only to places that served food and certainly would not include clubs.

Soon such policies were being considered across the rest of Europe and the rest of the world, with conferences being held in Scotland and Brussels to discuss how to swap tactics and establish 'best practice' – meaning that any new enforcement by one authority could be spread like bushfire to another.

Bravely some countries resisted the tide, with notable exemptions allowing smoking rooms or even smoking bars in countries such as Germany, Italy and Spain. Still, as I have seen with my own eyes in Trinidad and Tobago, where I worked for all of 2009, the pressure from the United Nation's World Health Organization is irresistible. Developing countries believe that one way of showing they are an advanced nation worthy of a seat at all the top tables is to introduce smoking bans – even though they are often only symbolic. In Trinidad the climate dictates that most people drink socially in the open air, often standing outside a bar with a bottle of Carib or Stag 'liming' with their friends, a lit cigarette in hand. Inside, the hot and sticky bar is empty but smoking is banned. How pointless but how 'First World'.

The same is happening with alcohol taxes, as they are hiked up around the globe – as I witnessed in Botswana even though displays of public drunkenness are rare.

While the globalisation of bullying shows that not only do we have to win the argument in Britain and then export it – just as privatisation of state corporations and the move to freer markets was exported after the defeat of communism in the 1980s – so we have to ensure that the bullying of our lives at a local level is also halted and reversed. The UK's devolved administrations, the Scottish Parliament, the Welsh Assembly and the Northern Ireland Assembly all are keen to carry on regardless of any UK change in mood and the local authorities beneath them are also unrelenting in believing they can push us around.

The Scottish Parliament at Holyrood remains one of the proudest defenders of bullying in Britain. Anyone who hoped that the replacement of the Labour/Liberal Democrat coalition by the Scottish Nationalists would lead to a flowering of individual freedom should have been given a straightjacket and committed, for the SNP's policies in opposition were, if anything, worse – and so the reality has proven with an SNP government.

Having been in the vanguard of Scotland's smoking ban the SNP has been leading the crusade in favour of minimum pricing of alcohol units, and despite some defeats in Parliament the 'Tartan Taliban', as the SNP is known to many, remains demonically committed to this position. Typically the SNP is being coy about what the minimum price would be – suggesting that it might be only 40p per unit – but all the professional advocates are calling for the price to be at least 50p if not 60p per unit. The reason for this is simple: at 40p per unit the cost of whisky and other spirits in the supermarket will generally not be affected, being just £10.50 for own-brand gin, but at 60p it goes up to £15.75, while Famous Grouse whisky would be £16.80 – well above what supermarkets charge currently.

Scotland not only produces £800 million worth of whisky a year, but is also responsible for distilling, bottling and packaging some 80 per cent of the UK's gin and vodka, including well known brands such as Gordon's, Tanquery and Smirnoff. The distilling industry argues that if the producing country of these drinks introduces a new price intervention then it will be a green light for other countries to up their taxes and import duties, hitting production and costing jobs.

The drink that receives the most opprobrium from Scottish politicians is, however, a tonic wine produced by monks in Devon called Buckfast – or Buckie in the colloquial slang. The sweetish sherry-like alcoholic drink, which includes caffeine, is a favourite of adolescents looking for a quick high and the detritus of empty bottles of Buckie can easily be found on the soulless barren council estates of west central Scotland. Ironically Buckfast is not cheap, selling at about £7.00 a bottle, so would not be affected by minimum pricing even if the rate is set at 60p. This suggests that the policy is about politicians being seen to be doing something even if it has no impact, and will ultimately require further political intervention – illustrating yet again that once the bullies have an idea in their mind they will not let the evidence get in the way.

The Tartan Taliban is concerned with more than tobacco and alcohol, having introduced an amendment into its own Criminal Justice Bill that will give local councils the powers to limit the number of lap dancing clubs in their area. (*Scottish Daily Express,* 17 June 2010). The aim of the supporters of this prurient paternalism is of course to set the limit at zero.

The proposed ban may yet be resisted after the intervention of Sara Vernon, who tabled a submission to Parliament on behalf of the International Union of Sex Workers saying, 'demand for this form of entertainment will not disappear. Closure of current adult entertainment venues will drive the practice into unlicensed venues, hotel rooms and domestic premises, greatly increasing the risk to dancers' safety.' Ms Vernon might be expected to know what she's talking about, as she wrote a 90,000-word PhD on striptease and strip club culture, including seven years as a 'participant-observer' (*Scottish Daily Express,* 17 June 2010).

After so many years of political correctness and holier-than-thou condescension that Scotland can show the English, the ideas are not restricted to the politicians but seep out from the pores of officials too. The Scottish government's quango Transport Scotland actually wants to stop construction workers on the new Forth Bridge from swearing whilst working on site (Dorothy-Grace Elder, *Scottish Daily Express,* 10 June 2010). It has told bidders for the contract that their workers 'will not use foul language'. This might seem a tad unrealistic on most building sites but who is going to enforce such a rule 300 feet up on the top of a column? The same Transport Scotland also has decreed that noise should be kept to a minimum so that the construction work does not upset the fish. Clearly some people have too much time on their hands – including some in local government.

In Edinburgh the city council is telling local pubs that they will be forced to close if they do not meet new building standards regulations that it interprets as requiring the same number of toilets for women as for men. The law states that there has to be one toilet for every thirty patrons, but Edinburgh Council has decided to assume an equality of 50/50 between male and female customers, so a bar with a capacity of 180 people will be required to have three toilets for ninety women.

The result is that some bars frequented almost exclusively by men will have to install additional toilets for ladies who never show up. The alternative is to have their legal capacity cut to fit the number of toilets – this would mean a bar with one existing ladies' toilet would not be able to have more than sixty customers even though its capacity might be three times that number and it has enough urinals and WCs for that many men. Many pubs are saying this will be the last straw that will put them out of business.

Are there women writing to the papers complaining about a shortage of toilets? Are they marching on the city council offices demanding action? No. If there are any complaints at all I imagine they are about the sanitation standards rather than the quantity of toilets. The council has the power to relax the regulation just as Glasgow did in 2009 but Edinburgh is unrelenting in its bullying of pubs. Previously it tried to limit the number of customers who would be allowed to stand in an effort to stop people buying rounds of drinks, backing down only after a public outcry (*Edinburgh Evening News*, 8 April 2010).

As I argued in my book, once one politician introduces a ban others rush to emulate it – a sort of herd instinct is adopted as politicians think, 'oh, we can do this too!' So, following Boris Johnson's ban on booze on the London Underground, we now have Scottish doctors arguing for an alcohol ban on all public transport across Britain. They have submitted a motion to the BMA's annual conference in Brighton saying such a ban will encourage more people to use public transport. This sounds like the same argument that banning smoking would lead to more people using pubs – a falsehood that we can now all see for ourselves.

Of course the fact that many people prefer to travel by train precisely so they can have a civilised drink on a long journey could mean that a ban would result in people returning to their cars – the exact opposite of the desired effect. The doctors did not specify if public transport included airlines but given that trains, ferries and coaches were included and are mostly privately operated, the ban could include long-haul flights too. Despite the lack of any evidence that there is a problem with alcohol on public transport this idea will be picked up by and become the latest cause célèbre for some politicians (*Scottish Daily Mail*, 17 June 2010).

So as we peruse the landscape, be it British, European, international or just down at the end of the street, there is some good news and some bad, or at least disappointing.

The issue is global and in the USA matters are likely to take a turn for the worst while Obama is in power, as he tries to extend the scope of federal government, especially in healthcare. This can only mean federal government taking an even greater interest in how individual American citizens live their lives. In the rest of the world the influence of the UN (WHO) and the EU is significant in driving developing countries towards bullying like the donor nations – it won't be hard to encourage them, for bullying has always been the natural disposition of military juntas and single party states.

The British government parties are incoherent in their approach and in partnership likely to be more so; while some aspects of the Bully State, such as ID cards, are in retreat, others, such as minimum alcohol pricing, are still on the horizon and new ones such as the Big Society are being developed. Meanwhile at a local level the bullying by devolved administrations and councils carries on unabated and generally unchallenged.

But still my glass remains half full. We should see the new coalition government as an opportunity – a chance to fill the vacuum of ideas and to win arguments all over again. We may not repeal some laws but we can begin to erode them at the margins by, for instance, licensing smoking rooms in pubs so long as they meet stringent air quality standards. That way we can have choice and that is all we ask – to be at liberty to make the informed decision for ourselves.

Where we do win, where we have made gains, it is because we have embarrassed, ridiculed and defeated the forces of control, often by groups across the political spectrum working together in single-issue campaigns or by convincing one of the parties it is to their advantage to change tack.

By raising the volume of debate and better co-ordinating the forces of true liberalism we can win small victories that, like Mao's long march, can lead to us to eventual victory.

Freedom and liberty under the coalition

Philip Johnston

Will the cause of individual freedom and liberty be advanced under the coalition after suffering so grievously at the hands of Labour over the past thirteen years?

To quote the former Chinese Foreign Minister Chou en-Lai, when asked what he thought had been the historical impact of the French Revolution, 'it is a little too early to tell'. We just don't know yet. But the auspices are excellent. They have made a good start. In fact, you only have to look at the list of measures lined up for repeal by the coalition to appreciate the full extent of the legislative lunacy we have witnessed over the past fifteen years.

It is also an indication of how the benchmark against which we measure our freedoms has altered compared to just twenty or even fifteen years ago. For instance:

- the fingerprinting of schoolchildren will be forbidden without parental permission (it is hard to believe it was even allowed, but it has become commonplace);
- the protection of historic freedoms through the defence of trial by jury;
- other than in exceptional circumstances, the DNA of innocent people will not be added to the criminal database;
- rights to non-violent protest will be restored;
- safeguards introduced to prevent the misuse of anti-terrorism legislation;

- a brake applied on the creation of new criminal offences, of which Labour managed to produce an additional 3,000 in thirteen years;
- further regulation of CCTV;
- ending the storage of internet and email records without good reason.

It is extraordinary to think that few of these existed at all before 1997, but let's not stop there. The vetting and barring scheme to be administered by the new Independent Safeguarding Authority, which will affect nine million people from this autumn, needs to be scrapped, as do many aspects of the Licensing Act 2003.

There is also an ominous silence about the promised free vote on the restoration of foxhunting, though it may well be the case that reversing the ban would not get through Parliament. And it is disappointing that Nick Clegg (a self-confessed secret puffer), who is in charge of this process, has ruled out amending the smoking ban. A simple revision would allow some landlords to designate their pubs as either smoking or non-smoking establishments, giving people – including staff – the choice of where to drink and work.

One perverse outcome of the ban, which was, after all, supposed to protect vulnerable people from the effect of passive smoking, is that many adults now stay at home to smoke, thereby afflicting their children with fumes they might otherwise have avoided. Another purpose was to prevent children seeing smoking and being tempted into the habit – yet, because smokers have to stand in the street, that didn't work either.

However, the importance of the promised Great Repeal Bill lies not just in what it contains but in what it symbolises: a decisive move, one hopes, away from the centrally-run, paternalistic social engineering of the past thirteen years.

While carrying out research for my book *Bad Laws* I visited the parliamentary archive – something I had failed to do in all the years

I worked as a Lobby correspondent. It is stored in Victoria Tower, which houses the real treasures of our country – its laws.

There are more than 1.5 million Acts of Parliament passed since 1497, including some of the seminal laws of the land, the very essence of nationhood and liberty: the Petition of Right 1628, the Habeas Corpus Act 1679, the Bill of Rights 1689, the Slave Trade Acts of 1807 and 1833, the Great Reform Act of 1832 and the Parliament Acts of 1911 and 1949.

They also contain a few best forgotten: the Dangerous Dogs Act 1991, the ID Card Act 2006, umpteen Criminal Justice Acts since 1997, the Licensing Act 2005 and a welter of legislation to restrict, rather than enhance, our freedoms, such as the ban on smoking or on making hostile comments about religion.

And it struck me going around the archive that if there is a fundamental difference between the laws passed today and those of yore, it is this: for hundreds of years the fight, both literally and metaphorically, was to advance the cause of personal liberty and to reduce the power of the state; in recent times, the reverse has happened.

When I was growing up there were two common phrases that you hardly ever hear today and which encapsulated a popular understanding of the sort of country we are, appreciated by people who never knew the works of Edmund Burke, Adam Smith, John Stuart Mill, A. V. Dicey or Isaiah Berlin.

One was 'It's a free country.' The other was 'There should be a law against it.'

We are no longer a free country, not in the sense that previous generations would have understood the phrase; and, whatever it is, there almost certainly *is* now a law against it. The point is that the two go together.

Liberty is freedom from the arbitrary exercise of the law, even if the people applying it believe they are doing it for your own good.

But Mill's dictum – that the only justification for restricting liberty is the prevention of harm to others – was long ago abandoned.

Today, government routinely restricts our freedom for what it judges to be our own benefit. We have ceded liberty under the law for security under the state. Most Britons now appear more comfortable with the paternalistic state of the present than the minimal state of the past.

Whereas our forefathers wanted to be left alone, we want to be looked after. Long gone is the world depicted by A. J. P. Taylor in the opening lines of his *English History 1914–45*: 'Until August 1914 a sensible, law-abiding Englishman could pass through life and hardly notice the existence of the State, beyond the post office and the policeman.'

The state does infinitely more than it did a century ago, but does it very badly. Above all, the state has lost moral authority, something it needs to recover. It can appear as both avuncular and bullying. More of its citizens have been reduced to dependency, circumstances that the state then exploits by convincing them that their interests lie in permanent client status. Instead of priding ourselves on a love of liberty, we acquiesce in our own servitude.

But being against the Big State does not mean being in favour of no state. State interference on its own is not incompatible with liberty; it can, indeed, be its protector.

It is a question of balance and proportion and we are in danger of getting it wrong; perhaps we already have.

This debate goes to the very heart of David Cameron's idea of a Big Society – a nebulous concept that people have found hard to define, not least Mr Cameron himself. He is searching for the words to articulate that idea, once bred in the bone, of what it means to be a free country.

That is why the Left dislike and deride it so – because it is the antithesis of big government and of paternalism, the idea that the state knows best how we should live our lives and how to spend our money.

But this we do know: when the state seeks to do everything, its citizens feel they need do nothing. Big government removes the obligation on its citizens of independent action, self-sacrifice and voluntary effort.

A free country is one in which the state does what its citizens cannot do for themselves, but no more – and stops trying to run their lives from the cradle to the grave.

If the coalition really is interested in freedom and liberty it must be prepared to relinquish a good deal of the power garnered by governments since the war. That is some task, especially when so much of it is wielded by Europe nowadays.

Reforms of the way Parliament does its business may help to ensure that legislation is debated properly. 2011 will be the first year since 1949 without a Queen's Speech because of the move to a five-year fixed term.

Why not go further and have just one Queen's Speech a Parliament? There could still be a State Opening every year, with all the attendant pomp and circumstance; but the annual requirement to find twenty or so Bills to put into the Queen's Speech becomes a frantic search for more and more things in which to interfere.

As Hobbes said in Leviathan: 'Liberties depend on the silence of the law.' A period of legislative peace under the coalition would be most welcome and would go a long way towards undoing the damage to liberty we have witnessed in recent years.

Immigration, asylum and civil liberties

Daniel Hamilton

Over the past decade, there have been few issues that have sparked as much debate, brought about as much exasperation or provoked so much fury as immigration. Politicians from across the political divide have been strong on rhetoric – from William Hague's denunciation in 2001 of the racketeers 'flooding the country'[56] with bogus asylum seekers to Alan Johnson's description of immigration as a 'strain that has been ignored for far too long'.[57]

The numerous problems facing the United Kingdom's immigration and asylum system are not ones that can be remedied with tough words, nor can they easily be solved by a newly-minted government minister with an evangelical determination to drive through 'reform'.

In this paper, I will examine a few of the ways in which the government can ensure a tough and uncompromising approach to the issue while at the same time protecting the civil liberties of all of those living in the UK – regardless of where they were born or which passport they hold.

It is often said that the worst kind of law is that created in the immediate aftermath of an emotional event which has had a remarkable impact upon the public consciousness. Gun owners would cite the stringent gun control laws implemented in Britain following the Dunblane massacre as one example, while many dog owners lament the introduction of the 1991 Dangerous Dogs Act following tabloid reports of attacks on children as another.

The phenomenon of government needing to be seen to do *something* in response to a crisis was strongly apparent in the United Kingdom in the months following al-Qaeda's attack on the World Trade Centre in 2001. In this case, the result was the Anti-Terrorism, Crime and Security Act – guillotined through the House of Commons as emergency legislation in November 2001, two months after the terrorist atrocities.

The Act empowered the Home Secretary to indefinitely detain foreign nationals if they '(a) believe that the person's presence in the United Kingdom is a risk to national security, and (b) suspect that the person is a terrorist'.[58] The Bill was struck down by the Law Lords in December 2004[59] with Lord Nicholls branding it an 'anathema in any country which observes the rule of law'.[60]

While the decision of the Law Lords ought to have drawn a line under the issue of detention without trial, the 2005 Prevention of Terrorism Act was passed as a direct attempt to circumvent the ruling. The Act, as passed, allowed the Home Secretary to impose so-called 'control orders' upon individuals 'for purposes connected with protecting members of the public from a risk of terrorism'.[61]

The scope of control orders is wide-ranging, including 'prohibitions or restrictions' on:

- The individual's 'possession or use of specified articles or substances'
- The individual's use of 'specified services or specified facilities, or on his carrying on specified activities'
- Their 'association or communications with specified persons or with other persons generally'
- Their 'being at specified places or within a specified area at specified times or on specified days'

Essentially, the Act awarded the Home Secretary the power to impose more stringent conditions on the movements and daily lives of individuals than those the Burmese military junta have placed on Aung San Suu Kyi. There are numerous examples of individuals placed under control orders who have found themselves subjected to Kafkaesque restrictions on their freedom only later to be fully exonerated of any wrongdoing.

In pursuing the war against terrorism, it is clear that the police and security services must have effective tools by which to monitor those they suspect of involvement in terrorist activities. Traditional forms of police surveillance and investigation would, I suggest, be a more effective way of fighting this battle than essentially alerting suspects to the fact they are being investigated!

Quite apart from the clear threat these orders pose to the civil liberties of individuals who have not been convicted or even formally accused of committing crimes, Alex Deane has eloquently illustrated their lack of effectiveness – suggesting that, of the forty-five imposed to date, seven of the individuals have absconded and the remainder have been discontinued.[62]

The coalition government have indicated that a review of control orders is currently underway. This review must find in favour of discontinuing this ineffective and unfair practice.

While control orders give the Home Secretary the power to detain an individual in their own home and forbid them owning mobile phones, the Terrorism Act of 2006 awarded the police the ability to jail a suspect for up to 28 days. The 28-day limit introduced in the Act represented a reduction from the 90 days originally proposed, following sustained public opposition. Such was the concern at the scheme that individuals such as Archbishop Desmond Tutu wistfully observed that '90 days for a South African is an awful déjà-vu because we had in South Africa in the bad old days a 90-day detention law'.[63]

The campaign to prevent the extension of the 28-day limit to 90 days undoubtedly represented a significant victory for the British civil liberties movement, galvanising into action many members of the public who had previously never given the issue particular thought. Among Members of Parliament from across the political divide, memories remain of the veracity of the letter-writing campaigns from their constituents opposing the scheme, as well as the organised rallies at Parliament which drew thousands to Westminster. The victory was, however, a hollow one.

It remains the law of the United Kingdom that a suspect who has not been formally accused or charged with any crime can be detained for 28 days. Despite the Liberal Democrats having pledged in their manifesto to reduce the 28-day limit to fourteen days, the coalition government has yet to announce any formal review of the policy. This Mugabe-style policy of trial without detention remains a gross infringement of civil liberties which must continue to be challenged in the months ahead.

Following the formation of the coalition government in May, both the Conservatives and Liberal Democrats spoke in lofty terms about how they had 'delivered' on their manifesto promise to abolish ID cards. At the time of writing, the House of Commons is currently debating the repeal of the 2007 Identity Cards Bill with a view to the process being completed by December 2010.

The government has not, however, been so proactive in the reversal of this requirement for foreign nationals, opting to retain biometric identity cards for non-EU citizens. The National Biometric Identity Service, which signed a seven-year service agreement with IBM in July 2009,[64] will continue to operate as it did under the previous administration.[65]

To date, the coalition government has defended its position on the continuation of stringent ID controls on non-EU nationals by blaming the realities of European Union law, in particular the snappily-named 'Council Regulation (EC) No. 380/2008 laying down a uniform format for residence permits for third-country nationals'[66] which demands that, under the auspices of the EU's 'harmonised immigration policy': 'The uniform format for residence permits should contain all the necessary… For the purposes of this Regulation, Member States shall take biometric identifiers comprising the facial image and two fingerprints from third-country nationals.'

Furthermore, the regulation demands that: 'The residence permit including biometrics will be produced as a stand-alone document'.

Such a provision has been transposed directly into British law through the 2007 Borders Act: *'(6) Regulations under subsection (1)(b) may, in particular, require the production or other use of a biometric immigration document that is combined with another document; and section 16 of the Identity Cards Act 2006 (c. 15) (prohibition of requirement to produce ID card) is subject to this subsection'.*

In short, EU law has ended the decades-old system in which the legality of a foreign national's entry to and residency in the UK was indicated by a 'vignette' sticker in their passport to a wholly more draconian system of fingerprinting, DNA swabbing and ID-card carrying.

While the coalition can validly claim to have taken concrete steps towards abolishing ID cards for British citizens and those living in the remaining twenty-six European Union member states, the scheme continues to remain in force for all other foreign nationals.

Each of the arguments offered as to why British nationals should not have to carry ID cards – which are outlined elsewhere in this publication – are equally applicable to foreign nationals.

I would, however, add one further observation.

The European Union has a population of almost 500 million people, taking in states as diverse as Denmark and Romania, France and Bulgaria, Spain and Latvia.

The EU shares porous external borders with states such as Belarus and Serbia – both of which have considerably higher levels of violent and organised crime than the United Kingdom. Hungary has awarded citizenship to all ethnic Magyars living in non-EU states, while Romanian government policy allows for all citizens of Moldova – Europe's poorest nation with an annual GDP per capita income of US$1,516 – to hold their passports.

None of the citizens of these countries require ID cards to live in the UK. Those from Australia, Canada and the United States do.

The pointless requirement for foreign nationals to carry ID cards must be discontinued at the earliest opportunity.

Both the Conservatives and Liberal Democrats fought the 2010 general election on an expressed platform of reducing the size of what former shadow Home Secretary David Davis has described as the 'database state'[67]. It is disappointing, therefore, that the coalition agreement reached by the two parties includes in it an expressed commitment to 'support e-borders' as part of the entry and exit requirements for those coming in and out of the United Kingdom.

According to the Home Office, the e-borders scheme exists in order to carry out checks on travellers before they begin their journey'[68] and to ensure that the immigration authorities are aware of those who are passing in and out of the United Kingdom. The scheme demands – under the provisions of the Immigration and Police (Passenger, Crew and Service Information) Order 2008[69] – the following pieces of information are, among others, recorded:

- The identity of the individual who has made the booking.
- The names of any other passengers who are included on the same booking.
- The means by which the ticket was booked, including the number of any credit or debit cards used.
- A note that the ticket booked is one-way (if applicable).
- The class of transport in which the passenger is travelling.
- The card number of any frequent traveller scheme used by the individual.
- Any personalised meal requests i.e. for dietary or religious reasons.

In total, the e-borders system logs forty-two different pieces of information about each traveller (fifty-nine if they are lucky enough to be under the age of eighteen).[70]

Each of the forty-two pieces of data obtained relating to each passenger are logged on a central database in Manchester which can be accessed by myriad government bodies, including the police, Home Office and UK Border Authority. While the exact number of individuals with access to the data archived under the e-borders scheme has yet to be determined, one only need to look at past examples of data loss by government departments to see the foolhardiness of storing such a diverse range of personal information about individuals on a centralised government database.

Such data security consideration comes before one even delves into broader concerns about privacy. Why, for example, should a state body retain a log of comprehensive details relating to an adulterous couple's weekend away in Paris? Why too does the government need to retain a record of an individual's personal dietary requirements? What need does it fulfil for the credit card details of an airline passenger to be stored on a government database?

In opposing centralised computer systems such as e-borders, there is always a risk of appearing to take a Neanderthal approach to new technology. Nothing can be further from the truth.

Nobody would argue that it is not wise for the immigration authorities to conduct such a due diligence exercise in order to guarantee both the safety of passengers and the integrity of Britain's borders. The e-borders system, however, crosses the fine line between ensuring safety and unnecessarily intruding on privacy.

In seeking to ensure the safety of individual flights it is of course logical for the names and birth dates of passengers to be cross-referenced not only against those of suspected terrorists, but also those with past histories of having caused disruption on aircrafts. But, beyond this, due diligence as to the safety of the baggage checked in by passengers and the effects they have about their person can easily be conducted via the existing scanning procedures. The collection of any additional information as under the current e-borders system is an invasive and unnecessary distraction from the core objective of ensuring the safety of air passengers.

The coalition government should, of course, take steps to negotiate Britain's exemption from the European legislation demanding the operation of the e-borders system. The removal of this system does not, however, remove the necessity for the UK Border Force to continue to operate a system for monitoring immigration into and out of the country.

In the case of EU citizens, it is clearly unnecessary for such information to be held by the government; just as it is unnecessary for information about their movements around the UK to be recorded.

For foreign nationals, however, an effective scheme can already be operated in the form of the rigorous checking of entry and exit visas – including inspections of passport stamps to ascertain prior dates of entry and exit, and also the other destinations the traveller has been to. By tightening regulations relating to the inspection of passports for non-EU nationals, one would ensure that individuals are able to present an account of their movements while retaining control of their own travel records.

Throughout history, the United Kingdom has served as a port in the storm for hundreds of thousands – if not millions – of people fleeing from intolerance, persecution and genocide. One only need think of the inspiring examples of the 21,000 Hungarians given shelter in Britain after the Soviet Union's crushing of the anti-communist 1956 uprising, the 30,000 Ugandan Asians who fled Idi Amin's regime for the UK in the early 1970s or the sanctuary given to gay Iranian teenager Mehdi Kazemi to be proud of Britain's contribution in this field.

As such, it is deeply regrettable that this noble legacy has, for the most part, been significantly undermined by the at times hysterical attitude of the British press towards the influx of 'bogus' asylum seekers from the Serbian province of Kosovo between 1998 and 2001.

Fed by the mass media, the 'court of public opinion' attempted to draw a moral distinction between those applying to remain in the UK on the grounds that their lives would be at risk if they did attempt to return to the province and those who simply wished to remain in the UK for economic reasons. Indeed, while the motives of many entering the United Kingdom from the province were undoubtedly economic, their choice of the UK as a settling point was largely due to a 1996 High Court ruling[71] that determined Kosovo's ethnic Albanians were a persecuted group that should en masse be granted leave to remain upon their arrival at a UK border. As such, all any Kosovan Albanian needed to do in order to enter the UK was to claim asylum in order to receive leave to remain.

In this respect, the view of the public towards this situation is analogous to a case of two individuals claiming income support benefits: one a poor single mother (the Kosovan genuinely at risk of persecution) and the other a wealthy businessman (the economic migrant). The first, in the eyes of the public, would be making a valid claim whereas the other would be cheating the system.

Kosovo aside, economic migration under the auspices of seeking asylum is a widespread problem.

In 2008 alone, a total of 3,505 asylum applications (not including dependants such as children or elderly relatives) were received from Afghans, 3,165 from Zimbabweans, 2,270 from Iranians, 2,255 from Eritreans and 1,850 from Iraqis.[72] While each of these countries suffers from considerable internal tensions, it is unlikely that each of these applications could or indeed *should* be justified on human rights grounds.

Is this really a problem though?

At the moment, it is – but with an honest approach to immigration, it wouldn't be. The system, as it presently stands, draws no real distinction between genuine asylum applicants and economic migrants.

When an application for asylum is received, the individual concerned is placed under the direct control of the state, with governmental and social service rules regulating where that individual may live (usually in a secure detention centre) and the type of employment that person is able to undertake (since 2002, usually none). The applicant is essentially constrained by a state straitjacket which limits their freedom of movement and excludes them from the labour market against their will.

Such a system fails to take account of the civil liberties of both the genuine asylum seeker and the economic migrant. All it does is ensure that more people than strictly necessary must enter the UK under the pretence of fleeing from violent oppression, subjecting themselves to unnecessary detention by the state and intrusive questioning about their personal lives.

The current system of assessing the validity of asylum applications should remain in place, with those whose applications are judged to be valid granted all the transitory benefits necessary to ensure their speedy integration into life in the UK, including integrated education for their dependants and appropriate language classes (where needed). With time, such benefits should be reduced as those awarded asylum demonstrate an increased proficiency in the English language and obtain relevant employment.

A similar arrangement should apply to those opting to *honestly* enter the United Kingdom for the purposes of economic migration; yet with the UK Border Force expressing clearly that the individual has no recourse to public funds or any of the transitory arrangements offered to those genuinely seeking asylum.

Such a reform would go some distance to correcting a system which at present focuses on regulating the physical and labour market mobility of immigrants, nudging it towards one guaranteeing that those who are economically active have the right to work.

Beyond the issue of illegal asylum applications, it is important to note the failings made by the United Kingdom in respect of the conditions in which genuine applicants have been held – and the steps that must be taken to correct them.

The most significant example of this is the ongoing detention of more than 1,000 children under the age of eighteen in asylum 'holding centres' – a practice which puts the UK in a league with sub-Saharan African states that also operate government-sanctioned detention of minors. Damian Green, the minister of state with responsibility for the Home Office, has announced that the practice will end at the earliest possible opportunity,[73] a move which must be warmly welcomed.

While much of the debate surrounding immigration is centred upon the misdeeds of immigrants in Britain, far less attention is paid to the crimes that are perpetrated against immigrants themselves. Chief amongst these is human trafficking – the world's fastest growing criminal industry, sharing close links with the narcotics trade, weapons smuggling and organised crime rackets.

Some may be surprised to see a book focused on the malign role of the state in infringing civil liberties calling upon the government to take more action in a particular area, yet there can be no greater infringement of the rights of the individual than a lack of freedom to determine one's own destiny. In the United Kingdom alone, the estimated number of people affected by the practice has increased from an estimated 4,000[74] in 2003 to 18,000 today[75] – a 450 per cent increase.

In 2006, the government of the United Kingdom signed the United Nations Protocol to Prevent, Suppress and Punish Trafficking in Persons, defining human trafficking as:

> The recruitment, transportation, transfer, harbouring or receipt of persons, by means of the threat or use of force or other forms of coercion, of abduction, of fraud, of deception, of the abuse of power or of a position of vulnerability or of the giving or receiving of payments or benefits to achieve the consent of a person having control

over another person, for the purpose of exploitation. Exploitation shall include, at a minimum, the exploitation of the prostitution of others or other forms of sexual exploitation, forced labour or services, slavery or practices similar to slavery, servitude or the removal of organs ...[76]

As the definition laid down in the protocol suggests, human trafficking is multi-faceted, encompassing both labour and sexual exploitation – abhorrent practices which run entirely contrary to any concept of Western-style civil liberties.

The approach to this issue of successive governments has been ill-thought-through to say the least – the most recent failure to act to stop trafficking being the closure of the Metropolitan Police Force's dedicated unit examining human trafficking crimes. A concerted approach to tackling the evils of trafficking requires the issue to be prioritised at the very heart of central government – including making central funding available to police forces in order to tackle its rise.

There are, however, solid steps that can be taken to ensure that a line is drawn under this issue – at the border. Steps must be taken to increase the inspection of the documents and travel plans of those coming from countries with high instances of trafficking, such as Thailand and Sri Lanka, as well as minors entering the United Kingdom either unaccompanied or without their parents.

While it may appear contradictory to argue for increased state vigilance in order to protect civil liberties, this is exactly what must happen in order to tackle human trafficking. While the state can intrude on liberty, it can also play a role in protecting it from enemies of freedom.

The Conservative Party entered the 2010 general election with a stated policy of reducing the annual rate of inward migration to the UK to 'tens of thousands, rather than hundreds of thousands'.[77] This manifesto pledge was implemented by Home Secretary Theresa May in May 2010 with the initial cap on the number of non-EU migrants able to enter the United Kingdom set at 24,000 for the period leading up to April 2011.

The reduction in the level of inward migration to the United Kingdom offers the coalition government a tremendous opportunity to get to grips with the problem of illegal or undesirable immigration. By effectively securing the border and conducting the type of due diligence required to stop terrorists and human traffickers before they even enter the country, civil liberties can be returned to everyone in the UK – regardless of where they come from.

The rule of law is a powerful tool. It can be abused to strengthen the hand of a powerful government or used effectively and selectively to protect freedom.

It remains to be seen which of these paths the coalition will choose.

Inventing new crimes and suppressing free speech

David Green

During the last decade or so several new crimes have been invented. The most pernicious have involved the suppression of the freedom to speak out without fear of police action. These new powers have been justified as necessary to combat 'hate crimes'. The new laws fall into two groups. First there are the 'aggravated hate crimes'. In these cases a crime such as assault is considered to be more serious if it is found to have been motivated by 'hatred' of a racial or other group. Second there are 'speech crimes'. In some cases voicing criticisms that members of politically defined groups dislike has led to conviction, including occasions when jokes have been made at their expense. Most objectionable of all, some people have been charged not so much for voicing criticisms but in practice for withholding approval of a type of behaviour. For example, it has been assumed that individuals who do not support the adoption of children by gay adults must do so because they 'hate' all gays, or that people who regard homosexuality as a sin must do so out of group hatred rather than religious conviction.

'Aggravated' offences

Hate crime in Britain was an invention of the 1998 Crime and Disorder Act. A search of the online version of Hansard (from 1803) for the phrase 'hate crime' reveals that it was first used in February

1998 in the House of Lords when the Crime and Disorder Bill was under discussion.[78] The 1998 Crime and Disorder Act created racially 'aggravated' offences, a group of crimes that were to be punished more severely if the court found that the offender had a racial motive.[79]

The dangers were understood when the 1998 Bill was debated. An article in The Times (3 October 1997) headed 'Blind Justice' said:

> The figure of justice is blindfold for a reason. Using the criminal justice system to make symbolic genuflections to political causes, however noble, only undermines the effective operation of the rule of law and fetters proper judicial discretion. Punishment should not depend on creating a statutory hierarchy of wickedness which elevates racial prejudice over any of the other ugly impulses towards criminality with which society must deal.

An earlier article in the *Daily Telegraph* (25 July 1997) had made a similar point. Headed 'Don't colour justice' it said: 'Is it any worse to mug someone because they are Asian, rather than simply for the sake of stealing their watch? Are not both crimes equally vile? Apparently not, in the view of the Home Secretary.'[80]

Since 1998 more groups have sought preferential treatment. The 1998 Act was revised by the 2001 Anti-Terrorism Act, which added the possibility of committing a 'religiously aggravated' crime. The Criminal Justice Act 2003 outlawed crimes aggravated on grounds of sexual orientation and disability (from April 2005).

Speech crimes

The most recent demand is for the law to be used to suppress opinion, including views regarded by most people as valid criticisms. The approach currently favoured by the police and the Crown Prosecution Service (CPS) is to use sections of the 1986 Public Order Act (as subsequently amended) that prohibit causing harassment, alarm or distress. Section 4 of the 1986 Act outlaws threatening, abusive or insulting words or behaviour with intent to cause a person to believe that immediate unlawful violence will be used against him. Section 4A was added by the 1994 Criminal Justice and Public Order Act, which came into effect in 1995. A person is guilty of an offence if, with intent to cause a person harassment, alarm or distress, he (a) uses threatening, abusive or insulting words or behaviour, or disorderly behaviour, or (b) displays any writing, sign or other visible representation which is threatening, abusive or insulting, thereby causing harassment, alarm or distress. Section 5 involves behaviour 'likely to cause' harassment, alarm or distress. It involves using threatening, abusive or insulting words or behaviour, or disorderly behaviour, or displays of writing and signs that are threatening, abusive or insulting, within the hearing or sight of a person likely to be caused harassment, alarm or distress thereby.

The freedom to speak our minds without fear or favour is always high up the list of things that the people of Britain will fight for. It is an important part of the live-and-let-live ethos that has typified this country for centuries. But there have always been elements who prefer force to freedom. We even had a law prohibiting blasphemy until 2008. The last person to be imprisoned for blasphemy was John William Gott in 1921. He was given nine months with hard labour, upheld on appeal in 1922. His crime was to have published an anti-Christian pamphlet called *Rib Ticklers*, which among other things compared Jesus' journey into Jerusalem on a donkey with the actions of a circus clown.[81]

Surely today we are more enlightened and yet, in April 2010, the law was used aggressively against someone rather like John Gott. Harry Taylor, a militant atheist, put some leaflets mocking Christianity and Islam in a prayer room at Liverpool's John Lennon Airport. He was not charged with blasphemy but with causing religiously aggravated intentional harassment, alarm or distress under the Public Order Act. The judge sentenced him to six months in prison suspended for two years, imposed a fine of £250, and required him to carry out 100 hours of unpaid work. In addition the judge imposed an ASBO prohibiting Taylor from carrying religiously offensive material in a public place.[82] Taylor's defence was that he was merely putting his own 'rational' view. And he could be forgiven for thinking that he had a right to do so. When Parliament passed the Racial and Religious Hatred Act of 2006, clause 29J entitled 'Protection of freedom of expression' had been inserted. It said:

> Nothing in this Part shall be read or given effect in a way which prohibits or restricts discussion, criticism or expressions of antipathy, dislike, ridicule, insult or abuse of particular religions or the beliefs or practices of their adherents, or of any other belief system or the beliefs or practices of its adherents, or proselytising or urging adherents of a different religion or belief system to cease practising their religion or belief system.

Parliament had made its intentions clear but the Crown Prosecution Service disregarded its wishes and used the looser provision of the Public Order Act as subsequently amended.

Ben and Sharon Vogelenzang were hotel owners in Liverpool who also found themselves accused of religious hatred. As a result of a conversation over breakfast with a female Muslim hotel guest, they were accused of a religiously aggravated hate crime and pursued by the police and the Crown Prosecution Service, contrary to the evidence. A 60-year-old woman, Ericka Tazi, who converted to Islam when she married a Muslim man, claimed that Ben Vogelenzang had compared Muhammad to a warlord when she wore a hijab on the last day of her stay at the Bounty House Hotel in March 2009. She also claimed that Sharon Vogelenzang had said that wearing the hijab symbolised female oppression. As a devout Muslim she felt insulted. However, the district judge did not accept Ericka Tazi's version of events. He referred to Mrs Tazi's conversation with an ambulance driver in which she said: 'they were taking the p*** out of me.' He thought the comment 'does not quite form the same religious view that was put to me on the stand'. Moreover, it transpired that a Muslim doctor had also been eating breakfast in the hotel and found nothing objectionable about the Vogelenzang's conduct. His integrity and courage saved the day.[83]

Throughout most of human history the suppression of unwelcome opinions has been normal and open societies in which we try to conduct arguments without violence have been a great human achievement. The new speech laws are an attempt to return to the primitive ways we have left behind. They have been allowed to creep on to the statute book because they have been portrayed as necessary to protect victim groups. How did it happen?

The growth of hate crime

The Cross-Government Action Plan on hate crime of September 2009 laid down a long-term vision, which assumed that some groups in Britain were 'targeted' by people who hate them. The government declared its hostility to any such targeting and promised to create 'an environment which discourages and condemns the prejudices, hostilities, discrimination, portrayals and other factors that enable and cause hate crime'. The perpetrators of hate crime would be punished by means of 'appropriate sanctions'.[84]

The battle over the Religious Hatred Bill in 2006 reveals the motives of some campaigners. The danger to freedom of speech was brought to public attention mainly by comedians who feared for their own safety because the sponsors of the Bill clearly intended to arm themselves with powers of compulsion that would enable them to silence unwanted opinions. The similar battle over free speech when Parliament debated hatred on grounds of sexual orientation exposed campaigners' motives even more clearly. Hatred on grounds of sexual orientation was outlawed by the 2008 Criminal Justice and Immigration Act, but the Act included a free speech amendment, inserted by the House of Lords. It said: 'For the avoidance of doubt, the discussion or criticism of sexual conduct or practices or the urging of persons to refrain from or modify such conduct or practices shall not be taken of itself to be threatening or intended to stir up hatred.' The government tried to remove the amendment and delayed implementation of the Act until it could repeal it. It tried to add a clause to the Coroners and Justice Bill but failed late in 2009. Consequently the law prohibiting the incitement of hatred on grounds of sexual orientation was finally brought into force in March 2010, with the freedom of speech protection included.[85]

Jack Straw, who pushed the Act through Parliament, claimed that there was no need to limit the power, given that there was no evidence that it might be abused. Two cases cited in the parliamentary debate proved him to be wrong but left the government unmoved. During the debate on the Coroners and Justice Bill, Dominic Grieve cited the case of two old-age pensioners living in Blackpool who wrote to their local authority to say that they did not approve of its giving money to a gay organisation. Grieve pointed out that, instead of getting a reply saying, 'terribly sorry. We were voted in, and this is what we believe in. We disagree with you,' they got a visit from two police officers telling them that if they wrote such letters again, they might be prosecuted. Grieve continued: 'they received treatment that makes me ashamed of the system that we seem to be creating in this country. We must ensure that such things do not happen. A sensible freedom of speech clause would be helpful, to reassure those who want to continue to express views that are legal.'[86] Grieve obviously saw the importance of free speech but also felt that he had to go out of his way to proclaim his wish to suppress hatred. Before mentioning the Blackpool pensioners he found it necessary to say: 'I want individuals who incite homophobic hatred to be prosecuted just as much as the Under-Secretary does.'

Fear of being called homophobic or a racist has got us tied up in emotional knots. Fear of false accusation is no basis for rational debate about the proper uses of force in a free society.

A House of Commons Library note cites another case from an article in the Ecclesiastical Law Journal by Professor Ian Leigh. In *Hammond* v. *DPP*, the conviction was upheld of an elderly street evangelist who preached in the centre of Bournemouth on a Saturday afternoon in 2001 while holding a large sign with the words: 'Jesus Gives Peace, Jesus is Alive, Stop Immorality, Stop Homosexuality, Stop Lesbianism, Jesus is Lord'. A hostile crowd of some thirty to forty people had formed, some of whom assaulted Mr Hammond by throwing water and soil at him. The police were called but Mr Hammond refused to allow the intimidation to prevent him preaching. The police decided to arrest Hammond for breach of the peace largely for his own protection, even though his opponents had been violent. In 2002 he was convicted by local magistrates of displaying an 'insulting' sign causing 'harassment, alarm or distress' contrary to section 5 of the Public Order Act 1986. Although he died soon after conviction, in 2004 Mr Hammond's appeal against the magistrates' conviction went ahead but was dismissed by the High Court, which rejected the arguments that his rights of religious freedom and free expression (under Articles 9 and 10 of the European Convention on Human Rights) had been violated.[87]

In the appeal Lord Justice May quoted Lord Reid in a House of Lords case of 1973:

> Parliament had to solve the difficult question of how far freedom of speech or behaviour must be limited in the general public interest. It would have been going much too far to prohibit all speech or conduct likely to occasion a breach of the peace because determined opponents might not shrink from organising or at least threatening a breach of the peace in order to silence a speaker whose views they detest. Therefore vigorous and it may be distasteful or unmannerly speech or behaviour is permitted so long as it does not go beyond any one of three limits. It must not be threatening. It must not be abusive. It must not be insulting.[88]

At the time the relevant law was the Public Order Act 1936. The judges in 2004 saw the law in similar terms, but disregarded the fact that the crowd had plainly caused a disturbance 'in order to silence a speaker whose views they detest'. In finding against Mr Hammond they encouraged illiberal groups to use intimidation to suppress the expression of opinions they dislike.[89]

Despite awareness of these powerful examples, Lord Bach, speaking on behalf of the government in the House of Lords, refused to withdraw the proposal to repeal the 'free speech' clause:

> The offence of inciting hatred on grounds of sexual orientation has a very high threshold. The offence will be made out only where a person uses threatening words or behaviour with the intention of inciting hatred. There are no circumstances in which the right to freedom of speech should justify such behaviour. The additional provision inserted 'for the avoidance of doubt' is unnecessary and could serve to cause confusion about the ambit of the offence. In our view it should be removed.[90]

The government failed to suppress the free-speech clause, however, and so we now have new laws prohibiting hatred on grounds of race, religion and sexual orientation with free-speech protections. However, the experience of Harry Turner in April 2010 suggests that they will not stop aggressive groups hell-bent on using police powers to suppress opinions of which they disapprove. The last time this kind of mentality became dominant in Britain was during the brief reign of the Major Generals in the 1650s, a period that has given Puritanism a bad name ever since.

The growth of prosecutions

From 1998 there was a steady growth in prosecutions until 2008/09, when the number fell for the first time. In 1998/99 1,602 people were charged with a racist crime. The number increased steadily to 7,430 in 2005/06. From that year the statistical series was altered to include crimes that involved religious as well as racial aggravation. The updated figures show that 8,868 defendants were prosecuted for crimes involving racial or religious aggravation in 2005/06. The number increased to 13,008 in 2007/08 but the Crown Prosecution Service Hate Crime Report, published in December 2009, shows a fall in the number of defendants prosecuted to 11,624. This was the first fall since 1998. As if to compensate, the government has increased further categories of crime: homophobic, transphobic and disability hate crimes. In 2008–09 1,406 people were charged with homophobic or disability related crimes.

The government has reacted by setting up systems to encourage people to report more 'hate' incidents to the police. The Cross-Government Action Plan on hate crime of September 2009 declared that the government's objective was to increase the reporting of hate crime.[91] The CPS website confirms that it defines a racist incident as 'any incident which is perceived to be racist by the victim or any other person' in order to 'increase the level of reporting of racist incidents'. Since 1996 there has been a 'steady increase every year'.[92] In addition, alleged victims are able to report incidents to third-parties, such as a local voluntary association, instead of the police.

The Cross-Government Action Plan knowingly exaggerates under-reporting. The main text says 'there is sufficient information from victim surveys to indicate the scale of the problem'. It compares police figures of 57,055 racist incidents with the British Crime Survey estimate of 207,000. But hidden in the footnote it says that 'a direct comparison between BCS and police recorded crime figures is not possible because police recorded crime only refers to four crime types whereas BCS estimates could refer to all crime types.'[93]

By March 2008 all forty-two CPS areas had Hate Crime Scrutiny Panels, whose role was to look at 'finalised hate crime case files' to ensure that correct policies had been followed. Also by March 2008 they had Community Involvement Panels, whose members include activists who 'challenge' racist and religious discrimination.

The forty-two Hate Crime Scrutiny Panels are made up of local victim groups with a lawyer as chairman to encourage alleged victims to bring forward more complaints. The first was established in 2004 (initially as a race crime scrutiny panel). These panels have become fishing expeditions for more business. The CPS defines itself on its own website as 'the largest law firm in the UK' and its attempts to search out opportunities to prosecute people for hate crime are more compatible with the attitude of a profit-maximising business than a public service.[94] The CPS is starting to resemble the law firms that advertise on television their ability to win compensation for people who tripped on the pavement. The advert would go something like this: 'Has anyone ever called you a bastard? Did he call you a black bastard? If so, call now and free of charge you could have the satisfaction of seeing him put in jail.'

Normally the government is very keen to show that it has reduced crime, but hate crime is different. The foreword to the CPS Hate Crime Report 2008–09, by Keir Starmer, says that the CPS has sustained racist crime prosecutions and 'increased the volume of homophobic and transphobic, and disability hate crime cases being prosecuted'. On the next page, however, there is evidence that in its anxiety to encourage reporting and prosecutions the CPS is scraping the barrel. There had been an increase in cases failing because of 'victim issues', including non-attendance at court and 'cases where the evidence of victims did not support the case'.[95]

The police have been caught up in the campaign and are urged to set up hate-crime units. The cross-government action plan makes it clear that 'no hate incident or hate crime is not serious enough to report'.[96] In London some officers privately complain that they are being required to define trivial spats between people as hate crimes, when they would prefer to deal with more serious offences. The purpose of a legal system is to replace heated demands for private vengeance with calm and collected justice. Instead of pursuing the common good, the last government abused its power to urge the Crown Prosecution Service to whip up demands for vengeance among victim groups who it hoped would display their gratitude at election time.

The premise behind third-party reporting and political pressure on the police is that ethnic minorities lack confidence in the police, but the most recent British Crime Survey of public satisfaction with the police found in 2008–09 that ethnic minorities had slightly more confidence in the police than white people. For example, in answer to the statement 'The police can be relied on when needed' only 46 per cent of white respondents agreed compared with 60 per cent of non-whites. When asked about their overall confidence in the police, 66 per cent of whites were confident and 71 per cent of non-whites. However, there was a difference between the perception of black and Asian respondents: 65 per cent of blacks were confident and 75 per cent of Asians. When asked whether the police do a 'good or excellent' job the results were similar: 53 per cent of whites agreed and 57 per cent of non-whites.

Questions about fairness revealed some differences. When asked whether they expected the police to treat them fairly, 65 per cent of white people agreed compared with 64 per cent of non-whites. This slight difference conceals a larger disparity between Asians and blacks: 70 per cent of Asians thought they would be treated fairly and 55 per cent of blacks. Respondents were also asked whether the police would treat them with respect. 84 per cent of whites thought they would, compared with 81 per cent of non-whites. Again there was a difference between Asians and blacks: 83 per cent of Asians thought they would be treated with respect and 77 per cent of blacks.[97] There are differences between the races, but they do not suggest a problem calling for a major and irrevocable change in society. And on the overall measures of public satisfaction non-whites were more satisfied than whites.

Impact on the police

The Hammond case provides some valuable insights into the police handling of hate crime. According to the court report, the constables who arrived on the scene behaved with the sensible pragmatism one would expect from British police officers. Strictly speaking they should have protected him from the violent crowd but, lacking the resources to do so, they did the next best thing and arrested him primarily for his own safety. It was only later that he was charged under the Public Order Act.[98]

The decision was made in 2001 at the height of police defensiveness following the Macpherson report. Most police officers were long-standing defenders of consensual policing and impartial justice, but by 2001 it was clear which way the wind was blowing. The Macpherson report was seized upon by Home Secretary Jack Straw to put pressure on the police to abandon long-standing principles of justice. Ambitious officers soon realised that the only way to rise through the ranks was to champion the new orthodoxy. One of the outstanding examples is provided by Matt Baggott, now Chief Constable of the police service in Northern Ireland, and former (2002–2009) Chief Constable of Leicestershire police. In the late 1990s he had worked as a staff officer for Sir Paul Condon on the Stephen Lawrence Inquiry. Condon put up a fight for impartial justice but was undermined by the government of the day and effectively forced to recant what had until that time been the mainstream view of policing. Baggott is on record as having said at the time of the inquiry that the mere fact that the killers shouted racist abuse did not prove the killing was racially motivated. Revealingly, his profile in *The Times* reports the incident as 'one of his few PR mistakes'.[99] By 2002 he had recognised the political realities and wrote the 2002 and 2003 editions of the Hate Crime Manual for the Association of Chief Police Officers (ACPO). (There was a more radical revision in 2005, which is currently under further revision and not to be found on the ACPO website.)

When Jack Straw, the former Home Secretary, published the Macpherson Report in February 1999 he made it clear that he regarded it as much more than an investigation of a botched police inquiry. I want this report, he said, 'to serve as a watershed in our attitudes to racism. I want it to act as a catalyst for permanent and irrevocable change, not just across our public services but across the whole of society.'[100]

This statement is quoted on the second page of the ACPO hate-crime manual as if the police had an obligation to act as catalysts for 'permanent and irrevocable change' across the 'whole of society'. Following the Home Secretary's lead, the ideal of impartial justice was scornfully dismissed. 'Colour blind' policing (in quotation marks to signify its implausibility) was defined as follows:

> 'Colour blind' policing means policing that purports to treat everyone in the same way. Such an approach is flawed and unjust. It fails to take account of the fact that different people have different reactions and different needs. Failure to recognise and understand these means failure to deliver services appropriate to needs and an inability to protect people irrespective of their background...[101]

Impartial justice was now 'unjust' and it's not surprising that many rank and file officers had difficulty accepting the new approach. But their concerns were given short shrift. They were to be 'retrained' or disciplined. But it was not easy for officers to work out how they could stay out of trouble. In one section of the manual officers were told to behave in a 'non-discriminatory and unprejudiced manner' and that they would be disciplined if they didn't: 'Anyone who is unable to behave in a non-discriminatory and unprejudiced manner,' said the report, 'must expect disciplinary action. **There is no place in the police service for those who will not uphold and protect the human rights of others**.'[102] However, on page seven such 'colour blind' (non-discriminatory) policing had been denounced. Perhaps aware of the paradox, an attempt to explain it was made on page nine:

> There was a time when to be passively non-racist was considered suf-
> ficient (i.e. the passive state of expressing no prejudice and engaging
> in no racially discriminatory behaviours). This is not enough. In a
> passively non-racist environment, racists can still thrive, discrimi-
> natory organisational structures and practices can still persist, and
> racism in the broader community can go largely unchallenged.[103]

An officer reading these passages could be excused for thinking that opposites were being advocated. Non-discrimination was a human right but discrimination in favour of ethnic groups was 'non-racism', which must be actively supported on pain of punishment. This double-think was the result of the quasi-religious fervour that infused the report. One section entitled 'the new agenda' said this:

> Hate crime is a most repugnant form of crime ... By working together
> against hate crime we can turn the tables; we can include the exclud-
> ed and liberate the fearful. Joint action across society can change
> attitudes and push racism, homophobia and other group hatreds
> outside the limits of acceptability. The police service is committed to
> making a significant contribution by taking positive action against
> racist and other hate behaviours.

But on the same page, under the heading 'The window of opportunity' the political – almost Machiavellian – character of the manual was revealed:

> Events such as the London nail bombings of April 1999, the terror-
> ist attack on the World Trade Centre in America and in particular
> the Stephen Lawrence Inquiry have raised the profile of racism and
> homophobia. There is now a political and social will, greater than
> ever before in this country, to confront and tackle prejudice and dis-
> crimination throughout society.

The murders present, according to the report, 'a unique window of opportunity for change'. The 'sharpened focus on racism and homo-
phobia has had a catalytic effect, stimulating the police service to

work with its partners and communities towards the common goal of bringing an end to hate crime.' And, 'with emotions running high and sentiments strong, there is energy to turn those sentiments into strategies.[104]

The police were also to be educators of the young, at least by 'disrupting' and 'neutralising' bad influences on young people, including (we must assume) their parents:

> A principal focus for pre-emptive prevention should be on the young, on whom our hopes for the future rest. Those bringing up the young pass on the infection of racism, homophobia and other group hatreds. Unpalatable as it is, hate incidents are taking place in the primary school playgrounds every day. Children who are below school age can give racist abuse. Whilst educators have a duty to confront and counteract this, they cannot turn the tide on their own. Police and other agencies should work to disrupt and neutralise the corrupting influences that play on the young.[105]

The police it appears had joined the culture war: 'Social tolerance towards hate crime needs to drop to zero. Such behaviour must be regarded as totally unacceptable. It must be marginalised and isolated from the mainstream. Hatred must be met by a hostile environment.'[106]

The police were to disrupt, neutralise and marginalise unwanted influences and to create a 'hostile environment'. They were to 'give the hate-motivated offender a simple choice: change your behaviour if you want to be accepted. Indulge in hate crime and face society's censure and our positive arrest policy.'

Never before in our history has police power been used by a political party to impose changes of attitude on the general population. The police have typically only enforced those conventions that were already widely shared. It seems that the over-zealous policy of arrests and prosecutions that was to follow was the result of a deliberate strategy of social engineering and animosity towards the majority:

Our ultimate goal is to eradicate hate crime. This is no overnight task. A more tangible goal must be to reverse the positions in society of the victim and the hate-motivated offender. The offender often enjoys the comfort and anonymity of working from within the fabric of society against victims who are isolated from the mainstream. Indeed, a common desire of the hate-motivated offender is to increase the isolation and hence the vulnerability of the victim.[107]

There was even confusion about the role of evidence. According to the 2002 Hate Crime Manual, the accepted definition of a racist incident had been provided by the Stephen Lawrence Inquiry, namely 'any incident which is perceived to be racist by the victim or any other person'. It was the basis for what the police would record and investigate. A paragraph in bold text rams the point home:

It must be clearly understood that to report or record an incident as racist or homophobic, evidence is not needed. Evidence is not the test. Perception on the part of anyone is all that is required. These aspects will then be recorded and investigated in addition to any (other) criminal offences which are being investigated.[108]

But on page nineteen the more temperate approach previously typical of the British police reasserts itself:

It is imperative that all efforts are made to ensure that there is no confusion in the minds of victims, witnesses, partners or the media between the definition used to record offences compared with the charging standards required to bring racially aggravated offences before the courts. The first is a perception in the mind of the victim, or any other person, that the offence is racist or homophobic, the latter must be based upon sound and objective evidence.

And on page fifteen officers are advised to apply a checklist to 'all your police decision making', including:

Best information: Make any decision against the best information reasonably available to you at the time. Ask, do not assume. Do not accept at face value: explore, examine and investigate.

Accountability: transparency – show the reasoning behind your action. To show it you must know it. Think through your decisions so
you can explain them.

So when it came to charging, evidence was still supposed to prevail.
However, as we have seen, cases like that of the Vogelenzangs were
pursued contrary to the evidence.

The most disturbing aspect of the Hate Crime Manual is the
blatant politicisation of policing. It should never be part of police
strategy to exploit emotions and turn them to advantage. And to
refer to the 1999 nail bombings and murder of Lawrence as providing a 'unique window of opportunity for change' was profoundly
misguided. It reveals a mentality on a par with the infamous claim
by Labour special adviser Jo Moore that 11 September 2001, when the
twin towers were burning, was a good day to 'bury' bad news about
the rail service. Three people were killed by the nail bombs and 129
injured. The bombing of the pub in Soho killed a pregnant woman
and severely injured her husband. It was interpreted as an attack on
gays, whose pressure groups exploited the furore to call for special
protections, but the deeper truth was that bombs in public places
might kill anyone. They are a reminder of our common humanity,
not a rationale for gaining preferential treatment for politically
active groups while sentiment is running high.

The same was true of the murder of Stephen Lawrence. The real
truth is that murder investigations in London at that time were
generally being handled incompetently. Off the record many senior
officers admit that murder inquiries at that time were shockingly
ineffective, regardless of the race of the victim. At almost the same
time that he was killed, Rachel Nickell was also murdered on
Wimbledon Common. That investigation was handled with absurd
incompetence, and the police made even greater blunders than in
the Lawrence case. The police did at least identify the murderers of
Stephen Lawrence but were unable to make charges stick in court.
In the Nickell case they wasted years pursuing the wrong person. If

there was a systemic problem at the time, it was poor quality police investigation, not racism. The message was one that should have united us all. Everyone was at greater risk because of police ineffectiveness. Instead the government of the day exploited it to impose their own political agenda.

Perhaps the most serious outcome was that impartial justice came to be viewed as white justice and the police were seen as the white police. It had never been true. The Macpherson report did not find 'overt racism' but it invented a weasel term – institutional racism – whose meaning could be varied to suit the occasion.[109] By exaggerating racism and claiming it existed where it manifestly did not, it also diminished the importance of real racism and real hate. In 2010 cases were brought to court that showed how a small number of bigots were inciting hatred and encouraging violence.

In April 2010 Nicky Davison, aged nineteen from County Durham, was convicted at Newcastle Crown Court of three counts of possessing information useful in committing or preparing acts of terrorism. He was a founder member of the Aryan Strike Force set up by his 41-year-old father Ian who had already admitted six charges, including preparing for acts of terrorism by producing the dangerous toxin ricin. Their group planned to fight against what they called the Zionist Occupied Government because they believed Britain had been taken over by Jews.[110]

In June 2010 two other neo-Nazis were convicted at Liverpool Crown Court of inciting racial hatred. Both had been charged with soliciting murder but were unanimously cleared of the more serious charge. Like Davison, Michael Heaton and Trevor Hannington were members of the Aryan Strike Force (ASF). The jury had been told that they left comments on the ASF website. Heaton said of Jews: 'they will always be scum, destroy 'em with whatever it takes'. He also wrote: 'I would encourage any religion or race that wants to destroy the Jews, I hate them with a passion'. He had posted four comments on the ASF website in 2008. In one he wrote that black people were 'less intelligent than other species', and in another that Jews were leeches and 'treacherous f****** scum'. Heaton's bedroom was adorned with flags and symbols of far-right movements, and a samurai sword hung above his bed. He was convicted of six counts of using threatening, abusive or insulting words likely to stir up racial hatred.

Hannington posted the message: 'Kill the Jew, Kill the Jew, Burn down a synagogue today! ... Burn the scum'. Hannington had previously admitted two counts of possessing information likely to be useful to a person committing or preparing an act of terrorism. And he pleaded guilty to inciting racial hatred with internet posts declaring that Jews were 'parasites feeding on others' and 'utterly evil sub-beings'. Flags bearing swastikas were discovered in his house and police found weapons including daggers. Before being closed, the ASF website changed its name to Legion 88 and then Wolfpack. The prosecution explained that the number eight refers to the eighth letter in the alphabet, H. So eighty-eight stood for HH, as in Heil Hitler.[111]

Only similar extremists would disagree with the prosecution of men such as these, but in the post-Macpherson years the police and the CPS lost their sense of proportion. Ben and Sharon Vogelenzang were charged with the same offence under the Public Order Act as Davison, Heaton and Hannington, when all the Liverpool hotel owners did was to have a discussion with a Muslim guest. At best, pursuing people like the Vogelenzangs, Harry Turner and the Blackpool pensioners is a waste of precious police resources, at a time when we face serious threats.

Worst of all, the outcome of the anti-hate campaigns has been a retreat from the liberal ideal of equality before the law, and the suppression of freedom of speech, until recently so central to our heritage of liberty.

Stereotypes, shibboleths and civil rights

Terri Dowty

> *Childhood placed at a tangent to adulthood, perceived as special and magical, precious and dangerous at once, has turned into some volatile stuff – hydrogen, or mercury, which has to be contained. The separate condition of the child has never been so bounded by thinking, so established in law as it is today.* [112]

When historian Marina Warner thus described childhood in her series of 1994 Reith lectures, appositely entitled 'Managing Monsters', she encapsulated perfectly our perpetually anxious, ambivalent attitude towards children and young people. Children represent our worst fears and our ideal selves. Their social position is that of prey or predator; cherub or demon. Rarely are they accepted into the grey area inhabited by ordinary citizens of average virtue. Indeed, whatever we perceive to be wrong with our adult-centric society is swiftly redirected from an opportunity to contemplate ourselves in the mirror into an educational programme to prevent children becoming just like us.

These split attitudes towards children create irrational prejudice against a view of them as subjects of rights and possessors of freedoms. To link 'children' with 'rights' in the same sentence is to provoke the inevitable response that they have 'too many' rights. All too often, the objectors are those who have never even considered the content of human rights conventions. They are strangely reticent when asked which of the articles contained, for instance, in the UN Convention on the Rights of the Child – ratified by the Conservative government in 1991 – should be curtailed. Freedom from discrimination or torture, perhaps? The right to a fair trial, or even to play? Nowhere in any convention is there mention of a right to resist bedtime, to create havoc in the classroom or to claim unlimited confectionery. Just as the Data Protection Act is inaccurately invoked to excuse administrative failures, vague mutterings about 'human rights' provide a lazy means of evading our real responsibilities towards children.

When a polarised attitude to children is combined with queasiness around acknowledging them as the subjects of rights, the ground is prepared for some pretty drastic infringements of children's civil liberties. The twin fixations of 'child protection' and 'delinquent youth' jockey for the top spot in the tabloid press, and public concern is directed towards protecting the cherub to the point of zero risk-tolerance, while the demon is curbed with draconian restriction. During the past decade, there have been unprecedented intrusions into children's ability to belong in society. We have seen dislike of children raised to a fetish and glorified by legislation, while fears for their safety have served only to create multiple intrusions upon children's privacy and underline their separateness from the rest of us.

The coalition government has made a promising start on reversing the objectification of children, but closing down one high-profile database is simply not enough when many others remain and the assumptions underpinning them are left unchallenged. Similarly, shedding the ASBO will do little to alleviate the alienation of young people if we cannot also unpick the tangle of problems tossed into the ill-defined basket labelled 'antisocial behaviour'.

To understand the extent of the complex web of systems that monitor children, it is important to know something of the context. We did not arrive overnight at a point where the privacy of children and their families is seriously compromised, and young people's freedom curtailed. Rather, it has been a subtle process of function creep, small changes that appear to be little more than semantic, and larger changes presented as the ultimate solution to media-inflamed fears about children's safety or dangerousness.

The school census and National Pupil Database (NPD)

As a perfect example of function-creep, it is hard to beat the introduction of the National Pupil Database. The Education Act 1996 empowered the government to collect aggregate, 'school level', data about pupils directly from schools. This was to facilitate planning and specifically excluded identification of individual pupils. That provision was subsequently amended by the Education Act 1997 to allow the collection of pupil performance information.

The following year, the School Standards and Framework Bill came before Parliament. In one of the final committee sessions, the government tabled an amendment to the 30th Schedule that turned 'school level' data into 'pupil level' data, thus transforming the provision into a power to collect personal information about each pupil. The data was to be specified in regulations and collected directly from school management systems via an annual school census. It would then be uploaded to the new National Pupil Database. No consent was necessary from parents or pupils because the legislation placed a statutory duty upon schools and local authorities to supply the information.

The census is now carried out every term and the range of data items has increased steadily. It includes information about each pupil's means of transport to school; the specific reason for each absence and for any exclusion – including alleged racist bullying, sexual misconduct or substance misuse. Bear in mind that a head teacher has only to be satisfied on a balance of probabilities that such behaviour has occurred. The information is held permanently on the database.

It is disappointing that the coalition government is currently expressing reluctance to repeal the relevant paragraph of the School Standards and Framework Act 1998, which would enable a return to the position where the only personal data collected was a strictly factual record of academic results.

Connexions

At the time that the National Pupil Database was being created, the Learning and Skills Act 2000 came into being. It provided for information about all teenagers to be collected and shared without consent across a wide range of health, education, social care and youth justice agencies in order to identify young people in the target age group, and to spot those who appeared to be 'disengaged' from education.

The Act also made provision for a new service: 'Connexions'. This brought together youth work, counselling and careers services in order to create:

> a much better support service, founded around personal advisers, to guide young people through their teenage years and help them get around the problems that might stop them from making the most of learning.[113]

Every young person was to be allocated a 'personal adviser' to carry out an in-depth personal assessment of the young person and broker access to services. This assessment process, known as the APIR (Assessment, Planning, Implementation and Review), considers all areas of a young person's life, including mental health, sexual behaviour and criminal offending, and seeks information about parents, family and friends.

Although 'Connexions' has fallen on hard times since the withdrawal of central government funding in 2007, and its future is uncertain, its initial establishment was highly significant: it provided a prototype for the whole 'Every Child Matters' agenda that was to follow, and every other information-sharing initiative since.

Every Child Matters

In November 2003 the Labour government published a green paper entitled 'Every Child Matters', setting out proposals to monitor all children from birth to eighteen in order to spot those who might need services. Although these proposals were presented as a child protection initiative in response to Lord Laming's report that year into the murder of Victoria Climbié, in reality they were the continuation of the government's 'Identification, Referral and Tracking' project that had already been announced in August 2002.[114]

The green paper redefined the phrase 'at risk' – previously understood to mean 'at risk of significant harm from neglect or abuse' – to mean 'at risk' of educational failure, substance misuse, committing criminal offences and a wide range of other undesirable outcomes. This subtle shift of definition passed unnoticed by the general public, who continued to believe that the whole initiative was a child protection measure, and the government was quick to invoke Victoria Climbié at the first sign of any protest.

The subsequent Children Act 2004 reconfigured local authority and health agencies into Children's Trusts, charged with working together and sharing information about children, and allowed for the establishment of children's databases by secondary legislation. As the Children Bill made its way through Parliament, the plans were scrutinised by the Joint Committee on Human Rights, who warned:

> ... if the justification for information-sharing about children is that it is always proportionate where the purpose is to identify children who need welfare services, there is no meaningful content left to a child's Article 8 right to privacy and confidentiality in their personal information.[115]

The Children Act 2004 spawned two national databases; unfortunately only one of them, ContactPoint, attracted attention but the public remains largely oblivious of the still-unfolding plans for the second, eCAF.

ContactPoint

ContactPoint was the name given to the national index of all children, accessible to an estimated 400,000 health, education and social care practitioners. It contained basic information about every child, details of their health and education providers and a contact list for every service that the child used. Quite apart from the enormous privacy implications, from the outset it was dogged by the security problems that inevitably accompany such large-scale databases.

The coalition government made good its pledge to scrap the entire system, and it was closed down in August 2010. Although this was a welcome development, work continues on ContactPoint's less-publicised sibling, the national Electronic Common Assessment Framework.

Electronic Common Assessment Framework (eCAF)

The Common Assessment Framework is a central feature of the 'Every Child Matters' agenda. It is a comprehensive profiling tool, to be used whenever a practitioner believes that a child needs extra services, or is not making satisfactory progress. The CAF practitioner's guide[116] gives a six-page list of assessment criteria, which includes information on every aspect of the child's physical, mental and emotional development, together with intensely personal information about the whole family and the practitioner's views on the adequacy of the child's parents. The information contained in the CAF is then shared with any other practitioner involved with the child. The coalition government is continuing the project, initiated by its predecessor, to construct the national eCAF database containing the personal profile of every child who needs services – an estimated four million children at any time, and half of all children over time.

All of the objections to ContactPoint apply even more strongly to eCAF. There is no such thing as a secure, large-scale database, and this ugly sister will contain information much more sensitive than names, addresses and phone numbers. Although CAF is described as a consent-based process, in practice Action on Rights for Children (ARCH) receives many calls from parents who have been told that they must agree to the completion of a CAF if they want to gain access to services. Practitioners also tell us that the rule in their own local authority is 'no CAF, no services'. Sometimes parents are not even aware that a CAF form has been completed until they are asked for their signature. To maintain that this is in any way consent-based is, at best, disingenuous.

Even where consent has been given, families are sometimes astonished at the opinions that have been recorded. One teenager was distraught to find that her worried silence following a disastrous set of GCSE results was misrepresented as a lack of concern, because the practitioner had failed to notice that she was terrified that her career plans were in ruins. A mother who took her seriously ill, disabled child to her local hospital's accident and emergency department found herself described as 'over-protective', implying that there is an approved level of protectiveness on such an occasion. Children and parents alike find that their reputation is ultimately at the mercy of an individual practitioner's particular bias, inexperience or snap judgement.

There are other problems, too: the government's information-sharing guidance asserts that children aged twelve or over 'may generally be expected' to give consent to data-sharing without the need for parental involvement.[117] This is simply not true. In 2009 ARCH, supported by the Nuffield Foundation, consulted numerous legal specialists in issues of consent, and found that there is no basis whatsoever in English law for the government's assertion – described by one senior legal academic as 'plucking a figure out of the air'. Worse still, a survey of local authorities revealed that on the basis of this guidance, the majority have adopted twelve as a de facto age of consent to data-sharing. This is unlawful, and the consent obtained is unlikely to be valid.

It is also worth noting that our survey found information-handling practices within most local authorities to be poor, and sometimes downright dangerous. Data protection knowledge was often inadequate and training in assessing a child's ability to give consent almost entirely lacking.

Despite our efforts to draw the attention of the previous government to our subsequent report, 'The law and children's consent to sharing personal data',[118] our findings were simply batted away and the information-sharing guidance remained unchanged. This is a completely unacceptable situation. If the coalition government seriously believes that eCAF is acceptable as a consent-based system, then it should at the very least waste no time in conducting a thorough review of the elements of lawfully valid consent.

Prior to the election, the Conservatives promised that they would be 'requiring new powers of data-sharing to be introduced into law by primary legislation, not by order'. [119]

If this pledge is to mean anything, it is important that the coalition government also reverses the data-sharing powers that already exist by repealing the relevant sections of the Children Act 2004 and the School Standards and Framework Act 1998. To do otherwise indicates that they are perfectly willing to use the pre-existing powers of which they apparently so strongly disapprove.

'Predicting' children who may commit offences

Another member of the personal profiling/risk-management stable is to be found in the youth justice sector, where there is increasing emphasis on monitoring, screening, and identifying children 'at risk' of delinquency.

Children aged eight to thirteen are referred to their local Youth Offending Team if they are thought to be 'at risk' of becoming offenders. Following referral, the child will be assessed using a screening tool called 'ONSET', developed by the Youth Justice Board (YJB) and described as follows: 'Onset promotes the YJB's prevention strategy by helping to identify risk factors to be reduced and protective factors to be enhanced. It also provides information which might be helpful in selecting appropriate interventions for those identified as needing early intervention.'[120]

If the child reaches the threshold for intervention, he will be referred onwards to a local prevention programme.

Should a child have already committed a criminal offence, he will be screened with the 'ASSET' tool,[121] another profiling system that calculates the likelihood of re-offending by allocating a score to various assessment categories. Since the introduction of the 'Scaled Approach' in 2009,[122] ASSET scores are submitted to an automated system that spits out the suggested sentencing recommendation that should be made to the courts, based entirely on the child's ASSET score.

No evaluation of the effectiveness of ONSET has ever been published, while the evaluation of ASSET was carried out by its designers. A recent report from the Centre for Crime and Justice Studies, which carried out a literature review of the available evidence, concluded that the current enthusiasm for prediction and the risk-management of children is seriously misguided. [123]

It is not only profiling tools, risk-scoring and databases that threaten children's privacy and freedom: the last few years have also seen a huge rise in the use of various kinds of surveillance technology in schools. Some of this is not new at all; rather, it is the result of diversification on the part of suppliers. Schools have emerged as a ready market, hungry for state-of-the-art technology with which to demonstrate their efficiency and modernity.

Biometrics

During the last decade, many schools have installed library, canteen and registration systems that monitor and analyse children's habits, such as their choice of reading matter or their individual school meal choices. Typically these systems use children's fingerprints, the justification being that this eliminates the problems created by lost library cards. Suppliers promote them as a means of addressing a catalogue of current anxieties, and advertising straplines include such assertions as: 'a cashless system is an effective anti-bullying tool'; 'The scheme promotes healthy eating'; 'Pupils are happy to borrow and return books'.

After undertaking a literature review of the use of children's biometrics, Dr Sandra Leaton-Gray of Homerton College, Cambridge commented:

> I have not been able to find a single piece of published research which suggests that the use of biometrics in schools promotes healthy eating or improves reading skills amongst children. I am concerned that these reasons are being given as a justification for fingerprinting children. There is absolutely no evidence for such claims.[124]

There is currently no requirement for schools to seek parental consent before taking a child's fingerprints; however, the coalition government has pledged to bring forward legislation that will make consent compulsory. This is a welcome move but, as with children's databases, the real challenge will be to ensure that any such consent is sufficiently informed to be properly valid.

The only information about biometric systems is provided by those who are selling them. No independent research has ever been commissioned and schools have so far been able to spend many thousands of pounds without any need to make a business case for the expenditure. Worst of all, no consideration at all has been given to the potential impact of habituating children to giving up their irreplaceable biometrics for such low-level purposes, although one head teacher did at least acknowledge the significance of taking children's fingerprints when he said:

All the measures to do with ID cards will possibly invade their privacy even further, but the world has no answer to terrorism without using these things and I would see us as getting them ready for the world in which they will have to live.[125]

It is not only the biometric data itself that is problematic. There is a more fundamental issue here about whether children should be subjected to this level of surveillance. When initial research was carried out on the first 'cashless catering' systems, Professor Ian Johnson of the Institute of Food Research observed that it: '... has demonstrated the ability of the system to identify individuals who persistently choose highly inappropriate meals. What a school does with that important health information presents society with an ethical issue.'[126]

Indeed it does, but the 'ethical issue' has never been debated in the five years since that initial research, and many schools in fact boast of their ability to deliver a complete print-out of pupils' canteen choices.

CCTV and webcams

A couple of years ago, a head teacher in Manchester justified his decision to install CCTV cameras throughout his school – including in the toilets – like this: 'they've definitely proved their worth because pupils know they're being watched 24 hours a day. There are cameras on the corridors, in all the communal spaces and outside on the playground.'[127]

Have we really reached a point where young people can be treated like prisoners? Apparently so, according to Dr Emmeline Taylor, who carried out extensive research into the use of CCTV in schools.[128] She found that most had at least twenty cameras, and their installation in school toilets was routine practice. A study by the London School of Hygiene and Tropical Medicine found the standard of hygiene in the majority of school toilets to be deplorable, but CCTV cameras were present even if soap and toilet roll were not.[129]

A more recent development has seen the emergence of Internet Protocol (IP) CCTV, which allows images to be monitored via the internet from a location remote from the school. The industry has reacted enthusiastically to the potential of the education marketplace:

> The current wave of new school building projects – and old school refurbishments – is one of the biggest and most exciting opportunities for our rapidly-emerging IP CCTV industry. The timing couldn't be better. Just when internet-based surveillance is becoming a mainstream solution, a ready-made, national customer base for it has emerged in the education sector.[130]

The coalition government has promised to improve the regulation of CCTV in public spaces, and it is to be hoped that they will also address its unregulated growth in schools. As Dr Taylor points out: 'The dearth of concrete legislation permits ever more invasive surveillance practices to be introduced in schools. Pupils are definitely the most surveilled non-criminal population.'[131]

It is not only schools in which cameras are proliferating: there is a growing trend towards the use of webcams in pre-school settings. Parents, and others nominated by them, are able to log on to a dedicated website at any time in order to watch their toddler at play. Since the camera covers the entire room, all observers see every child and adult present. While advertising material focuses on webcams as a way of fostering parental involvement in their children's lives, a Danish study of the use of nursery webcams concludes that they are a useful means of bridging the gap between 'traditional society' and 'radicalised modernity' and could help parents who experience 'difficulties accepting the decreasing importance of the family in the socialization of the child.' [132]

Although webcams are seen as important for parents, and as an effective means of promoting a political agenda, children are, paradoxically, invisible in this equation. No attention is paid to the potential problems of allowing large numbers of people to observe the daily lives of children too young to offer consent. Quite apart from any child protection implications, there is no apparent recognition that webcams undermine the dignity of a baby or toddler by turning them into the equivalent of a cute YouTube clip. Moreover, the assertion that they permit 'parental involvement' is simply misleading: one-sided observation cannot constitute a reciprocal relationship; it merely reinforces the idea of a child as a passive object of adult scrutiny. One can only imagine the confusion a small child might feel were his parents to comment on the events of his day when they had not actually been present.

No matter how much the education business is left to individual head teachers, when schools and nurseries are routinely breaching children's privacy and encouraging them to consider relentless surveillance a perfectly normal state of affairs, they are carrying out a form of social conditioning that affects us all. Head teachers and school governors are ultimately responsible to the public for the values that they instil in their pupils.

Antisocial behaviour

In recent years a new offence appears to have slouched into existence: it is 'being fifteen in a public place'. A recent survey found:

A third of residents living in Youth Crime Action Plan areas believe

that teenagers 'hanging around' is in itself antisocial behaviour, according to a new government survey ... When asked to rank the most
significant problems in their community, teenagers hanging around
and litter were the top concerns.[133]

It would seem that little has changed, then, since the publication of
the White Paper that preceded the infamous Antisocial Behaviour
Act 2003:

It is important that communities are not afraid to use parks, playgrounds, streets and shopping centres. Young people gathering together in groups can be very intimidating to the public ...In the year
2000, 32 per cent of respondents to the BCS cited teenagers hanging
around in the street as a big problem in their area.[134]

In order to assuage this anxiety, a raft of measures was introduced
to spare the public the sight of young people hanging out together.
There were dispersal zones, curfews and ASBOs; parenting orders
and fixed penalty notices. Young people were to be directed to
'diversionary activity', implying, with all the subtlety of a thrown
half-brick, that inside every teenager lurked a criminal merely
awaiting an opportunity. Few adults would tolerate having to
conduct their social lives entirely through evening classes, but that
was the proposal for teenagers, who did not have adults' option of
meeting friends at the pub.

The term 'antisocial behaviour' brings to mind Humpty-Dumpty's
assertion in *Alice in Wonderland*: 'when I use a word, it means just
what I choose it to mean'. The most dangerous aspect of the Act
was the lack of definition: whether an action is antisocial depends
entirely upon the perceptions of those who witness it. Thus, behaviour that might be viewed with indifference in Tottenham could
earn someone an ASBO in Taunton. The Act had a particularly
serious effect upon young people, whose existence had already
been identified as a threat to civilised society, because it legitimised
irrational prejudice and suspicion.

Meanwhile, things that were already offences were downgraded to 'antisocial behaviour', meaning that there was no longer much difference between the young person whose delinquency actually needed serious intervention and the one engaging in noisy horseplay with friends. Every news item on antisocial behaviour was accompanied by film footage of teenagers committing criminal damage or hurling abuse at passers-by. The message was clear: young people had become 'feral'. Suddenly it was open season, and perfectly acceptable to drive all teenagers off the streets.

Enter the 'Mosquito', surely the most antisocial device ever created. It emits a nasty, high-pitched whine that can be heard only by those younger than their mid-twenties. Shopkeepers use it to prevent groups of young people hanging about near their shops, where their presence might alarm or distress customers. In June 2010, The Council of Europe recommended it be banned, saying that: 'inflicting acoustic pain on young people and treating them as if they were unwanted birds or pests, is harmful and highly offensive.'[135]

One determined young man, who is on the autistic spectrum, succeeded in persuading the Co-op stores to stop using Mosquito devices altogether. Many people with autism have heightened noise-sensitivity, and his local Co-op's use of the Mosquito caused him such acute pain that he was unable to use his local High Street: 'as a teenager I was always going to hear it,' said Paul Brookfield, nineteen. 'But as I had autism it was heightened. It was a high-pitched whizzing, whirring. I've heard of cases involving some people with autism who can't go anywhere near a store because it actually makes them sick.'[136]

Any child can hear the sound. This includes babies, who are completely unable to explain their distress to oblivious parents. It is appalling that young people face such unashamed discrimination, and even more alarming if the war on 'feral youth' has reached a point where babies and young people with disabilities can be regarded as little more than collateral damage.

Lack of consideration for children's rights and liberties has combined with a naive and ill-informed fascination with new technologies to destroy the freedom and privacy of children, and also of their families. The process has been subtle, and public resistance has been overcome by casting it as some kind of comprehensive safety exercise. It is time to reverse the trend by bringing children back into mainstream society.

As adults, we all have an interest in ensuring the socialisation of our younger generation. Although some seem to believe this equates only to having the power to deliver a 'good ticking-off', such behaviour is of itself antisocial if it is done solely to establish the ascendancy of our own wishes, and offers lamentable role-modelling to children. Rather, we have the duty to explain, to listen, to demonstrate courteous behaviour, to make the limits clear but also to understand that learning involves making mistakes. We are, after all, the grown-ups here. We are not children's aggressive rivals, determined to assert our superior strength or knowledge, which is exactly what we become when we attempt to make children disappear from society.

If children are to grow up with a genuine sense of right and wrong, they need our help in learning how to make rational, moral decisions. If we confine ourselves merely to observing them like specimens in a jar, we create a situation where children base their behaviour solely on the likelihood of being observed and facing punishment or intervention. That is not any kind of genuine morality.

Children also need to be present and visible in society. The balance has become seriously skewed between a child's right to protection from harm, and the equally important right to enjoy adult company and play their part alongside everyone else. We cannot protect children by placing them in some kind of separate reservation and observing them through binoculars, nor by repeatedly invading their privacy with our 'interventions', however well-meant they may be.

Finally, even if one views the rights of children and young people with complete indifference, self-interest at least should dictate that they are the business of everyone. Plans for the National Identity Register, for example, did not come out of thin air. Hived off by the shibboleth of 'child protection', or avoided because of their alleged dangerousness, children and young people have provided an abundant supply of crash-test dummies for intrusive and restrictive policy initiatives.

Do we in any case want to live in the kind of society that a lack of respect for children's dignity, privacy and freedom will create? As Wilson Mizner once observed, 'always be nice to people on the way up; because you'll meet the same people on the way down.' The next generation will be rising to power as we decline into our dotage. They will choose our care homes and staff our hospitals. They will be the ones deciding whether or not our Age Concern lunch club is bristling with CCTV cameras, our mobility scooters are permitted in shopping centres or details of our faltering continence are available on the internet. There will be little point then in bleating about dignity and human rights if we have failed to bequeath any sense of their importance while we still can.

A licence to interfere

Josie Appleton

Proposed reforms to the licensing laws would make them even more authoritarian and killjoy than they already are – no mean feat. The Liberal–Conservative coalition government's proposals were whisked out for a brief consultation in August 2010. The anodyne title of the consultation ('Rebalancing the Licensing Act') and the rhetoric of 'empowering communities' are little more than pretty wrapping: the content is sinister stuff.

Far from empowering communities, the proposed changes would increase the power of local councils, the police and other authorities, who will be removed from necessary checks and balances. Far from rolling back New Labour's hyper-regulatory regime, the proposed changes would roll it out much further and faster.

After the Licensing Act 2003, New Labour created a network of licensing committees, based in each local authority, to issue licenses to sell alcohol to pubs and other premises. This replaced the previous system of licenses issued by local magistrates. In theory, replacing magistrates with local councillors could have been a good thing – except that the Licensing Act set out four 'licensing objectives', which meant that the committee started to play a much more interfering role in licensed premises.

The objectives were wide-ranging: 1) the prevention of crime and disorder; 2) improving public safety; 3) the prevention of public nuisance; and 4) the protection of children from harm. In pursuing these aims, licensing committees have imposed petty conditions on pubs and bars that have little to do with genuine public order or legality issues. At the Manifesto Club, we have had cases reported to us of pubs asked to install CCTV cameras or CRB-check their staff, put up 'responsible drinking' notices, search customers, or install a 'Think 30' ID check policy. These same licensing committees were responsible for issuing licenses for what the Licensing Act termed 'regulated entertainment', covering everything from live music to the mere possession of a piano, not only in licensed premises but in village halls and old people's homes.

If this current government is committed to civil liberties, as it claims, then the powers of licensing committees should be reduced and not massively increased, as this consultation document proposes.

In our view, the problems with the government's proposals are as follows.

Overturning principles of due process

The Lib-Con consultation document proposed allowing licensing authorities to bring cases for licence removal before themselves. It also suggests reducing the burden of proof required for a licensing authority to remove a pub's or bar's licence – and that licensing authorities hear their own appeals, rather than the appeal being heard in a magistrate's court as it is at present. Finally, it suggests enacting licensing authorities' decisions as soon as they are made, rather than pending an appeal.

These proposals go against the basic elements of justice: that a person is innocent until proven guilty; that a state authority must have a very good reason before stopping people from doing things; that an appeal is heard by a different authority from the authority that made the original decision. These proposals essentially give licensing authorities unchecked powers to close down, or impose their conditions on, licensed premises, without being subject to due process.

Accepting the police's word as truth

The consultation document proposes that licensing authorities accept all representations from the police – for example, to close down a bar – unless there is strong evidence to the contrary. This is a big shift from the current situation, where evidence from the police is generally treated with the same weight as evidence from other bodies.

This is a worrying development. The police have a very particular set of interests, which do not marry with those of civic interest groups. The police, if given the choice, would doubtless not have any bars or nightlife at all, since this would mean less crime and rowdiness and a quieter life for them. In Barking and Dagenham, two police officers put in twenty-two applications for licence review in the course of a single year; there were even local supermarkets on their list. Should their opinion always prevail? No. The police's views on these matters must always be tested and weighed in courts or by other independent bodies, not only for their truth but also for their reasonableness when countered against other social interests, such as members of the public wanting to be able to buy beer at their supermarket.

Empowering the health police

The consultation document suggests allowing health authorities to bring licence review cases. It also suggests designating 'health harm' as the fifth 'licensing objective'.

Most local health authorities would no doubt be too busy treating patients to get involved in licensing proceedings. But there is an element of the medical establishment which, like the police, has a particular set of interests that are not necessarily the same as the general public's. Statements from the National Institute for Health and Clinical Excellence (NICE) and other health bodies show a growing penchant for interfering in people's liberties for the alleged sake of our health – for example, NICE's recent call for a minimum alcohol price and for a complete ban on alcohol advertising.

From a pure health perspective, it might be better not to drink at all and to be in bed early every night. However, we do not organise our lives solely around our physical well-being, which is why it is better that doctors do not get too involved in politics. Giving health authorities more political powers would encourage the authoritarian strand of the medical establishment. As a licensing objective, it would also give licensing committees even more powers to interfere in city nightlife.

Over-penalising premises for under-age serving

The Lib-Con consultation document proposes greater penalties to close, fine and review the licenses of premises found to be serving under-age customers.

The official obsession with preventing all under-age drinking is an impossible and counterproductive errand. As Dolan Cummings showed in his Manifesto Club report, '28¾: How Constant Age Checks are Infantilising Adults', the main result of 'Think 25' policies has been to force people in their late twenties and thirties to carry their passports to the supermarket. Any tightening of penalties will encourage the constant ID-checking of young adults.

Furthermore, there has been a long-standing practice in Britain of landlords turning a blind eye to 16- or 17-year-old drinkers, so long as they behaved themselves. This arrangement meant that young people tended to be socialised into responsible and adult drinking. A further crackdown on under-age drinking will not stop under-18s getting hold of alcohol: it will just mean that they drink in a more childish and unchecked manner, away from adults and adult institutions. By any account, a local pub is a far better place for a 16- or 17-year-old to encounter alcohol than the corner of a local car park.

Banning cheap booze

The consultation document proposes setting a minimum price on alcohol or banning 'below cost' selling.

It is not the government's business to set a price for alcohol, or for any other product. For a start, 'below cost' would be almost impossible to define, since different licensed premises have different 'costs'. Underlying these policies, though, is an implication that excessive drinking is solely the result of cheap alcohol, and that the only answer is to pinch people's pockets. In practice, the reasons why people drink to excess.owe far more to social and existential factors than to price.

Regulating spontaneous social events

The consultation document proposes increasing the regulation of what are known as 'temporary events', with the proposal that holders of temporary events must give longer periods of notice. It also proposes that the police have more time in which to object to applications, and that the number of applications that can be made by one person or in one area are limited.

There is already too much bureaucracy covering applications for 'temporary events' – a category that includes carnivals, village fêtes, public concerts, beer festivals, and so on. Temporary events are essential and spontaneous parts of community life; it should not be too onerous for members of the public to organise these events, even if they lack expertise in licensing regulation or other forms of local council bureaucracy. The proposal to increase the regulation of temporary events, requiring more procedures, greater notice and more potential for objection from the authorities, would greatly increase the administrative burden and make it harder for local events to go ahead.

And finally...

On the plus-side, the one good thing about the consultation document is that it suggests repealing the so-called 'mandatory conditions', which are two bits of law tacked on to the Licensing Act by the New Labour government (one was enacted in April 2010, the other is due to start from October).

The mandatory conditions that entered in April 2010 prohibited 'irresponsible promotions', banning everything from prizes of free alcohol, offers of cheap alcohol around sporting events, or provision of free/cheap alcohol through use of promotional flyers. This condition was an inappropriate intervention into pub life. Why shouldn't a pub be allowed to give alcohol as a prize for a pub quiz, or have '2 for 1' offers? The Happy Hour is a traditional part of pub life. Again, it should not be the business of government to tell pubs and bars how they should promote their products.

The second set of mandatory conditions, which will be introduced on 1 October 2010, will require each licensed premises to have an Age Verification Policy and to request photographic and holographic ID from anybody who appears to be under the age specified in the policy (normally twenty-one or twenty-five). This condition will lead to yet more young adults being regularly ID-checked, which seems counterproductive for a government that has abolished ID cards.

At the Manifesto Club, we support the repeal of both sets of mandatory conditions – and the binning of the whole Licensing Consultation Document, from its sorry start to its still-worse finish.

Freedom and the European Union

Simon Richards

At the formal launch of Big Brother Watch on 18 January 2010, two people gave speeches: David Davis and Tony Benn. There could not have been two more appropriate speakers; David Davis has championed traditional British freedoms, while Tony Benn has been a passionate advocate of liberty and democracy. While David Davis rightly – and powerfully – challenged the authoritarianism of the last Labour government, it is to Tony Benn's long-standing opposition to British membership of the European Union (EU) that I wish to turn.

There has been no better exponent of the single most fundamental objection to the European Union than Mr Benn. Others have exposed the vast cost of the EU and the damage the Common Agricultural Policy does to developing countries denied fair access to the EU's markets, but nobody has been clearer, more consistent or more articulate than Tony Benn about the fundamentally anti-democratic nature of the European Union. The point he has made again and again is that, whereas the electorate can change the British government by voting in general elections, no such mechanism exists for calling the unelected European Commission to account.

It is not my intention here to detail all the arguments for leaving the EU, but simply to argue that, however much damage the last Labour government's assault on civil liberties did to traditional British freedoms, the danger the EU poses to those freedoms is far more serious. The point is not that the EU's position on civil liberties is necessarily more hostile than that Labour government's, but that, unlike any British administration, it is both unaccountable and fundamentally hostile to the British system based on habeas corpus.

In the short time since Big Brother Watch was launched, there have been major changes in British policy as a result of the general election. So, for example, Labour's identity card scheme has been scrapped and there have been many other instances of respect for individual freedom by the coalition government. Of course, much more remains to be done, but these changes have demonstrated that British parliamentary democracy can still work – at least within the limits imposed by our membership of the European Union.

Contrast this with the threats to our traditional freedoms from the EU. There is no change there, other than a relentless accumulation of more EU control over our lives and our laws. Gordon Brown was kicked out of office after the last general election; no such change ever takes place in the EU. It is the ultimate corporate state, immune from the hostility of the people it purports to represent. That is why the EU's assault on our freedoms is so much more serious than any ill-considered anti-terror legislation David Blunkett pushed through Parliament.

Many may accept that, in its accountability, the EU is fundamentally flawed, but they might still question whether its anti-democratic nature poses a threat to our freedom. The answer lies in the European Arrest Warrant, the European Investigation Order, the European Public Prosecutor and the European Gendarmerie Force. These are not figments of the imagination; they are all either up and running or announced and being introduced.

Of course, most British politicians – not least the coalition government – remain in complete denial about this EU onslaught on traditional British freedoms. The same politicians told us that the Lisbon Treaty would not be signed without a referendum, that there would never be an EU diplomatic service with its own Foreign

Minister and that there would never be the EU-imposed taxes being discussed even as I write this.

Let us take a look at each of the main instruments by which the EU is exerting power over member states and their citizens. Each, on their own, would give cause for concern. Taken together, they provide the unelected and unaccountable European Commission with a panoply of powers to circumvent member states and to enforce the will of the EU over individuals throughout the EU empire, riding roughshod over traditional British legal safeguards for the individual and for defendants. As if the European Arrest Warrant, European Investigation Order and European Public Prosecutor were not in themselves a formidable enough threat, looming behind them all stands the European Gendarmerie Force, a body of armed quasi-military units ready to do the EU's bidding by intervening across national borders. Thus all the mechanisms of an unelected, unaccountable, supra-national police state are already in place.

The European Arrest Warrant

The case of 'The Derby Two', David Birkinshaw and Matthew Neale, offers a good of example of the European Arrest Warrant (EAW) in action – and why it should concern us.

Birkinshaw and Neale, two British citizens, were accused in Riga, Latvia, on very tenuous evidence, of assaulting an auxiliary policeman, and sent off to Riga under the terms of the European Arrest Warrant. They were held in appalling conditions for an indefinite period, and denied the rights which we take for granted in Britain. Acquitted last year, they had to go back to Riga for a second time, because the prosecutor decided to appeal against the acquittal.

The European Arrest Warrant is quite different to extradition, which has long been an accepted part of international law. In extradition cases there is a range of safeguards for the citizen. In particular, a UK court has to agree that there is a material case to answer before allowing extradition, and may form a view about the reliability of the judicial system in the other country, but with the EAW, the safeguards are set aside, and grave injustices can follow, as we see in the cases of David Birkinshaw and Matthew Neale. Not just they, but any one of us, on the whim of a foreign magistrate, can be dragged off to jail in Latvia, or Bulgaria, or (in future, perhaps) Croatia or Turkey, and we have no protection at all.

Roger Helmer MEP, who has taken up the case of 'The Derby Two' and attended the appeal hearing in Riga, Latvia has described the EAW as 'a grave threat to our historic British liberties'. As he writes,

At the appeal hearing on 27 May 2010 there was no substantive evidence of wrongdoing whatever by 'The Derby Two'. During the hearing, the Prosecutor withdrew the appeal in the case of David Birkinshaw – effectively an admission that he was innocent, that they had no contrary evidence, and that the appeal should never have been brought. But perversely, she did not withdraw the appeal in the case of Matthew Neale.

This case has been hanging over the two for two years. It is now set to go on for a further five months. It has caused huge anxiety and distress to the two men and their families, not least to David Birkinshaw's three-year-old daughter, who can't bear to hear the word 'Latvia' spoken.

At least David Birkinshaw's confirmed acquittal should have been some cause for celebration, but after all the trauma, and with their friend Matthew still caught in the net, David and his fiancée Rachel (who was with him in Riga) were too shell-shocked to celebrate.

Roger Helmer concluded,

I believe that this case perfectly illustrates what is wrong with the EAW. It is a form of extradition, but it sets aside all the normal legal safeguards that should apply to extradition. First of all, no one should be extradited unless the alleged offence is sufficient to justify it. Extradition, in other words, should be proportionate. In this case, David Birkinshaw, now acquitted and innocent, has suffered two years of desperate anxiety. He has spent three months in jail. And he has been hit with costs and loss of income amounting to tens of thousands of pounds. That is far more than we could have expected his penalty to be even if found guilty. It is wholly disproportionate.

Secondly, no one should be extradited unless a British court has established that sufficient evidence exists to establish a prima facie case. There was no such evidence in this case. I am confident that if the UK Crown Prosecution Service had considered the case, it would have decided against bringing it to court on the grounds that it had no realistic prospect of success.

Thirdly, no one should be extradited to any country unless that country's judicial system can guarantee broadly comparable standards and safeguards to those available in the UK. As we have seen in this case, that does not apply in Latvia – nor in Hungary, nor in some other EU countries. It is bizarre that we won't deport Islamist terrorists to Islamic countries for fear that their human rights may be infringed, yet we happily send British subjects to other EU countries where, as with the Derby two, they suffer manifest injustices.[137]

The European Investigation Order

The European Investigation Order (EIO) is a partner to the European Arrest Warrant.

On 27 July 2010, Theresa May, the Home Secretary, announced in the House of Commons that the United Kingdom would be adopting the EIO. As Alex Deane, Director of Big Brother Watch, has explained on the Big Brother Watch blog,

> The EIO is intended to make it easier to gather evidence on another member state's soil. Amongst other things, it would grant foreign police the right to carry out the 'real time' interception of communications, monitor a person's bank account, demand bodily samples, DNA or fingerprints from a person in another EU state. They would be able to order British officers to conduct undercover-spying missions, and pursue people for 'crimes' which are not recognised in UK law – such as the Portuguese offence of criminal defamation.

In the House of Commons, Dominic Raab MP warned that:

> Britain should not opt into this half-baked measure. It would allow

European police to order British officers to embark on wild-goose chases. It would force our police to hand over personal information on British citizens, even if they are not suspects and the conduct under investigation is not a crime in this country. And it gives foreign police law enforcement authority on British soil. The Order won't help tackle crime – it will waste police time and ditch safeguards that UK citizens expect from the British justice system.[138]

The European Public Prosecutor

Christopher Gill, Hon. President of The Freedom Association, was amongst the first to recognise that, with the Lisbon Treaty in force, after its repeated rejection in referendums in France, the Netherlands and Ireland, the EU would move rapidly to introduce a European Public Prosecutor. On 25 January 2010 he observed that:

> It would be comforting for British people to believe that the EPP would be like our own Director of Public Prosecutions, overseeing the work of the Crown Prosecution Service, who in turn oversee the investigative and prosecutory role of the police, and acting as a check and balance or restraining influence. Sadly the reality is very different because a European Prosecutor is more like a Chief of Police, who drives investigations forward, with the powers of a judge (for they are all members of a career judiciary). They wear judicial robes but they carry out a police function – in point of fact the uniformed police execute their commands and do their legwork for them. They have frightening powers and take the initiative in ordering house searches (the dreaded knock on the door in the small hours of the morning); the arrest of suspects; the interrogation of suspects; the imprisonment of suspects (potentially for months at a time, with no public hearing) etcetera.[139]

The European Gendarmerie Force

The European Gendarmerie Force (EGF) is described, on its own website, as 'an initiative of 5 EU Member States: France, Italy, The Netherlands, Portugal and Spain, aimed at improving the crisis management capability in sensitive areas.' Romania has since joined the EGF. Again, in its own words, the EGF,

> ... responds to the need to rapidly conduct all the spectrum of civil security actions, either on its own or in parallel with the military intervention, by providing a multinational and effective tool. The EGF will facilitate the handling of crisis that require management by police forces, usually in a critical situation, also taking advantage from the experience already gained in the relevant peace-keeping missions. Based in Vicenza in the 'Generale Chinotto' barracks, the EGF HQ is now developing a comprehensive and coherent operational system, which will permit [it] to be ready in case of prompt deployment to crisis areas. EGF['s] goal is to provide the International Community with a valid and operational instrument for crisis management, first and foremost at [the] disposal of [the] EU, but also of other International Organizations, as NATO, UN and OSCE, and ad hoc coalitions.[140]

As Tony Bunyan, the editor of Statewatch, has commented:

> The creation of a European paramilitary force, the EGF, adds to the growing list of bodies, agencies and forces spawned by the EU over which there is scant accountability, scrutiny, transparency or openness. Para-military police are by their very name and nature trained to use force beyond that normally available to police forces and require greater not less oversight.
>
> Everyone can understand the need to provide resources across borders for natural disasters and say, for hijacking where specialist help may be needed. But what are the limits, whether inside or outside the EU? Will the EGF be used for border control and the Special Task Forces for public order (for example, the G8 summit in Genoa in 2001 when there were massive anti-globalisation riots)?
>
> Where are the mechanisms for accountability? Should there not be provision for the European Commission to produce an annual report on the reason, use and deployment of such groups? Should not national and European Parliaments be expressly given the task of scrutinising the use of such groups?[141]

There we have it, then – the full apparatus of EU control over our lives is now in place, granting our new, unaccountable overlords the ability to ride roughshod over traditions the British have held for hundreds of years. In 2015 we shall celebrate the 800th anniversary of Magna Carta, but the rights enshrined in that historic document, from which generations of Britons have benefited, are no more, because our time-honoured system that a defendant is innocent until proved guilty has been shoved aside by the supremacy of EU law, based on the continental system under which people may be imprisoned merely on suspicion by members of judiciaries who also act as investigators. Such is the betrayal of our most fundamental rights by a generation of politicians who have surrendered our birthright in return for the illusion of power at a succession of EU summit meetings.

The excesses of Tony Blair's 'War on Terror' are already being undone – at least to an extent – by the coalition government. The EU's legal hold over the British people will only be undone by regaining our freedom to set our own laws, outside the European Union.

Criminal evidence and civil liberties

Julian Huppert MP

A wide range of people, with diverse motivations, are interested in civil liberties. One of the principal reasons, which probably attracts the most people, is that there is a direct effect on their everyday lives; I see people in my constituency surgeries who are interested purely because they have been caught up – stopped and searched under section 44 powers, for example. It is absolutely understandable that they care about the matters that affect them.

Then there are those who take a broader interest, and become involved in campaigning across a wider spectrum of issues, even those that do not directly affect them. However, this category itself can be split into two groups. Broadly speaking, one group is interested in removing laws that affect 'people like me' – in this country, they tend to be white, middle-class males (to stereotype somewhat), and their focus tends to be largely combating rules that affect white, middle-class males. Recently, this has included a focus on traffic monitoring (leading to the announcement recently that speed cameras will be removed from public roads) and on bin monitoring.

The other line comes from an even broader human rights perspective, focusing on the idea that all people are fundamentally human, and deserve a broad spectrum of protections as a result. This is my position, and is perhaps best exemplified by the campaigning organisation Liberty (I used to be on their National Council, not coincidentally). Their priority is more on helping those most in need of help, regardless of their background. Recently, this has included a focus on issues such as control orders and immigration policy. This is a principled position, beautifully (and chillingly) described by Martin Niemöller in 1946:

> They came first for the Communists,
>
> and I didn't speak up because I wasn't a Communist.
>
> Then they came for the trade unionists,
>
> and I didn't speak up because I wasn't a trade unionist.
>
> Then they came for the Jews,
>
> and I didn't speak up because I wasn't a Jew.
>
> Then they came for me,
>
> and by that time, no one was left to speak up.'

Central to this position is the Human Rights Act (HRA). This Act entrenches in law the European Convention on Human Rights, and ensures that cases can be heard initially in the UK. It has made a huge difference to the standing of fundamental rights in this country, and is much to be welcomed. It has had some criticism, but closer inspection reveals that many of the stories about it are simply untrue. For ideological reasons, various aspects of the right-wing press have taken a position against the Act, seeking to portray it falsely as only helping criminals and terrorists; whereas in fact it defends all of us.

However, this line appeals to those who are uninterested in civil liberties, and also those who are only interested in human rights for 'people like me'.

However, the Conservatives announced prior to the 2010 election that they plan to repeal it. This would be a serious blow to all of us involved in human rights. It is also rather astonishing – the European Convention on Human Rights was largely written by British lawyers on the instructions of Winston Churchill. The idea at the time was that we would make Europe adhere to good British principles, so that they would not fall back into ill behaviour and war. It is bizarre that a Conservative party wants to dismantle Churchill's legacy, although it is to be hoped that Lib Dem influence and pressure from those Conservatives with an interest in the area, such as Ken Clarke, will mean that we do not go down that path.

Limits to liberties?

However, whatever the motivation for an interest, the real challenge is around the limits to these rights and liberties.

We all accept that there are some limits; few people would deny that the power of arrest is in itself a proportionate response, even though it does restrict liberty. For me, trained as a scientist, this raises fundamental questions of how to collect evidence; my starting point would be that in the absence of clear evidence as to how any infringement of civil liberties is proportionate and clearly beneficial, the presumption ought to be that it is disproportionate and not accepted.

Of course, some rights, e.g. the Article 3 right against torture, are not subject to limits; it is never acceptable to torture another person – it is never proportionate. Some people do make arguments against it, coming up with theoretically interesting *Gedanken* (thought experiments), such as imagining that torturing one individual could reveal the location of a bomb that would otherwise kill millions. The flaw in this analysis is that it is well known that torture does not produce reliable information, and so even in that highly theoretical instance, torture is not supported.

But most rights have some limits, and in many cases these are also necessary to allow the rights of others to exist. So the question is then to establish what a reasonable level of constraint is.

One classic example in this area in the UK has been the ongoing discussion about how long terror suspects may be held without charge. The Labour government sought to increase this time period from 48 hours to 90 days, arguing that it may not be possible to charge people in this intervening period. Ultimately, the situation is that the time period was increased to 28 days; this power was recently renewed for a further six months after a brief debate in the House of Commons.

But how should one determine the length of time? Clearly, an indefinitely long time period would be the most effective way to catch suspects and to have long enough to investigate them under all circumstances; how do we weigh this against the infringements of civil liberties, and the risk that long time periods may actually increase the risk of terrorism as a response to an overbearing state?

I argue that what is needed is evidence. One should start off with a minimal time limit – it is fairly trivial to make a case, for example, that a five-minute delay before charge is reasonable. For non-terrorist cases, there must be a review after six hours of detention, and then a series of escalating processes to an absolute maximum of 96 hours, which would require at least two appearances in a magistrate's court.

For the purposes of this discussion, let us assume that this process is proportionate. Then the question is: for a terror suspect, is there sufficient evidence of a requirement to detain pre-charge for longer? In general, very little evidence to support such a claim is ever presented; if one reads the transcript of the most recent debate, on 14 July 2010, there is essentially no evidence presented for any positions; there are 'longer' camps and 'shorter' camps. In the absence of reliable evidence, then the presumption should be for shorter periods of pre-charge detention.

Indeed, this is the solution that other nations have reached; Liberty has performed a detailed analysis of other countries' approaches to the same problem, and they have in general all gone for figures of up to a week, with two days in the US and five in Spain, both of which have been subject to serious terrorist attacks.

Forensic evidence; the balance between errors

Another area where there is a careful balancing act to perform is in criminal justice; deciding whether someone is to be found guilty. There are two errors that we wish to avoid, as in all such problems. False positives, where we find someone guilty when they are not, and false negatives where we let them go incorrectly. True positives and true negatives are cases where we get the verdict right.

Everyone wants to minimise both errors, but unless you introduce new information, decreasing one necessarily increases the other; if you want to be absolutely sure of convicting the guilty, you must accept getting some innocent people caught up in the net. It is generally accepted that one should err on the side of releasing people, so we have developed a requirement of 'beyond reasonable doubt', so that we knowingly release people who probably were guilty. But how much worse is it to convict the innocent than free the guilty? 100 times? 1000 times? A million times? This determines how much doubt we can tolerate, and how many total errors we make.

However, quantifying probabilities is normally challenging – in most cases you couldn't ask a jury to calculate the chances of someone being guilty, and then see if it is over (say) 99 per cent. We do this on gut feeling instead.

But for some kinds of evidence, we can more sensibly look at the chances of errors. We can calculate for many types of forensic test just how likely we are to be wrong.

However, we are very bad at then understanding what this means, and juries in general have a tendency to over-estimate the importance of such statistics.

One tragic example was in the Sally Clark case, where two of Sally's children died, and it was alleged that they had been murdered. Incorrect statistical advice implied to the jury that the chance of two Sudden Infant Death Syndrome cases was one in 73 million – almost certainly enough to convict – whereas in fact the true figure was many orders of magnitude lower.

Indeed, we often make huge errors, and are seduced by data that confirms our hunches. Let me give one intriguing example, modified from Professor David MacKay's book *Information theory, Inference and Learning Algorithms*. Note that while the figures presented are not accurate, the conclusions are:

> Two people have left traces of their own blood at the scene of a crime. A suspect, Oliver, is tested and found to have type 'O' blood. The blood group of the two traces are found to be of type 'O' (common, 60 per cent of the population) and of type 'AB' (rare, 1 per cent of the population).
>
> Does this support the prosecution claim that Oliver was at the scene?

Many people would believe that this was evidence that Oliver was on the scene, although probably not prove that it was definitely him. In fact, when the figures are correctly analysed, it turns out that this information in fact makes it less likely that Oliver is a suspect, although only by a bit (see the book for full details).

As well as errors in understanding statistics, many of the errors made relate to the fact that forensic tests are taken to show more than they in fact do. A DNA sample found at a crime scene may be evidence that an individual was present at some stage, but it cannot in general comment on whether someone was there at the time of the crime.

An additional problem is that while we are getting better at analysing samples, we are also pushing the technologies to the limits of their ability. Low copy number DNA samples allow us to identify tiny traces of DNA, but at the cost of making many more errors, making the risk of mis-identification much higher.

And the technology itself makes people not consider explanations they would consider with more familiar systems. If a prosecution case rested on finding a gun in someone's back garden, any defence lawyer or jury could understand that it might have been planted there, and so hopefully would not convict based solely on that. However, a DNA sample is generally held to be more reliable and unfakeable.

In fact, however, this is wrong. DNA testing looks only at a handful of positions in the genome, and reports on how many copies of a particular sequence are found at each of those. It is fairly easy to copy those sections using a common technique called PCR, and hence to produce a fake sample. This was shown experimentally by Frumkin and his colleagues from the forensics company Nucleix. Given a sample of someone's hair, it is possible to produce a large blood (or saliva etc) sample that would match their DNA sample. This would take only about twenty-four hours to do, and requires little specialist equipment and minimal cost. Courts need to be aware that this is possible.

If there is a DNA database, it is even easier – if one knows what someone's entry on the database looks like, then a sample can be made almost as easily without having access to the person themselves.

Ways forward

I have tried to present a vision of civil liberties issues that combines both values and beliefs with evidence and statistics; both are required to take rational steps forward. Value judgements and our underlying philosophy allow us to set out what our aims and intentions are – how much liberty we may trade for how much security, for example – and then evidence allows us to correctly reach those goals in a rational and consistent way.

Evidence without beliefs gives an answer without knowing the question, whereas beliefs without evidence give questions but no answers. We need to ensure that we fit both question and answer together.

How UK internet regulation is killing business and stifling freedom

Dominique Lazanski

Other chapters in this book are concerned with clear-cut invasions of personal privacy by various parties, including the government. Everything from personal data collection to CCTV monitoring demonstrates obvious examples of infringement on one's personal life. This chapter, however, is going to focus on a not-so-obvious breach of personal privacy. Internet regulation by the UK government has a less apparent and immediate impact on a citizen's day-to-day life. The passing and implementation of internet regulation has unintended consequences that are wide-reaching for businesses and internet users alike. This chapter will focus on two specific internet regulation issues, one already passed into law and one likely to be brought before Parliament in the near future: the Digital Economy Act of 2010 and the issue of Net Neutrality.

In this chapter I will set out the history of the Digital Economy Act as it developed and was passed in the waning days of the last government. I will show how this piece of legislation remedies several problems, but creates more issues than it provides solutions. I will also discuss the debate around Net Neutrality in the US and look at how that debate is shaping up in the UK and the EU. Finally, I will provide some thoughts on what impacts both issues have on the big brother state and how a government can remedy – or even remove itself altogether – from the business of internet regulation.

Digital Economy Act 2010

The Digital Economy Bill was first introduced by Peter Mandelson
and came into law as the Digital Economy Act (DEA) by Royal
Assent on 12 June 2010. The Digital Economy Bill was passed last
April in a last-minute, poorly attended parliamentary session prior
to the election. The Act that was developed includes a wide range of
policy issues, from wireless spectrum use to the digital switchover
to the re-classification of video games. For the most part, the DEA
updates various out-of-date policies regarding current use and
practice in the digital industries.

The most contentious part of the DEA is sections 3 to 16, or the
Online Infringement of Copyright. This part of the Act legally
enabled the ability to track down illegal file sharers and, after three
cease and desist notifications, created the ability to limit or disconnect the infringer altogether. The DEA also provided for a general
prosecuting process outside of judicial determination. The Internet
Service Providers' Association (ISPA), speaking on behalf of the
ISPs, called this the worst kind of government intervention and
meddling with private companies and private industry. Even the
CEO from TalkTalk publically announced that the company would
not comply with the Digital Economy Bill's regulation.

At issue here are the specific steps in implementing this process.
They are:

First, in order to implement network monitoring the ISPs themselves must incur the costs of making the monitoring happen.
The government is now telling businesses how they must spend
their money. ISPs will be forced to change how they conduct their
business too, moving from being simply internet providers and
becoming internet monitors as well.

Second, the government intends to 'provide for backstop powers
for Ofcom to place additional conditions on ISPs to reduce or
prevent copyright infringement ...' Essentially, the government will

allow Ofcom to dictate and control how the ISPs monitor and cut off their users.

Finally, there will be a 'trigger mechanism' which would give ISPs and rights holders incentives to make this whole thing work. The idea of a 'trigger mechanism' was vague enough that a consultation by the Department for Business, Innovation & Skills (BIS) was held to further define what this is. In flushing this out in the consultation BIS decided that it would be best to give the Secretary of State the power to grant Ofcom the necessary authority it needs to not only demand the suspension of user accounts, but to force ISPs to give over data and information on those users. This means that the government would circumvent due process and give power directly to Ofcom to make legal decisions about how we use the internet.

Furthermore, Business, Innovation & Skills has come out with additional clarification on exactly how the costs of prosecuting will be divided. Under a proposed code of conduct outlined earlier this year, however, rights holders will send ISPs the IP computer addresses of those people caught illegally downloading. Then those ISPs will send warning letters to the registered owners of those computer addresses. The rights holders then can demand the contact information of those infringers in order to prosecute them for illegal use of their material. The proposed code of conduct suggests that after three warning letters in one year, the copyright infringer can be put on the list of users that can be requested by rights holders. It is the cost of this process and the following legal administration that will be incurred by ISPs at 25 per cent of the total cost. Rights holders will pay 75 per cent of that cost, but ISPA and the ISPs that they represent believe that the rights holders should carry the full burden because it is in their best interests.[142]

At the time of writing this chapter, Ofcom just closed a consultation on a code of practice called the Online Copyright Infringement Initial Obligations Code. This builds on the BIS recommendation and seeks to create some sort of quality assurance for allegations made against people who have infringed copyrights by illegally downloading music or media. Furthermore, the code provides for smaller ISPs and mobile operators to be exempt and allows for exceptions to be made as the process of prosecuting takes place. Recommendations as a result of this consultation will be available by the end of 2010 and a definitive code of practice will be published by 8 January 2011.[143]

The problem with tracking rights violators is that it is very possible and quite likely that other people free ride on or hack into wi-fi that they don't own. A recent study by CPP showed that 25 per cent of wi-fi networks are unprotected and another 25 per cent are easily hacked. This means that half the 40,000 wi-fi networks that CPP sampled for the report were easy to connect to. It really is quite easy to get on the internet at someone else's expense.

Tracking rights violators who illegally download media is absolutely dependent on the wi-fi that they are connected to. In order to track these people, ISPs must use IP addresses. IP addresses are a unique number identifying the location and owner of a specific broadband or cable connection. If the wi-fi of a specific owner is hacked unknowingly and illegal downloading takes place, the owner of the wi-fi is responsible for the situation and not the hacker who, mostly likely, will not be discovered. It can be argued that accounting for this very situation would take far more time and money than anyone can spare. Are ISPs and rights holders going to spend all of their time tracking down some teenager who downloaded the new McFly single while surfing the internet at their local coffee shop? The rationale seems completely misguided.

The music industry had a big part to play in the development of the Online Infringement of Copyright section of the DEA. Persistent discussions, or lobbying, went on between the Conservative shadow ministers at the time and executives from the major music labels. The music industry blames the growth of illegal downloading of music as the main reason why they are seeing revenue fall.

According to recent figures released by the music industry, a solo musician would have to sell 143 self-pressed albums or 12,399 individually downloaded tracks from iTunes or Amazon per month to reach minimum wage.[144] This means that physical sales are still the way to go to make cash. This doesn't even take into account sales of gig tickets or merchandise. In spite of the reality of these numbers, the music industry has chosen to litigate and not innovate its way out of the technological disruption that has caused massive but positive changes to their business model. Lobbying future government ministers to pass a law like this was a step backwards for the business, but a step forward for increased surveillance.

In spite of all of the issues discussed above, the Digital Economy Act, its code of practice and, ultimately, the disconnection of users is going full steam ahead. We will see clarification on issues like exactly how ISP subscribers will be indentified – either by the rights holders sending IP addresses that they track on file sharing services, or by the ISP watching IP addresses themselves – and the standardisation of notification letters as in the Ofcom consultation document. However, other issues will remain uncertain. What is the future of wi-fi? What is the economic impact on ISPs and legal purchases of online media? And how will privacy be assessed and maintained?

There is no doubt that the development and use of wi-fi will be greatly impacted. Back in the late 1990s, the inhabitants of San Francisco created an open and free wi-fi network by allowing unlimited and linked access to wi-fi networks across the city. This happened because thousands of Silicon Valley employees demanded more flexible and accessible internet access, and it was just not available at the time. This project and the constant demand for wi-fi access across the city spurred the investment and development of it in subsequent years. This is just one of a thousand similar examples, but it demonstrates that this kind of problem-solving and encouragement of technical innovation would not happen if people were afraid of being prosecuted by the government if an unknown user illegally downloaded copyrighted material. So in short, wi-fi ubiquity and innovation will be impacted as an unintended consequence of the DEA.

Additionally, there has been no widespread economic assessment. Specifically, will the cost of prosecution balance the net economic benefit to the rights holder? Is so much content being illegally downloaded that thousands upon thousands are being lost? Does it make any sense to require so many different parties – from rights holders to ISPs – to bear the costs of man-hours and administration to see every single prosecution through? How will this regulation impact the bottom line and infrastructure investment? All of these questions are just a sample of the financial assessments that have yet to be made.

And what of the ISPs themselves? All of these new legal requirements create undue burdens on ISPs. ISPs are being disincentivised one requirement at a time to engage in providing internet access. By taking away the opportunity and resources to innovate within their own business on their own time, ISPs will slow down investment in new technologies or, worse, leave the industry altogether. This means that the UK won't see new or cheaper ways to get online across the whole country and the UK won't see new jobs and businesses created as a result of technological innovation.

Finally, the issue of privacy is a big one. If the government, rights holders, and ISPs can track you down and prosecute you based on the knowledge of how and what you do online while you are online, then where does it stop? If the Secretary of State can disconnect you from the internet based on varying degrees of evidence, then where does it end? The protection of one's privacy online is growing increasingly difficult due the open nature of the internet itself. One of the benefits of the internet is the vast amount of knowledge and communication that goes online. However, if the government can snoop on you at home by using an ISP then that is going a bit too far. But if the government can disconnect you altogether than that is disproportional. Sure, there will always be the exception to the rule. Few do engage in gross, widespread illegal downloading. Prosecution, however, should involve the rights holder and the rights infringer themselves in a court of law and not involve hundreds of other people whose time is better spent doing what they know best.

The Digital Economy Act, its code of conduct and the future litigation may only be the beginning. Further regulation of the internet is about to take place in other forms as well. Let's take a look at another contentious issue that may change the internet as we know it today.

Net Neutrality

Net Neutrality is a relatively new debate in the UK and the EU. In the US, Net Neutrality has taken on a life of its own. The debate is heated and protracted, with President Obama weighing in during his election campaign with the promise of a fair and open internet for all. The principles are clear enough, with both sides falling into distinct camps. But what exactly is Net Neutrality?

Net Neutrality is a misnomer for a concept that isn't neutral at all. Proponents of Net Neutrality argue that regulation or some sort of government intervention is a necessary requirement in order to ensure that the traffic on the internet remains balanced. Effectively, people looking to log on to their email or view a YouTube video should be able to do that equally. The internet traffic to one site shouldn't take precedence over the internet traffic to another.

At first and in theory, this might seem like a good idea. People will be able to access content from anywhere else in the world, at the same time, with the same ability. Fantastic. But what happens when (for example) a user buys a film on iTunes and wants to download it, and another customer who gets their connection to the internet from the same company wants to log on and check their email? Should both of these actions be treated equally?

The answer is no. More bandwidth is required to download a film than is required to check email. Network providers like BT, Verizon, TalkTalk, and AT&T know this. They also know that if they treat all network traffic equally, they are likely to have many angry customers who are accidentally disconnected from their internet just as their film finishes downloading.

The prioritisation of internet traffic by companies is called 'network management'. Companies who provide access to the internet for their customers do this all time – and have done so since the early 1990s. Managing internet traffic is complex, but in doing so companies can provide access for all their customers specifically when they need greater or lesser bandwidth. Customers do not often see the end result unless network speed slows to a crawl or shuts down altogether.

Proponents of Net Neutrality claim that all internet traffic needs to be treated equally so that the freedom and the spirit of the internet are preserved. Sir Tim Berners-Lee, the inventor of the World Wide Web, weighed in on this: 'there are a lot of companies who would love to be able to limit what web pages you can see, and governments would love to be able to slow down information going down to particular sites'. He went on to say,

> The moment you let Net Neutrality go, you lose the web as it is. You lose something essential – the fact that any innovator can dream up an idea and set up a website at some random place and let it just take off from word of mouth. You can end up helping humanity and make a profit out of it once you've got a domain name.

Berners-Lee is usually right in all things internet-related, but here he is wrong for a very simple reason: this would *limit* access to the internet, because Net Neutrality is government regulation of the internet. Any government – or even the EU for that matter – would have to pass a series of laws and legislation limiting the commercial ability of public and private companies who provide internet access. This means that the management of their own business for the benefit of their customers would be regulated by the government – and not by industry standards as it is today in the UK. Furthermore, customers who today can change internet providers if they are receiving poor service or pay more for greater broadband would no longer be able to switch to a different provider because, effectively, all providers would have the same and equal quality of service. This is 'equality' achieved by dragging everyone down to the same low level.

In the US, this debate has been taking place for a heated five years. The term originally derives from as early as the 1860s when telegrams were not intercepted or otherwise delayed in their transmission and thus 'neutral'. However, the term Net Neutrality has only recently been linked to equality, fairness and best practice in the US.

In the last five years in the US, various kinds of legislation on Net Neutrality have failed to be passed by Congress. However, intense amounts of lobbying have taken place in order to push both sides of the agenda. Most recently, Congressman Waxman proposed to enforce Net Neutrality on all wired connections to the internet and leave wireless spectrums out of the debate. Republicans, however, refused to support yet another attempt at proposed legislation – the sixth effort in five years.

While the debate is now back in the hands of the US's Federal Communications Commission, ISPs in the US continue to weigh into the debate as online television, film, and music streaming grow at a quick enough rate to impact internet speeds and bring up the issue of paid prioritisation.

We in the UK enjoy choice in how to connect to the internet, unlike our American friends where provider consolidation has left few options in ISPs. In a sense we are a bit luckier at the moment because the issue of paid prioritisation – at the heart of the Net Neutrality debate in the US – has not yet hit epic proportions. ISPs in the US propose to allow for content providers to bid or pay for priority over another, lower-paying provider. In turn, the customer will choose how much they want to pay for certain levels of access. A tiered approach to pricing and purchases occur when it comes to broadband access, with the most expensive option always allowing for the greatest broadband speed.

None of this seems as evil as the pro-Net Neutrality campaigners believe. The cost of creating, maintaining, and offering the technical capabilities of a highly complex system of access to the internet is as it should be – a pay for play situation. The more you pay the more broadband width you can gain access to. There is nothing wrong with that. The only exception comes when ISPs actively defraud the customer with a lesser service than advertised. And in the US, a limited number of ISPs to choose from means less choice.

In the UK, we do not have the same issue. As stated above, we do have a number of small, medium, and large providers ranging from BT to Virgin to BE Broadband. In spite of what the BBC might say on their internet blog,[145] we can and do choose to change providers when we no longer like the service, move house, or end our contract. It is that easy – we have an open and competitive market that allows for both investments in technologies and choice for consumers. Don't be fooled otherwise.

The EU provides the UK with more difficult issues when it comes to Net Neutrality. While the UK may not pass or adopt new legislation around Net Neutrality in the immediate future, the UK may be subject to future EU regulation. Currently, under the EU Universal Service Directive, ISPs and related communication service providers must allow for a 'minimum set of services of specified quality to which all end-users have access, at an affordable price in the light of specific national conditions, without distorting competition'.[146]

Effectively, within reason ISPs must provide reasonable access at reasonable prices regardless of access speeds and the equality of the traffic. So, ISPs in EU member states can continue to manage their network traffic as they see fit within their business goals and provide for a variety of tiered access options to suit all levels of customers. The Universal Service Directive was updated in 2009 and the revision took into account current issues being debated at that time.

At the time of writing, the European Commission's Public Consultation on the Open Internet and Net Neutrality in Europe closed on 30 September 2010. We are currently awaiting the results of the consultation, scheduled for a late 2010 or early 2011 announcement.

The internet is free and open as it is – except when governments get involved. Look at China and Iran – 'Net Neutrality' need never be a debate in those countries because the government already regulates their internet. Let's not call this debate 'Net Neutrality' – because it is not. Let's call it '**net regulation**'. The internet will be fine without government intervention, just as it has been so far. Just look at all of the entrepreneurs who have built businesses and created jobs and contributed to the growth of the economy.

Conclusion

Both the Digital Economy Act and Net Neutrality are contentious subjects. Both require research to understand and debate to appreciate the complexity of each issue. We in the UK are at the early stages of the enactment of the Digital Economy Act and the code of conduct has yet to be published. At the beginning of 2011 we will see changes to technology, the law, and ISP business practice as a result of rights holders, who are primarily major record and film companies, battling rights cases out in the courts. There is no doubt that the ramifications of these cases will impact how UK citizens get online and even if they *will* get online in the remotest of areas. Investment by ISPs will slow down and ISPs will become heavily burdened with new regulations and new administrative tasks.

The Net Neutrality debate is still in its infancy in the UK and the EU. We are fortunate enough to have a variety of ISPs making sure that their voices are heard in opposition to major changes. Network traffic management is at the heart of their business and there will be a great deal of campaigning before any kind of law that requires widespread traffic equalisation happens. The debate will be long and protracted, but both the UK and the EU will learn from the often bitter US debates that have been fought on this subject.

The common link between the Digital Economy Act and Net Neutrality is the regulation of the internet. Big Brother in the form of government would love to increase control over personal data online or monitor network traffic beyond the current state of national security surveillance. The internet is the last vestige of a truly free and open platform on which people can voice their views, buy or sell a product, and stream a film. Individuals, private companies, educational institutions, and governments have all contributed to the growth of the internet and benefit greatly from the wide diversity of information, communication activities, and purchasing that can take place across the globe. Regulating and taxing the internet are issues the government has been and will continue to be involved in.

Individuals and private industry can and will innovate, build better networks, and provide better codes of practice than the government. The best way to solve the complex and overregulated issues involved in the Digital Economy Act and the Net Neutrality debate is to make sure that the government keeps their hands off the internet.

A land of liberty?

Leo Mckinstry

Britain used to be renowned as a land of liberty. It was a country without an over-mighty government or petty interference from the state. According to the great historian A. J. P. Taylor, the only officials that the average Victorian citizen might encounter were postmen and policemen.

But that world of freedom and personal responsibility has now vanished. Under Labour, we entered a new age of oppression by officialdom, where our lives are increasingly ruled by an army of tax-demanding, fine-threatening, clipboard-wielding, form-issuing, camera-watching, lecture-giving, finger-wagging bureaucrats. Over the last decade, the relationship between the citizen and the state has been completely inverted. In a healthy democracy, the government should be accountable to the public for its actions. Yet today the British public is increasingly held to account by an arrogant government, which grabs much of our income, tells us what we should eat, demands entry to our homes, ascertains our ethnic origin, checks constantly on our movements, and even monitors what we are saying. Bullying masquerades as concern for our safety, social engineering as the drive for fairness and equality.

Thankfully, the new coalition government is starting to dismantle some of the worst excesses of Labour's central control. One of the new administration's first acts was to abolish the wretched, unwanted National Identity Card scheme, for which no clear justification had ever been given. One moment ministers argued that an ID system would improve access to public services; the next that it was essential for our security against terrorism. But these specious claims were a sham. Our society will function far better without this vast alien machinery of intrusion. Other early measures have proved equally useful, like the restoration of democracy in the planning process, thereby loosening the grip of Whitehall, or the reduction in the heavy-handed vetting procedures for those doing voluntary work with children. And, unlike Labour, the Tory–Liberal Democrat coalition is not seeking powers to monitor every single email we send, a step that again was dressed up as necessary for our security but in practice was another hammer-blow to privacy.

But there is still a long way to go. The tentacles of the intrusive state are too long, too powerful, to be hacked back immediately. Moreover the culture of Big Brother continues to permeate our civic life. It used to be said that 'an Englishman's home is his castle'. Not any more it isn't. The last government passed 420 laws giving officials the right to enter our homes for an astonishing range of causes from council tax evaluation to checks on the energy output of fridges. In addition, Labour created no fewer than 3,605 new criminal offences in the last twelve years and passed nearly 3,000 new laws, not counting the deluge of EU regulations that the state's bureaucracy so eagerly imposes on us.

All this frenetic activity is profoundly alien to the spirit of our country, which used to regard state intrusion into the lives of the citizenry as a foreign concept. The commissar was a continental creature, not a figure to be seen on the streets of England. Indeed it was precisely this tradition of liberty that brought so many genuine political refugees to Britain, from nationalist radicals in the mid-nineteenth century to the Jews fleeing the Nazi regime in the 1930s. But now all that has changed. We seem increasingly willing to accept the obliteration of our freedoms in the name of equality or environmental awareness or public order or national security or anti-racism or whatever other fashionable dogma is used by the power-hungry bureaucrats.

I will never forget once talking to a great friend of mine in the late 1980s about the different cultures of Germany and Britain. We had been at university together, and he had subsequently emigrated to Frankfurt to take up a job there in the advertising industry. On one of his periodic returns to London, he told me about some of the intriguing aspects of everyday life in his adopted city. To my amazement, he said that every household had to sort out their rubbish into three different receptacles: one for ordinary waste, one for paper, and one for other recyclable material. The three containers were then emptied on successive weeks. Anyone failing to comply, such as putting the wrong rubbish in a certain bin, was liable to a heavy fine. This all struck me as absurd, typical of the Teutonic eagerness to submit to authority. 'It's never going to happen in Britain,' I confidently told my friend.

How wrong I was. Within less than twenty years, the once straightforward municipal task of emptying the rubbish bins has been turned into an ideological obstacle course. Weekly collections have been replaced by fortnightly ones throughout much of the country. Brutal sanctions have been introduced to punish even the most minor infringements of complex regulations. Those who have inadvertently failed to comply with the new schemes are treated far more ruthlessly than serious criminals like burglars, drug abusers or shoplifters. In one outrageous case, a woman from Stockport was fined £700 just for putting her container out on the wrong day. In another case, a Leicestershire man was fined for putting a piece of junk mail in a public litter bin near his home, because the unwanted document was classified as 'domestic waste', while in Burnley a 78-year-old pensioner with multiple sclerosis was threatened with a £1,000 fine and a criminal record after he mistakenly put an empty juice carton in a container meant for cardboard.

Not content with such bullying, the state has gone even further, fitting spy chips to more than two million wheelie bins in order to monitor the amount of garbage thrown out by individual households. The technology is widely seen as a precursor to 'pay-as-you-throw' taxes, by which the levy will be determined by the amount of waste produced. At the same time, local authorities are recruiting growing armies of recycling enforcement officers to ensure that householders are subscribing to the new regime. Even neighbours are being encouraged to spy on each other to promote compliance, a sinister echo of the old communist regimes of Eastern Europe. The absurdity of all these aggressive recycling initiatives is that they are based on the politically correct notion that global warming is on the verge of destroying our planet. But not only is this concept seriously discredited, for contrary to what Al Gore may say, the science is certainly not settled, but just as importantly, the modern state shows contempt for the recycling regime that it so rigorously enforces on the public. Material so carefully and earnestly sorted by the household is frequently just jumbled together in the back of refuse lorries, while large quantities of goods intended for recycling are just left in warehouses or are shipped off to China, causing more environmental damage.

So much of this sort of bullying is just gesture politics mixed with officialdom's twin desire for more control and more of our money. The same applies to the rash of speed cameras which have spread across the country, their appearance motivated more by the cash than road safety. Yet cameras, like CCTV, have helped to make the British the most heavily monitored people in the Western world. Again, just as bin chips have little to do with protecting the environment, so all this surveillance has done little to improve the public's sense of safety. This is hardly surprising, since violent crime is at record levels. CCTV is a limited deterrent because offenders know that, even if they are caught, they have little to fear from the justice system, so cameras give only the illusion of protection.

'It's a free country' used to be a common saying about Britain. But in our politically correct age, even one of the most basic liberties of all, freedom of speech, is under threat. The modern state's determination to require absolute obedience to the official creed of equality means that those with unorthodox views are threatened, ostracised, even punished. British criminal law used to concentrate on deeds. Now, in its obsessive embrace of so-called anti-discrimination, it covers words and even thoughts. The attitude of today's metropolitan elite was perfectly captured by Andrew Marr, now one of the stars of the BBC, formerly a left-wing commentator. In an article in *The Observer* in February 1999, Marr wrote of his belief in the 'vigorous use of state power to coerce and repress' for the sake of crushing racism.

'It may be my Presbyterian background, but I firmly believe that repression can be a great, civilising instrument for good. Stamp hard on certain "natural" beliefs for long enough and you can almost kill them off,' he continued. That is exactly what the zealots in officialdom try to do over every controversial issue from gay rights to mass immigration. When family campaigner Lynette Burrows dared to question, during a BBC interview, the practice of adoption by gay couples, she found herself being questioned by the police. The same happened to a woman from Norwich who complained about her taxes being used to support a gay pride march. Today's police are also infected by the neurotic attachment to so-called anti-racism and diversity. After Channel 4 had bravely made a documentary in 2007 exposing the activities of extremist Islamist preachers in some of Birmingham's mosques, the West Midlands police decided to act. But instead of investigating these dangerous fundamentalists, the police wrote to the Crown Prosecution Service asking if the Channel 4 producers could be taken to court for inciting racial hatred. The CPS, while backing down from legal action, issued a statement attacking Channel 4 for 'undermining community cohesion'. It was a disgraceful stance, one that ultimately cost the CPS and the West Midlands police a hefty sum in damages, but the case showed how far our law enforcers have abandoned any belief in freedom of speech.

This illiberal approach was exposed even more graphically by the
scandalous arrest in 2009 of Tory frontbencher Damian Green for
daring to challenge the Labour government over the failure of its
immigration policies. Such bullying of an MP is unprecedented in
the modern history of our country. This was the sort of conduct
we expect in Mugabe's tyranny in Zimbabwe or Putin's regime in
Russia, not in a supposedly open parliamentary system. Thanks to
Labour's authoritarian instincts, a mild-mannered politician could
be banged up for nine hours, have his mobile phone confiscated, his
computer seized, his home raided, his private correspondence with
his wife taken, and his office ransacked, simply because he is deemed
to have caused embarrassment to the government by exposing ministerial deceit and incompetence. Far from committing any genuine
offence or undermining security, Green actually performed a public
service by using leaked Home Office documents to highlight the
government's spectacular ineptitude and dishonesty on the issue
of immigration, including the employment of illegal immigrants
within Whitehall.

But in the twisted political culture built by Labour, exposure of
institutional failure became an offence against the state. Such action
not only betrayed an arrogant disdain for the privacy of the individual and the integrity of the Commons, but also made a mockery of
police claims to be overstretched. No member of the public reporting a burglary or an assault ever receives a fraction of the attention
devoted to Green, whose arrest involved no fewer than twenty-seven
officers. Moreover, with 13,000 dangerous Islamic extremists at large
in Britain and jihadists with British links reportedly operating in
Afghanistan, the Counter-Terrorism Unit surely has better uses of
its time than examining a Tory MP's love letters to his wife.

Few nations have ever been so obsessed with race and diversity as
modern Britain is. Only apartheid South Africa can match British
officialdom's eagerness to classify, categorise, and control the
population on the basis of ethnicity. The state's bureaucracy is now

suffused with training programmes, diversity co-ordinators, race commissions, monitoring exercises, and awareness initiatives, all designed to ensure correct thinking among the citizenry and the workforce. Indeed it is impossible now to get a job in the public sector without openly affirming one's faith in the official doctrine of equal opportunities. And the regime has been strengthened by the Equality Act, one of the last pieces of legislation passed by the Labour government, with shamefully little opposition from the Tories. Harman's 'Equalities' Bill was something straight out of George Orwell's novel *1984*. In the book, the Big Brother state machine puts contradictory slogans at the heart of its propaganda, such as 'slavery is freedom' or 'war is peace'. This practice, known in *1984* as 'double-think', was turned into a political reality by Harriet Harman. The claim that 'discrimination is equality' could not be more Orwellian, because the central purpose of her proposed legislation was to force employers to favour women and ethnic minorities in recruitment and promotion. In effect, she wanted the state to institutionalise prejudice against individuals purely because of their gender or the colour of their skin.

It was the government's task, she said, 'to play our part in fashioning a new social order'. The phrase 'a new social order' is one that was used by socialist dictators throughout the twentieth century, including Chairman Mao in China and Pol Pot in Cambodia. Under the Equality Act, every company will become subordinate to the commissars of the officialdom's discrimination industry. In a new climate of fear all too reminiscent of communist East Germany, organisations and firms that are deemed to be insufficiently enthusiastic about the ideology of equality will have to undergo heavy-handed inspections. 'We will shine a spotlight in every workplace,' said Harman, in unmistakable tones of socialist menace. Taxpayer-funded bureaucracy will expand remorselessly to carry out all the gender audits, diversity assessments, action plans and training exercises demanded by the legislation.

Even in the new age of austerity, the civil service and local government is still brimming with equality zealots thrilled at the opportunity to throw around their weight. One of the most alarming new weapons in their bureaucratic arsenal is the practice of 'contract compliance', whereby any firms bidding for work in the public sector will have to prove their diversity credentials. This kind of ideology bullying of private enterprise was first dreamt up by hard left councils, like the GLC, in the 1980s. Now it has become a key part of the governance of Britain. And 'contract compliance' represents an enormous power, since £175 billion is spent every year by the public sector on goods and services provided by private contractors. The process will be overseen by the classic apparatus of the politically correct state machine, with well-paid diversity bureaucrats sitting in judgement on the operations of private companies.

This has become the pattern of modern Britain. Where once the state existed to protect the vulnerable and provide certain essential services, now it seeks to dictate our actions, our thoughts and our lifestyles. The government is by far the nation's largest advertiser, spending over £540 million a year on propaganda about climate change or puerile instructions on how to exercise. The buses in my town of Margate now carry the fatuous slogan, 'Go green and save the planet.' We are surrounded by warning signs, official injunctions and safety notices which treat us like helpless children with no sense of personal responsibility. 'Caution: hot water', say the taps in the public toilet, while in one Midlands local authority area ramblers are urged to wear fluorescent lifejackets when they take a walk by the river. In the same vein, the government, working in league with the EU, has sought to ban the traditional lightbulb that has been illuminating our homes since the 1880s. Soon, in the name of saving the planet, we will all have to use fashionable new low emission devices. Only in the twisted mindset of a green zealot would the bulb's inventor, Thomas Edison, be transformed into an enemy of the people. Moreover, there is no proof that the low energy types are any less environmentally damaging than traditional ones. Indeed, some experts claim that, because of the amount of mercury they contain, they are actually more dangerous.

Furthermore, the government's much-trumpeted concern for the protection of the environment is undermined by its mania for development. And here too, in trying to concrete over England, the Big Brother state can be seen in brutal action, riding roughshod over local democracy, destroying green spaces, and encouraging greed from developers. I have direct experience of this destruction in action. Three years ago my wife and I moved to the small village of Westgate on the Kent coast.

At first everything seemed ideal. The property itself, a modest three-storey Edwardian terraced house, had appeared to be good value, priced at a fraction of what a similar place in London would cost. Westgate had a romantic appeal, its atmospheric seaside charm enhanced not only by the period architecture but also by the evocative cry of the numerous local seagulls. Indeed, during a visit to Westgate, Sir John Betjeman felt sufficiently moved to write a poem about the village, 'where those minarets and steeples pierce the open Thanet sky'.

For us, by far the best feature of our street was the large Victorian house next door, sitting in the middle of a handsome tree-lined garden. Once a doctor's surgery, the distinguished villa gave the neighbourhood a leafy, tranquil feeling.

Yet the day after the removal vans had left, our dreams of a peaceful abode by the sea were shattered. A letter from the council dropped on our doormat informing us that a developer had taken over the property next door and had put in a planning application to demolish the period house, rip up the grounds and build two blocks of flats.

I greeted the news with a mixture of incredulity and despair. On the one hand it seemed preposterous that this destructive plan might succeed. After all, we lived in an official conservation area

which meant that the local architectural heritage should be protected. On the other hand, I was only too aware of the government's
fixation with new development, all in the name of supposedly
meeting 'local housing need'.

Wishes of residents, environmental concerns and respect for
history would all count for nothing in the face of socialists' bureaucratic bulldozer. And so it turned out. That letter from the council
was the start of a grim saga which has ultimately resulted in an act
of centrally-dictated vandalism. When the application for the two
apartment blocks was first submitted, the local authority, Thanet
District Council, immediately rejected it. But the developer was not
to be thwarted. Three further applications were submitted, each with
minor amendments; much to our relief, they too were all rejected.

But then the undemocratic fare deepened. The developer put
forward an appeal to the unaccountable quango, the government's
£55 million Planning Inspectorate, which oversees around 30,000
planning cases a year. Naively, I thought that the Inspectorate might
take account of the strength of local feeling and the need to protect
the local environment. Not a bit of it. A creature of Whitehall,
the Inspectorate quickly approved the developer's plans and condemned the property for demolition. There was nothing we could
do. We, the local residents, were allowed no right of appeal against
this outrageous decision, even though the developer's bosses could
appeal as much as they wanted. So now, thanks to the cocktail of
Stalinist central control and developers' avarice, we are living next
door to a building site rather than a pleasant period home.

Again, this is another area where the coalition government holds
out some hope for the future, as the regional housing targets have
been abolished and a central role in the planning process has been
restored to town halls.

All the Big Brother activity does not come cheap. As the state
expands, public spending grows out of control, swallowing 53 per
cent of GDP. So we have become trapped in a vicious circle where

the power of officialdom requires ever more revenue to maintain its operations, so taxes have to rise. But the increasing burden of taxation only exacerbates the influence of the Big Brother state, with the government growing more ravenous, more intrusive in its quest for our cash. In the early 1960s, the average skilled worker paid just 8 per cent of his income in tax and national insurance. By 2010, that figure has risen to almost 30 per cent.

A century ago Lord Rosebery, the last Liberal peer to hold the Premiership, prophetically saw the world that would exist today. In a speech at Glasgow University in July 1908, Rosebery declared,

> The modern cry is, 'Let the Government have a finger in every pie,' probing, propping, disturbing. Every day the area of initiative is being narrowed, every day the standing ground for self-reliance is being undermined; every day the public infringes – with the best intentions no doubt – on the individual. The nation is being taken into custody by the state.

We have only just started to reverse this century-long trend. There is still a mighty long way to go before we have our freedoms back.

Google street view: a systematic intrusion on privacy

Alex Deane

It is easy in the fight to protect privacy to believe that the threat comes solely from the state. But there is another front in the battle: the private sector is just as capable of intruding into our private lives as government. Google is an enormous company running many products and platforms, each of which poses potential privacy issues – not least the world's most popular search engine. I will confine myself here to discussing Google Street View.

There are two separate issues with Street View. First, the fact that the cars which created the images also, in the course of preparing images for Street View going 'live', captured data from members of the public who happened to be using wi-fi as they passed by. They collected over 600 gigabytes of such data in the UK alone, in preparation for the programme rolling out nationally in March 2010. Secondly, there is the question of whether Street View is intrusive per se.

On the first question, as I understand it from Privacy International's experts, the code that enabled the capture of data by cars from unknowing people as they trundled through neighbour-hoods was written in such a way that encrypted data was separated out and dumped, specifically sifting out and storing the vulnerable unencrypted data on Google hard drives. If true, this goes well beyond the 'mistake' promoted by Google, and PI would seem to be right in their contention that Google intentionally breached the privacy of many people's communications (it was a complaint from PI that led to the ongoing Metropolitan Police investigation into Google).

Some maintain that what Google did was 'standard operating procedure' for software engineers – that if one needs a component for some purpose and it's served by an available component which also performs other irrelevant tasks, you use it anyway. Perhaps so. I would be surprised if this is normal, but I don't know if this is indeed 'standard operating procedure' or not. It seems to me that if that is 'SOP' then it is wrong. In any case, the argument 'I do wrong because others also do so' is worthless.

Equally, arguing that people somehow 'deserved it' or have no right to complain because the data was transmitted via public networks and wasn't encrypted is fatuous. We don't encrypt our mail or our telephone calls, but they come with a legitimate expectation of privacy; our internet usage and email is just the same. Many people use public networks, sharing their access with friends or colleagues – sometimes because it's convenient; sometimes because they don't know how to protect their wi-fi. Certainly, they should do so – but it hardly relieves the wrongdoer of culpability if the victim happens to have been more careless than some others. That logic says that your grandmother shouldn't leave the house as she's so easy to rob.

Google's wi-fi intrusion has supposedly been looked into by the Information Commissioner's Office. To be precise, the ICO sent two non-technical staff to Google's headquarters – the heart of perhaps the world's most technologically advanced company – looked at a small sample of data taken from what Google chose to show them, and promptly issued a press release effectively clearing the company of any wrongdoing, in the middle of a formal police investigation.

Our ICO now effectively refuses to investigate Google whilst counterparts in countries like New Zealand, Australia, Canada, Germany, France, the Czech Republic and Italy all pursue the company on this very point and the authorities in South Korea physically raid

Google's offices there. Thirty-eight states in the USA have united to probe the company's behaviour, alongside a thumping class action.

In Britain alone the Commissioner has whitewashed the company's wrongdoing. The ICO has really let British people down. We deserve better from those who are given the responsibility of protecting our privacy. After all, the Metropolitan Police are currently investigating Google over this issue; if the allegations against Google merit an investigation by the police, who have to consider the criminal standard of fault, how can those allegations plausibly be said not to merit an investigation by the ICO?

Sadly for our privacy, but tellingly in terms of the ICO's uselessness, the assurances they gave have now been proven wrong by Google itself. Regulators in Canada and Spain have both accused Google of breaking their respective national laws, and in October 2010, when faced with such persistent criticisms, Google announced (strategically confessed?) that it *had* actually collected more complete personal data than previously admitted.

So the ICO may have to re-initiate their investigation after all, rather than acting as apologists for those they're supposed to police. But that will only be possible because the ICO's previous guidance was stymied by other proceedings. In May 2010, the ICO foolishly asked Google to delete the data it had collected from wireless networks, which would have hidden forever what they'd snatched and denied their victims knowledge of what was stolen (even though really reassuring said victims that the data was genuinely dispatched would be difficult, given the underhand way it was acquired in the first place) – but that process of destroying evidence was thankfully halted when the police began their separate investigation.

To be fair, Google is hardly the only offender in privacy terms. Facebook and the social networking media more generally also have privacy questions they need to answer. But of all the providers and organisations working online, Google is the only one I know of to have roamed the streets taking data from the airwaves. That does put them in a special category.

The Street View car data seizing apart, like most companies in the online space, Google can generally defend its products when challenged about privacy or intrusiveness by pointing to the implied or explicit consent of users to surrender or generate data which will be retained by the company. But this does not apply to Street View images, which are of homes whose homeowners have not consented to having such images shared, and of members of the public who have not consented to having their bodies displayed. And unlike the data-seizing issue, Google of course denies having done anything wrong in running Street View per se.

That is a question we ought genuinely to consider. It is my view that Street View is intrusive per se (perhaps particularly so when packaged with Google Earth). 'It's nothing you couldn't see walking along the street', the company's defenders say, as if we are all ten feet tall and have panopticonic vision which permanently records everything around us in glorious Technicolor, beaming it to the internet for later review at our or anyone else's leisure. In this time of catering for every conceivable minority interest, I suppose it's nice when a company does something for burglars. Or indeed for murderers, such as Steven Hodgson, who used it to target his victim's home this year before breaking in.

Then there are the more everyday privacy issues, like two instances in March and June 2010 where they showed images of naked little boys. Then there are the sort of unpleasant and unfortunate moments in time which are bound to occur when images are captured everywhere: Ashleigh Hall's family were very upset by images of her captured on Google Street View shortly before she was killed by the man who had stalked her on Facebook. Indeed, at the most unhappy end of the spectrum, several dead bodies at the scene of accidents have been captured and screened online by Street View in Brazil – from which the trauma and upset caused for families and loved ones can only be imagined. Each time, of course, Google says that what happened was a regrettable accident and the image is removed. But the burden is all on us to do something about it, having had our privacy infringed. They take masses of pictures of us and our property without our consent and without giving us notice, and then tell us that if there are problems or if we object, it's up to us to identify those problems and make those objections proactively. This is the wrong way round. It's their responsibility. They respond that an opt-in system would make Google Street View unworkable. That may be so. But their business concern is not my priority.

For many, Google's Street View cameras are an upsetting invasion of privacy. People are not consulted before Street View arrives in their town or asked if they approve of images of their homes and bodies being put online, and yet Google relies on the public to point out where it has gone wrong. And despite the automatic face-blurring function that the programme runs when images of people are captured, many can be identified by distinctive groupings, by hair or clothing – and of course the actual image is sitting somewhere unblurred in Google's archives. Big Brother Watch supporters have told us of their concerns about (for example) images of their homes and gardens being online, showing the distance of their gate to the child's paddling pool or the motor bike in the garage, the angles from which the pool or the bike can be seen from the house, the type of alarm they have.

We live in a world of technology, in which everyone seems to share everything. It seems to surprise those like Google, who live and work in the tech bubble, that people mind such intrusions. I think that they genuinely didn't foresee the problems that have arisen from Street View, because the notion that one might wish to opt out of such public living is alien to them. But – strange as it may seem to say it in this age – anonymity is not a crime.

Let us be fair to Google. There are many who will like Street View and want to use it, and there are checks in place which can and should be used. But it ought to be much easier for those who dislike the idea of being in perpetual public view to opt out. From what Big Brother Watch hears from our supporters, I think that there is a generational disconnect in play, with those most likely to be upset by Street View being those least likely to know how to go about getting themselves off the site. In this context, it was reassuring that Big Brother Watch received this undertaking from Google: anyone without internet access can write a letter to Google and have their house removed. This is important, because those trying to do so online often continue to struggle. The button to 'report a problem' is translucent and tiny, in the corner of the image displayed. It is hard to find. It is often effectively camouflaged, as it blends into tarmac and appears at a point on the page at which tarmac very frequently appears. Those who tend not to use the internet very much anyway would therefore almost certainly find it impossible to complete the opt-out process (as feedback from BBW supporters has confirmed). Google asked me what I would suggest to help them improve things in light of the negative coverage surrounding their launch in the UK in March 2010. I pointed out this specific issue to Peter Fleisher, their Global Privacy Counsel. He agreed that this was a problem. But nothing has changed.

It's pleasing that, unlike councils and national government, Google at least cares enough about public opinion to enter into a dialogue with critics. But I think that it's plain from the above that Google needs to take far greater responsibility for what they do – and that they need to be punished severely in the wi-fi capture case, which almost certainly constitutes the largest invasion of privacy ever carried out in the United Kingdom.

For those who do use the net and are troubled by Street View, Big Brother Watch has published a step-by-step guide to removing one's home or image from the site on www.bigbrotherwatch.org.uk.

Freedom is a strength

David Davis MP

In politics very few battles are ever won outright. Typically the clash of ideas sways back and forth between the contesting groups, with no clear winner, often for centuries. We have seen this most obviously in the last century in the contention between the capitalist and collectivist views of economies, with each having periods of pre-eminence lasting decades. Yet the battle of ideas in British politics over the freedom of the individual, over liberty under the law, seems to have ended in a conclusive victory. Both the parties in the coalition government are committed to ending the stream of authoritarian measures emanating from the last government. Even the Labour Party, the source of much of that incompetent authoritarianism, maintains an embarrassed silence on the subject. Most of the minority parties reject the authoritarian agenda.

So can we now relax? After all the government has abolished ID cards and started a full review of counter-terrorism legislation. They are going to enact a great Freedom Bill to eliminate vast swathes of unnecessary heavy-handed legislation.

So we have won the argument, and, apparently, the political battle. Why should we not now just move on?

The reason is the same as the one that led Thomas Jefferson to say that 'the price of freedom is eternal vigilance'.

The people who, as ministers and civil servants, eroded our freedoms did not do so out of malevolence. They did so because the pressures and temptations of government and politics made their actions seem rational, even irresistible.

In the first instance the actions were popular. ID cards were popular with 80 per cent of the population in the early days. In the battle over 90-day detention without charge, and then 42 days, over 70 per cent of the population at first supported the then government's policy. Now a combination of argument and events has reversed the public view. Nevertheless, authoritarian answers to intractable problems can often be attractive to the public, and that has not changed.

But it is not just about following the polls. It is more subtle than that.

So why else do governments do this? Why do they set about taking away our liberties and our privacy? Why do they appropriate our identities? It is not just Labour governments (although it has been worse in recent years). Is it misplaced machismo? Were David Blunkett and John Reid and Jacqui Smith going on an exercise to look tough on terror and make the opposition parties look weak? Of course it is partly that, but it is also based on something else. It is based on fear. Fear of failure. Fear of the *Daily Mail* headline when they cannot quite do what they promised to do about crime or immigration, or most particularly preventing terrorist attacks. These so-called tough policies are actually driven by the fear of difficult headlines. They are not tough, they are not courageous: they are actually cowardly.

And what did ministers do? After their initial attempts failed – targets, central controls, all of that – in desperation, they reached out for the nearest glittering toy, the nearest piece of magic that would solve their problem. These technological fixes included ID cards, databases, face recognition programmes, number-plate recognition programmes, biometrics, cameras, DNA databases, electronic surveillance of all sorts. Robert A. Heinlein once said 'to a primitive people any sufficiently advanced technology appears magic'. There is no more primitive group of people than ministers in a funk, and, naively, they saw these technological tricks as magic.

And so, piece by piece, they have eroded our liberty, our privacy, our control of our own identity, one tiny step at a time. Every action was apparently reasonable. So, slowly, without realising it, almost by accident, we lose our freedom. We acquired it by accident; if we are not careful we will lose it the same way.

Many otherwise intelligent politicians think that liberty is an indulgence, that it does not matter in times of recession when more material concerns press on people. I once had a conversation with a journalist who said 'now that people are afraid of losing their job and savings, losing their mortgage, houses, pensions, isn't this liberty thing just a luxury'. So I said to him 'well you tell me, when was the last time that liberty collapsed in Europe?' He looked at me and I could almost see the penny drop. 'Oh' he said, 'the 1930s, the Great Depression. I see what you mean.'

That slightly thoughtless mindset is actually not that uncommon, even in Britain, the home of modern liberty.

Indeed the British people, as we all know, are terribly casual about liberty. They treat it carelessly, like a very old, very comfortable suit of clothes that they have had for a very long time. Because, that is precisely what it is. Only when it is under very visible threat do they react. Then they come out and are willing to die in their hundreds of thousands to defend it. But to get British people to react, we have to make the threat obvious and clear.

One of the first sophisticated politicos to be cavalier with our freedom was Jack Straw. He recently said Britain is not a police state. He was right. This is not a police state. If it were, many of us would be locked up. We wouldn't have the right to debate. But that does not actually let the previous government off. It does not let them off the casual, careless corrosion of our freedoms that has been going on for the last decade and more.

The proper response to Jack Straw is not with an answer but with a question. That question is, when does Britain become a police state? When the government knows everything? When the government knows everything about every citizen anywhere in the country? When they know our every text, our every email, our every web access, our every phone call? When they can track every citizen through their car, to wherever they are in the country? When the police are able to enter your computer and search it without you even knowing about it? When virtually any state organisation can put you under surveillance without supervision or control, even including local government? When the police can arrest you for heckling the foreign secretary? Or for wearing a 'Bollocks to Blair' T-shirt or reading out the names at the Cenotaph. Or when the police can arrest you for photographing a London Bobby?

So is that a police state? Or does it become a police state when MPs are arrested simply for doing their job of holding the government to account and, yes, occasionally embarrassing them. Or, very much more seriously, is it a police state when the government colludes in or condones torture as an act of policy? Is that a police state? Are we there yet? And if the answer is no, now let's turn it round and say how many photographers do we arrest before it becomes a police state? How many innocent people on a DNA database before it becomes a police state: a million, as now, or two million? How many days do you lock people up without charge before it becomes a police state? Forty-two? Ninety? And while you ponder that, remember that 90-day detention without charge was the first number picked by South Africa under apartheid. It then became 180 days, and then it became indefinite. I am glad to say that state fell and was replaced by a better one. But many people suffered wrongful imprisonment before it did.

I don't know the answer to those questions. But I do know this: every erosion of our freedom diminishes us as a people, as a nation, as a civilisation. I also know this, that when the time arrives that we do know it is a police state it will be too late.

Because of course it will then be too late to do anything about it: the death of liberty would lead to the death of dissent. Because justice demands two views, the end of dissent would mean the end of justice. And our country will not be the same again. That is the reason why we had the fight when we did: to stop the rot before it did irreversible harm.

Now, we have had some spectacular victories: the political defeat of 90 and then 42 days and with it the collapse of the authoritarian agenda; the eventual defeat of ID cards; the legal defeat of the DNA database of innocent people, the massive retreat on the communications database that the government has had to undertake. Even David Blunkett gave a lecture on the dangers of the database state. But Blunkett's very partial change of heart tells us something important, because although David Blunkett is an authoritarian to his very fingertips, he is also an acutely clever politician. He can sense a change of wind almost before anybody else.

This has been, and will continue to be, a fateful battle, for freedom is not just an abstract virtue. It defines our society. It defines the spirit and soul of our nation and it defines our civilisation. Freedom of speech is the midwife to the freedom of thought, which is the parent of creativity. That is why we had Newton, Shakespeare, Faraday and all the other great geniuses in our history; probably more than we deserve to have had, given our size. It is what creates character, energy, vigour and integrity. Freedom from oppression gives you dignity, individualism and character. It is one of the reasons that many of our country's institutions of democracy and justice have often been successfully copied around the world.

So freedom is not abstract. It is very real. It makes us what we are. In the context of the government and the government's actions, we should recognise that freedom is not a weakness. Freedom is a strength. That is why as a British Member of Parliament I say to myself, what is the point of Britain if it does not adhere to the freedoms that made it? What is the point of Parliament if it does not uphold its most sacred trust as a guardian of our liberty? What is the point of government if its principles aim to maximise fear and minimise our freedoms?

If we forget this sacred trust to defend freedom under the law, it seldom stops there. We find other civilising instincts become corroded. These rights are fundamental, not limited to citizens of the United Kingdom, but there for everyone.

Tony Blair famously announced after 9/11 that the 'rules have changed'. In truth this appears to have meant 'the rules have gone'. The willingness to dilute the commitment to liberty and the rule of the law which has for centuries been the hallmark of our civilisation has led to a carelessness of moral standards on a wider front. This can best be seen in the acceptance of torture, and the government treating the courts as irritants that get in the way of the execution of policy.

Everybody accepts it is necessary for intelligence agencies to breach the law from time to time. Bribery and blackmail are all part of the tool kit of the clandestine world and nobody should be too prissy about this.

The rules to allow this were never designed to allow torture, however. Furthermore, when crimes are committed, the courts are entirely within their rights to publicise that fact. The government, regardless of what they might think, are answerable to the courts. Their attitude, of using bogus security arguments to keep secret evidence of wrongdoing, is simply wrong.

These torture cases highlight that the fundamental operation of the law is being thwarted by the persistent withholding of information and the repeated assaults on the courts. Whitehall even went so far as placing political pressure on the judges, peddling lines that served to make them appear as dupes of al-Qaeda.

This attitude towards anyone who criticises them or asks for answers is both arrogant and contemptuous.

It was even implied that our courts were alone amongst the judiciary of America's allies in their challenge to torture and rendition. This was also not just wrong, but ignorant in the extreme.

The courts in Canada, Germany and Italy had been vigorous in upholding the rights of suspects not to be abducted and tortured. They also proactively put into the public domain information about the actions of their own and America's intelligence services, where appropriate. Our courts by comparison were courteous to the point of deference.

The Canadian courts went so far as to release video footage of one alleged terrorist, Omar Khadr, being interviewed by Canadian intelligence officers in Guantanamo, showing him breaking down in tears.

The German courts appointed a prosecutor to issue arrest warrants for thirteen CIA agents relating to the case of Khalid el Masri, a Kuwaiti-born German citizen. El Masri was picked up by the CIA, tortured and then dumped penniless in Albania.

In Italy, the courts found twenty-three CIA agents guilty of abducting another suspect in Milan and taking him to Egypt for torture.

Are the Americans really going to cut off cooperation with these countries just because their courts upheld the standards that we are all supposed to believe in?

The United Kingdom rightly sees itself as the home of democracy, freedom and the rule of law. British lawyers created the constitutional framework for German law. Yet our governmental mindset changed so much that they viewed as intolerable court actions that were viewed as mild in allied nations.

It is of course true that the stories of rendition and torture are a propaganda gift to our enemies. The authors of that gift, however, are the members of Western intelligence agencies that precipitated those barbarous actions, and all those who acquiesced in their doing so.

It is now apparent that the loss of our moral compass, which complicity in torture came to symbolise, undermined the very aims these policies were designed to achieve. From control orders to Iraq, time and again the British government has made itself the best recruiting sergeant for terrorism.

We should not underestimate how difficult it is for governments to change the strategy and policies that balance public security and individual freedom. There are many agencies within the state that have strong vested interests in authoritarian measures. Much of this arises from the entirely understandable 'safety first' approach of most bureaucracies. No policeman, no prosecutor, wants the slightest chance of a terrorist atrocity on their watch. They are tempted to press ministers for every extra power, every extra piece of data, no matter how minor the advantage to the state and no matter how major the intrusion on the rights of the citizen.

Thus control orders were introduced to deal with foreign terror suspects who could not be deported. Now they are used entirely for British citizens or residents. 28-day detention was designed to catch dangerous terrorists, but has simply penalised the innocent.

And there are many other policies that also serve as propaganda to our enemies, perhaps none more so than the creation of secret inquests.

The Labour government tried to give itself the ability to have completely secret inquests, with no jury and a judge appointed by a minister, in the 2008 Counter-Terrorism Bill.

The rationale for Labour's assault on our inquest system was supposedly 'national security'. If it was really necessary to put secret evidence into court, then I believe we should have security-vetted juries and present only the secret part of the evidence, 'in camera'; a method which was used in a number of super-secret spy trials in the 1960s.

Again, these proposals were defeated, partly because everybody began to realise that their main aim was reducing political embarrassment rather than maximising military security.

So, battle won after battle won, where have we got to? Have

we, as I suggested at the beginning of this chapter, won the war? Philosophically, yes. Politically, almost entirely. Practically, within the walls of Whitehall, mostly. But as I write, the news comes through of the death of Thomas Bingham. As a judge he was a bastion of liberty, and at a convention two years ago I heard him quote Latimer, as he and Ridley were led to be burned at the stake. 'Be of good comfort, Master Ridley, and play the man! We shall this day light such a candle, by God's grace, in England, as I trust shall never be put out.'

Tom Bingham lit such a candle of freedom. Today it burns bright, but I suspect the next generation, like all before it, will have to work hard to keep it alight. And I am sure they will.

If you want to roll back the 'state', the 'state' includes the EU

Stephen Booth

The European Union's Lisbon Treaty, forced through Parliament despite the broken promises of a referendum, paves the way for far greater incursions into the lives of European citizens and threatens to shift yet more power from national governments to the murky and unaccountable EU law-making apparatus. Reassessing the UK's level of cooperation with Europe therefore needs to be a vital part of the coalition government's pledge to reverse the state's incursions on civil liberties witnessed over the last decade. In fact, over the next four years, the government faces tough choices in Europe that have potentially profound and long-lasting repercussions for civil liberties and the judicial and criminal system in this country. It is no good to fight for our civil liberties at home while closing our eyes to the ever-increasing role that Brussels plays in our lives.

The intention to bolster the EU's role in justice and home affairs was marked in 2010 by a 13 per cent budget increase for this area (higher than any other),[147] the allocation of two European Commissioners (one for Home Affairs and one for Justice, Fundamental Rights and Citizenship) where there was previously only one, and the agreement of a five-year plan of new measures, known as the 'Stockholm Programme'. The Lisbon Treaty also gives the European Commission greater powers to initiate new legislation, and the European Court of Justice unprecedented new powers to enforce it. Lisbon also allows for the creation of a European Public Prosecutor to independently launch investigations and prosecutions. As the Lord Chief of Justice Lord Judge said, 'the development of the European Union, and the extended jurisdiction of the European court in criminal matters, will have a significant impact domestically. Twenty years down the line, where will we be?'[148]

There is a tempting tendency, especially prevalent in the UK media, to portray all EU directives and regulations as foreign intrusions on our lives. However, we must acknowledge that much of the European cooperation in this area over the last ten years was a result of either the acquiescence, or at the behest, of the British government. The previous government often talked a good game on protecting national sovereignty over judicial, legal and policing matters from EU interference. It claimed the UK's 'opt in/opt out' arrangement secured in negotiations on the Lisbon Treaty as a victory for 'the British national interest'. However, the tough rhetoric and claim that the UK could 'pick and choose' which justice and policing policies it opted into was in fact a smokescreen. In practice, the Labour government's record was mixed to say the least. While at times it failed to even engage in crucial negotiations, at others, it drove policy by exporting its domestic doctrine to the rest of the EU. Both embody failures to stand up for the best interests of individual citizens.

For those in favour of extending or cementing the power of the state, the advantage of the EU is that it is akin to policymaking via the back door. And unlike on a national level, once power is handed over, it is nearly impossible for citizens, or indeed future governments, to get it back. If you think rolling back the state in the UK seems difficult, it is near impossible once twenty-six other governments are involved and the European Commission becomes 'guardian' of the whole project. Sovereignty is ceded on the quiet in return for new EU laws, which can be implemented while bypassing national democratic debate and, more often than not, media attention is limited – given the glut of domestic 'big brother' stories, journalists seem unable to keep up with the threats to our civil liberties coming from or via Brussels. A House of Lords report made the point in 2006 that when interior ministers from the EU's six largest member states – also known as the G6 – met at the German Baltic resort of Heiligendamm on 22 and 23 March 2006: 'they discussed almost every aspect of EU policy of interest to them, and in many cases reached firm conclusions on the action which should be taken, and the timetable for it. However in the United Kingdom the meetings went almost entirely unnoticed.'[149]

Law making at the EU level simply introduces another tier of government and is therefore a step further removed from the citizen, reducing transparency and accountability. In addition, the EU's commitment to 'ever closer union' and constant tendency to centralise, regulate and assume power often precludes any rational cost-benefit analysis of the impact that the goal of 'increased security' has on individuals' liberty.

At the same time, we must also recognise that there are occasions when, in a globalised world, with the threat of terrorism and more cross-border crime, regional or bilateral cooperation on justice and security issues is warranted. The EU may play a role in some cases but, given the drawbacks to policymaking at this level, it should only do so if strictly necessary and if, after proper democratic discussion, the benefits of increased security or reduced crime are judged to outweigh the limitations on individual and national freedoms.

However, the struggle to have a rational discussion about the EU's impact on civil liberties is hindered by the polarised nature of the debate on the EU more generally. Those who question the rationale or merits of a particular proposal are soon labelled 'anti-European' and are presumed to be questioning the EU's very existence. This is clearly a very dangerous context in which to make such important decisions as it allows policymakers and politicians to use the tarred brush of 'euroscepticism' to dismiss legitimate concerns about the power of the state over the individual. It is no wonder then that the lack of a mature debate has left us with a legacy of EU measures that are needlessly disproportionate and which have often left civil liberties by the wayside.

There are two recent cases of EU legislation that stand out as shining examples of the dangers and pitfalls of pursuing justice and security policy at the EU level: the European Arrest Warrant (EAW) and the Data Retention Directive.

The EAW, which was agreed in June 2002 in the aftermath of the 9/11 terrorist attacks in the US, and came into force in the UK in January 2004, removes the right of UK courts or government ministers to refuse extradition of British citizens to other EU states.[150] It covers not only terrorism but also a list of thirty-two very broadly defined offences which are not subject to the principle of dual criminality – the principle that an alleged crime is considered an offence in both the requesting and extraditing countries. The list includes: computer-related crime; racism and xenophobia; swindling; racketeering and extortion; piracy of products and sabotage.[151] Furthermore, a 2009 change means that member states may no longer reject a request for extradition if the person concerned has been tried in their absence.[152] The UK strongly supported the EAW, with Prime Minister Tony Blair saying in 2002: 'it is manifestly in this country's interest to have a procedure that is a fast-track procedure for extraditing people to this country from European countries... what this will do is simplify the procedure enormously.'[153]

Removing obstacles to the prompt extradition of terror suspects is one thing but the EAW's scope is so wide that there is an unsatisfactory level of legal protection against the extradition of citizens suspected of committing all manner of other offences. The EAW is now routinely used for offences that are either innocuous or where there is certainly no obvious need for a fast-track procedure that overrides member states' legal systems. For example, when looking at an EAW extradition case involving the alleged purchase of a stolen mobile phone in Poland worth about £20, which would be highly unlikely to lead to a custodial sentence in the UK, Lord Justice Maurice Kay noted: 'one is becoming used to European extradition cases for less serious offences than used to come before the courts for extradition, but in my reasonable experience of cases under the 2003 Act I have never seen one quite as low down the calendar as this.'[154]

The EAW is based on the principle of 'mutual recognition' of other member states' judicial and legal systems, effectively making the decisions of foreign judicial and law enforcement authorities binding on the UK. To repeat the point, it is far from clear why Europe needs a fast-track system of extradition that goes beyond cases where the suspects present a serious and imminent risk to public security. In cases of a less serious nature, there is no reason why there shouldn't be proper safeguards that allow member states to ascertain whether their citizens, or other EU citizens for that matter, have a case to answer before they are shipped off into foreign custody.

In April 2010 Ian Bailey, a British former journalist suspected in connection, but not charged, with the murder of a French filmmaker in Ireland in 1996, was detained by the Irish authorities under an EAW issued by a French judge.[155] French lawyers argued that they had jurisdiction over the case, citing the French Constitution, which states that murder cases involving French citizens in any part of the world can be brought in front of the French courts. However, the Irish Director of Public Prosecutions had decided not to prosecute Bailey for the murder. Therefore, in practice, the French extradition request amounted to a breach of the double jeopardy principle, enshrined in the European Convention on Human Rights (ECHR), as well as the Irish Constitution.

If Bailey were to lose his fight against extradition, the Irish authorities would have deported someone whom they believed did not have a case to answer under Irish law to face charges in another country. Leaving aside the specifics of Bailey's case, this example illustrates the potential that the EAW has to under-cut long-established national legal systems and traditions. Another controversial piece of EU legislation, the Data Retention Directive, which was agreed in 2006 and implemented in 2009, is a prime example of a UK government initiative that has been exported to the EU. The directive was tabled after the Madrid bombings in March 2004 and then fast-tracked under the British EU Presidency after the London terrorist attacks in July 2005.

The directive requires telephone operators and internet service providers to store data concerning every phone call, text message, email and website that their users access and make it available to government authorities. Although this does not include the content of emails or a recording of a phone call, it tracks the correspondence between citizens. UK authorities, including local councils as well as the police, can access this data under the Regulation of Investigatory Powers Act (RIPA). A report compiled by Sir Paul Kennedy, the Interception of Communications Commissioner, revealed that in 2008 a total of 504,073 requests were made to access communications data, the equivalent of one request every minute.[156] The report also disclosed that hundreds of errors had been made in these 'interception' operations, with the wrong phone numbers or emails being monitored.[157]

Because the data retention legislation derived from the EU it was allowed to pass through Parliament as secondary legislation, meaning it was subject to little or no scrutiny by MPs, practically handing the government a blank cheque to legislate. The then shadow Security Minister Baroness Pauline Neville-Jones warned, at the time, 'The government cannot expect us to support an instrument where there is such uncertainty over what it will do and how it will work in practice.'[158] It was only when the government attempted to 'gold plate' the directive, by introducing measures over and above the EU requirements, that it hit the headlines. The government's plan to build a central database to hold all the communications data, which would have required primary legislation, was greeted with sufficient public outrage[159] that the proposal was eventually shelved.[160]

The second major concern from a civil liberties point of view is the Data Retention Directive's legal basis in EU law. The European Commission, backed by a ruling from the European Court of Justice, decided that the directive should be brought in under single market rules rather than the justice and home affairs provisions in the EU treaties, thereby removing national vetoes over the proposal and also any future amendments to it.[161] The UK, desperate to put the legislation in place, was seemingly willing to give up its veto and, at the same time, agreed to a precedent whereby new EU laws which ostensibly relate to security and justice could be justified on the legal basis of rules governing the EU's internal market (in this case telecommunications). Such a casual approach to the rule of law would, understandably, not be tolerated nationally and it is alarming to say the least that the government was not held to account for this potentially far-reaching decision.

With the Lisbon Treaty now in place, the European Commission and national ministers have wasted no time in pushing for more cooperation in judicial and criminal matters in the shape of a new five-year programme, known as the 'Stockholm Programme'. The proposals, brought in under the Swedish EU Presidency in late 2009, will see a sharp increase in measures designed to share information on citizens across the EU. Beatrice Ask, the Swedish Minister for Justice, said at the time that, 'There is distinct need to work out an EU master plan on information exchange between law enforcement authorities.'[162] Other measures include the transfer of criminal proceedings and trials among EU member states.

The EU is also entering into more agreements with third countries such as the US to share citizens' data for counter-terror investigations. In February 2010 the European Parliament voted to end an agreement, reached between the EU's twenty-seven national governments and the US, to hand over details of European citizens' bank transactions over fears that there was insufficient protection for personal data.[163]

There may well be a good case for sharing such data in order to fight serious terrorism but shouldn't national parliaments be debating whether their citizens' data is handed over en masse to foreign countries rather than the European Parliament? There are people who argue that the European Parliament's greater powers, granted to it under Lisbon, will ensure that citizens' interests are better represented. However, these people should be reminded that only thirty-five per cent of the UK population and only forty-three per cent of the EU population turned out to vote for their MEPs in 2009.[164] This is no basis for effective representation.

But the key development over the next few years will be the increasing role of the European Court of Justice in Luxembourg. Under the rules of the Lisbon Treaty, the Court's jurisdiction is due to be fully extended to justice and policing legislation for the first time from 1 December 2014. This clearly marks a major transfer of power to the European courts as they would have the last say in these matters. The ECJ is not only unaccountable to citizens but, as we have seen with the Data Retention Directive, it also has a habit of making judgments that only serve to increase its powers and those of the other EU institutions.

However, the UK does have a choice in this. Under a provision in the Lisbon Treaty, the UK has until 1 June 2014 to decide whether it wants to remain a part of the vast majority of EU justice and policing legislation already in force by choosing whether to opt in or out en bloc (for EU asylum and immigration measures there is no such choice). As a result, in December 2014, if the government decides to opt out, the bulk of EU justice and policing laws will no longer apply to the UK, or, if it opts in, these laws will fall under the jurisdiction of the European Court of Justice.[165]

This ticking time-bomb, left by the previous government,

represents a huge decision, which will not only have an enormous impact on the legal system in this country but could also prove politically explosive for the new coalition government. It is widely known that the Conservatives and the Liberal Democrats do not see eye to eye when it comes to Europe, but this is especially the case when it comes to EU cooperation in justice and policing. The Conservatives opposed the European Arrest Warrant when it was first proposed and, before entering the coalition agreement, pledged to 'return powers' from the EU over criminal justice.[166] The Liberal Democrats, on the other hand, pledged to: 'keep Britain part of international crime-fighting measures such as the European Arrest Warrant, European Police Office (Europol), Eurojust, and the European Criminal Records Information System, while ensuring high standards of justice.'[167]

The fragile coalition between the two parties on this issue will therefore be continually tested, not only in making the 'big decision' in June 2014, but also as the European Commission proposes new initiatives or as it tries to amend existing legislation – any such amendments are automatically brought under the jurisdiction of the ECJ. While the Conservatives will still be granted the opportunity to make good on their pledge to opt out of EU criminal justice measures in 2014, it will only be on the EU's terms: the UK is either in, bound by the jurisdiction of the ECJ, or it is out altogether. The latter option would of course play well with the party faithful but it is unlikely to do so with security advisers, the Crown Prosecution Service and civil servants who have no doubt become attached to many of their new powers.

However, on balance, it would surely be in the best interests of citizens to take this opportunity to revaluate the UK's involvement in the EU's criminal justice and policing agenda and embark upon a new relationship that has been thoroughly debated in this country. And, just as importantly, if the new government is serious about rolling back the 'state', the 'state' also includes the EU. Future governments are likely to want to cooperate with their European partners on these issues, albeit probably not the ECJ, but any future agreements would have far greater legitimacy if they were properly debated and scrutinised by national politicians, the media and the public at large. Scaremongers will say that, if the UK were to once snub the EU by opting out, other European governments would refuse future requests for cooperation. This is the regrettable attitude that got us into this mess in the first place and ignores the fact that, when it puts its foot down, the UK is big enough to get most of what it wants, most of the time. Governments should have the courage to debate these issues with their citizens and then use this as the basis to enter into agreements with other countries. It is the least citizens should expect.

Liberty lost, democracy denied: the dual attack on Britain's tradition of freedom

Dominic Raab MP

In November 2008, as I finished writing *The Assault on Liberty: What Went Wrong with Rights*, an effort to describe New Labour's unprecedented dual attack on the British tradition of freedom, I asked myself a simple question: will it get worse?

On the one hand, we had witnessed a torrent of arbitrary legislation, whipped through Parliament on the wafer-thin pretext that it would make us safer from crime and terrorism. After proposals to extend detention without charge that even the former head of MI5 called 'draconian'; the introduction of the intrusive and recklessly vulnerable ID cards scheme; the stretching of surveillance powers, designed for counter-terrorism, but used to trail children home from school to check their catchment area; with half a billion wasted on more CCTV cameras per person than any other country (that produce just 20 per cent of usable footage); and having amassed the largest DNA database on the planet, but failed to improve detection rates – what more could the government do? How long before the notoriously apathetic British public awakens from its slumbers, and pushes back on the creeping authoritarianism of the state, which is robbing the citizen of his most basic freedoms without making an ounce of difference to public safety?

At the same time as our fundamental freedoms are pawned off all too cheaply, the British idea of liberty has been surreptitiously attacked on a different front – conflated, as swathes of other comparatively minor grievances, claims and interests were shoehorned into the ever-elastic language of inalienable, unimpeachable and judicially enforceable 'human rights'. Unaccountable judges at the European Court of Human Rights in Strasbourg – half of whom were not judges before their appointment – took it upon themselves to re-write the European Convention, carefully agreed between European governments in the aftermath of the Second World War. The result was to upgrade swathes of public service entitlements – including claims to social services, NHS treatment, welfare payments and even policing – to the status of constitutionally-guaranteed rights. The Human Rights Act has exacerbated the 'rights inflation', giving free rein to the most active of judicial legislators. Judges at home and in Strasbourg happily usurped the role of elected politicians, democratically accountable for debating and determining the delicate balance of public service priorities. Compounded by a growing compensation culture and mind-numbing applications of health and safety rules, New Labour's approach to human rights had become all things to all people – was there anything left we didn't have a 'right' to?

Liberty Lost

Eighteen months later, the dilemma is slowly dawning – but, under Gordon Brown New Labour's bandwagon just kept on rolling. Remember those blood-curdling assessments of the terrorist threat, backed up by ministerial statements that the police would be swamped under the 28-day pre-charge detention limit if it was not extended? Recent Home Office data shows these claims were nonsense at the time. Swamped under the 28-day limit? Hardly, as in almost four years now, no one has been detained by the police for longer than 19 days, let alone 28, whilst the head of MI5 has publicly stated that 'late-stage' terrorist planning has declined.

In 2010, ID cards were rolled out by stealth, as Labour ministers quietly ditched claims that they can stop crime, benefit fraud or terrorists. Instead, they boasted that the new IT made them a safer travel document and guaranteed access to services for the young and elderly. Even these diluted claims crumbled, as banks rejected ID cards and the new ID Commissioner warned that the ID cards database remained prone to abuse, inherently 'vulnerable to people who are stupid or corrupt'.

Meanwhile, stop and search under counter-terrorism powers sky-rocketed – from under 4,000 in 2001 to over 250,000 in 2009 – yet just 1 per cent lead to an arrest (let alone charges or a conviction). In one ludicrous case, TV presenters doing a sketch for a children's show were apprehended – wearing flak jackets, dark glasses and brandishing pink and turquoise hairdryers.

We are no safer as a result of this creeping authoritarianism. In a withering attack, former head of MI5, Dame Stella Rimington, exposed the fraud in Labour's claim to be trading freedom for security: 'it would be better that the Government recognised that there are risks, rather than frightening people in order to be able to pass laws which restrict civil liberties, precisely one of the objects of terrorism: that we live in fear and under a police state.'

This was followed in 2010 by the Joint Committee on Human Rights, who bluntly reported that: 'since September 11th 2001 the Government has continuously justified many of its counter-terrorism measures on the basis that there is a public emergency threatening the life of the nation. We question whether the country has been in such a state for more than eight years.'

The assault on our liberties has been matched by Labour's erosion of the justice system, rendering it less fair, and more flimsy. There has been a concerted drive to shortcut proper British justice, coinciding with an exponential increase in the use of 'instant justice' – including cautions and spot fines. The magistrates' courts used to deal with the overwhelming majority of criminal cases. That provided a judicial check on police and prosecuting authorities, but also – as a result of their independence and impartiality – entrusted the judiciary with proper sentencing powers unavailable to the police. Yet, since 1997, seventy-three courts (around 10 per cent) have been closed – whilst half of all criminals now avoid court altogether.

Over-reliance on spot fines risks arbitrary justice, because there is no check on police or council officers. The Magistrates Association recently spoke out against the over-reliance by police on cautions and spot fines – warning that it is a 'certainty' that some officers will misuse the powers. Equally, increasing numbers of over-zealous parking wardens – sometimes now paid on a commission basis – fine anything that moves. Seventy-six-year-old great-grandfather Ron Padwick was fined £75 because his parking permit was the wrong way round (although perfectly legible). Residents have been fined for overfilled wheelie bins. Even an ambulance was recently fined, as the driver stopped off to pick up medicine.

Whilst innocent law-abiding citizens may be vulnerable to jobsworth council or police officers abusing their powers, excessive reliance on 'instant justice' lets more serious criminals off the hook all too lightly. Around 40,000 assaults each year are now dealt with by a caution – a formal slap on the wrist – with the figures for 2009 including an instance of rape and a man who glassed a pub landlady. The government is effectively using spot fines to tax – rather than punish – criminal behaviour, with one thief given twelve spot fines for shoplifting rather than being properly prosecuted in court (where sentencing powers are stronger). Government-sanctioned 'pay-as-you-go hooliganism' undermines public trust and police confidence. In August 2009, rank and file police officers led by the Police Federation accused the government of 'dumbing down' the criminal justice system, leading the Director of Public Prosecutions to call for a review.

If spot fines have been used to side-step the justice system – and have allowed offenders to circumvent proper punishment – 2010 saw the first criminal trial in England and Wales in 400 years to dispense with the jury. The jury is an ancient bulwark of British justice, dating back to Magna Carta, connecting the complex machinery of justice with the real world. Our history is littered with cases of juries acquitting people prosecuted under bad law or in the interests of justice (which are not always the same as the dictates of law). The Labour government tried – and failed – to remove juries from complex fraud trials and sensitive coroners' inquests. However, in January 2010 the jury was dismissed for the trial of four men accused of a £1.75 million robbery at a Heathrow warehouse. Three previous trials had collapsed, with evidence of jury tampering, allowing prosecutors to apply to dispense with the twelve jurors. The logic could not be more perverse. First, having pumped billions into resourcing the police and endowing them with a wide array of new powers, why – for the first time in British history – are they uniquely incapable of putting together measures to protect the integrity of the jury? Why did our law enforcement capability in this area collapse in 2010, to justify shelving one of the ancient pillars of our justice system? The Lord Chief Justice – in a BBC interview on the subject in October 2009 – argued: 'those who say that no price is too much are overlooking that you have to choose between hospitals and schools and armour for our troops in Afghanistan, and all the other demands on public money.'

This public – and political – defence of government policy is both remarkable and flawed. Since when were judges democratically accountable for setting public service priorities? Ironically, the expansive approach to human rights definitions – via judicial legislation under the Human Rights Act – has imposed onerous new financial burdens on police, the NHS, social services and councils through judicially-divined 'positive obligations' (see below). But, the financial case for dispensing with the jury in this case is punctured by the £22 million squandered on the three trials that collapsed beforehand. Is it being seriously suggested that adequate juror protection, in the first trial, could not have been achieved at a fraction of that cost, thereby saving the expense of three subsequent trials? The removal of the jury is not a trade-off between principles of justice and protecting the public, but the symptom of a breakdown in law enforcement. A dangerous precedent has been set. It is only a matter of time before we see further attempts to remove juries, unless the existing legislation is repealed – just at the time when other countries including South Korea, Japan and China are drawing inspiration from the British jury model to strengthen safeguards in their own criminal justice systems.

When it comes to surveillance, the government has consistently overstated the crime-cutting benefits – and is now regularly caught being economical with the truth. Take CCTV. We have more CCTV cameras per person than any other country, and cases of palpable abuse – like the CCTV camera placed in a bedroom at a residential family centre to spy on the parenting skills of a young couple. From a law enforcement perspective, a 2005 Home Office report found that CCTV 'had little overall effect on crime levels', a police study in 2007 found that 80 per cent of CCTV footage is not fit for purpose, while a report by the Metropolitan Police last year found that one crime was solved for every 1,000 cameras. Despite the evidence – produced by the Home Office itself – ministers serially, and casually, exaggerate the impact of CCTV. In one particularly stark example, at Prime Minister's Questions on 18 June 2009, Gordon Brown nonchalantly claimed that 'in the most recent experiment, in central Newcastle, CCTV reduced crime by 60 per cent' – remarkable and ground-breaking figures, if true. It took three months for the government to disclose the source of the claim. Far from being recent research, the study was published in 1995. Far from cutting overall crime by

60 per cent – there was a 56 per cent drop in *one* crime, in *one* part of the city – the city-wide results showed a mere 2 per cent fall in burglary, and 8 per cent rises for criminal damage and theft. At what point does this amount to lying?

When it comes to intrusive surveillance conducted by town halls and quangos, state snoopers have expanded their remit still further – from dog fouling, bin crimes and policing catchment areas – to undercover riverside surveillance of anglers engaged in the nation's favourite sport, and following paper boys to check their licences (I was blissfully unaware such licensing existed). Yet, only 9 per cent of such authorised surveillance investigations lead to any sort of caution, fine or prosecution – an astonishingly poor return on the millions of pounds of precious law enforcement resources invested in this way.

Meanwhile, the Labour government continued its drive towards a 'presumption of guilt'. It proposed a vetting system to force community volunteers to prove they are not paedophiles, and micro-chipping every dog in the land and compulsory canine insurance for every owner to tackle a small number of people using dogs as weapons. Bit by bit, the citizen is becoming more accountable to the state – when British democracy is based on the reverse. Whilst the Information Commissioner warns against 'hardwiring surveillance' into our society, the gains in terms of public protection have been minimal, despite the billions invested in amassing such an enormous apparatus of state surveillance.

Democracy denied

So liberty matters – and the government's pretence of a trade-off between liberty and security turns out to be a con. But liberty is not the only thing that matters in our democracy – it is a pillar, but not the only one. We also value the rule of law (based on clear and predictable rules), the separation of powers between those who make and those who interpret the law and, perhaps above all, democratic accountability – the basic notion that law-makers should be directly elected representatives. Nor, for that matter, is liberal democracy the only thing we value in life. As the great British thinker Isaiah Berlin recognised: 'everything is what it is: liberty is liberty, not equality or fairness or justice or culture or human happiness or a quiet conscience.'

Freedom from abuse by the state is no magic wand for good schools, hospitals or finding the right balance between public service priorities. In fact, this was the original Marxist critique of liberty and liberty-based rights against the state. Marx's disciples viewed the post-revolutionary state as a redeemer, the iron fist redistributing wealth and engineering social equality, crushing individual dissent if necessary along the way. Liberals – in the philosophical, not party political sense – see the state as a threat; socialists see the state as their saviour.

If liberty was the principal source of the British tradition of human rights, a much wider notion of 'human rights' has now been co-opted by the various new brands on the left – socialists, social democrats and other hybrids. The British tradition of liberty that inspired the likes of Locke, Mill and Berlin was based on 'negative freedom', protecting the individual from the state. The novel idea of 'positive freedom' was expanded to incorporate anything else a person might value to build a good life, from personal entitlements like social services to collective goods like the environment, and shoehorned into a more elastic concept of human rights, which has increasingly come to represent all things to all people.

In reality this evolution started in the 1970s, as the European Court of Human Rights in Strasbourg – dominated by continental judges with a more socialist philosophy – abandoned the idea that its role as a court required it simply to apply the law, and began to usurp a law-making function. As of 2007, a majority of the judges in Strasbourg had no judicial experience before taking office there, which may partly explain the lack of judicial discipline. Some on the left welcome judicial innovation. As James Welch (Legal Director at Liberty) celebrates, 'Strasbourg has not let its interpretation of the convention be held back by the language or the intention of the drafters. In the court's words, the convention is a "living instrument" which has to be interpreted in the light of current conditions and standards.' Great, if you are a human rights NGO, bringing test cases against the government. Liberty's raison d'être is to test the boundaries of, and expand, human rights law – and that role has its place. But Liberty does not – and does not pretend to – represent the wider public interest. Nor can the judges – they are not democratically mandated, or accountable, for the novel legislative role they have conjured out of thin air.

Lord Hoffman, at one point the country's second most senior judge, has been a leading critic of these developments. He points out that Strasbourg 'has been unable to resist the temptation to aggrandise its jurisdiction and to impose uniform rules on Member States ... laying down a federal law of Europe'. The practical result has been a steady stream of cases over the last thirty-five years, whereby Strasbourg has developed the concept of 'positive obligations' – many of which are simply public service entitlements dressed up as constitutionally-guaranteed rights. We have seen a litany of new human rights to policing, social services and NHS treatment.

In one case, a drugs-trafficker with AIDS wielded his right not to be subjected to 'inhuman and degrading treatment' – originally inspired by Nazi atrocities during the Holocaust – to block his deportation, and force the government to let him remain in the UK in order to receive medical treatment on the NHS.

As a result of new human rights to policing – notionally based on the right to life, originally designed to prevent extra-judicial execution by dictators and despots – police are being forced to divert an increasing amount of time and resources to provide witness protection to gangsters giving evidence in mafia trials.

This inevitably displaces the police resources allocated to protect law-abiding members of society. It has been estimated that British police now spend £20 million a year protecting gangsters from each other, a perverse prioritisation of finite law enforcement resources.

Against this backdrop, the Human Rights Act (HRA) – brought into force by the Labour government in 2000 – has only made the 'rights inflation' worse. First, because the UK courts have interpreted section 2 of the HRA as a duty to match the case law produced by Strasbourg under domestic law, even though the European Convention imposes no such obligation to follow 'precedent' under international law, and few other civil law countries on the continent adopt such a strict approach. And, second, section 3 of the HRA allows UK courts to overrule the will of Parliament in their application of human rights. As one former Parliamentary Counsel described the practical effect, section 3 'instructs the courts to falsify the linguistic meaning of other Acts of Parliament, which hitherto has depended on legislative intention at the time of enactment' – giving domestic judges a broad licence to re-write British law to give effect to new rights made in Strasbourg.

In some areas, the UK courts have gone even further than Strasbourg. Strasbourg has banned deportation if there is a real risk of torture, but – as the House of Lords itself notes – Strasbourg has not blocked deportation on wider grounds. In contrast, the UK courts now regularly refuse to deport criminals if it disrupts their family life. An investigation by the *Sunday Telegraph* in 2009 estimated that at least fifty foreign criminals had resisted deportation in the past year on human rights grounds, most by claiming some sort of family rights.

Elsewhere, the number of illegal traveller sites has increased by over a half since the HRA became law, as many claim a human right to override planning law and camp on areas of greenbelt or outstanding natural beauty.

Some welcome this expansion of rights – beyond their protection of liberty. In 2009, the Labour government toyed with going even further, by enacting a string of new economic and social rights – including to NHS services, education and housing. Others, like Mary Robinson, go further still – arguing that climate change is as much an issue of human rights as a global challenge, because it violates 'the basic human rights of millions of the world's poor to life, security, food, health and shelter'. But why, then, stop there? If we are seduced into such an elastic approach to human rights, what don't we have a right to?

There are at least five good reasons to stop – and scale back – the ballooning expansion of human rights. First, at a philosophical level, once human rights start protecting more than liberty – or negative freedom in Berlin's sense – the floodgates open. There is very little that we want in life that cannot – somehow – be shoehorned into the language of human rights. Yet human rights are, by definition, meant to be a limited number of core freedoms – or, in Lord Hoffman's words, an 'irreducible minimum' of rights to liberty and respect for everyone – that government or Parliament cannot override. They have a sort of trump card status – in that, constitutionally, they out-rank the wider collective interest. That is one reason to keep the list of human rights relatively short. If we upgrade every claim, entitle-ment and social or economic aspiration to the status of a guaranteed human right, we dilute the value – not to mention credibility – of all human rights. The juxtaposition of a few individual rights to inviola-ble freedoms protected from the wider public interest – legitimately pursued by democratic government – collapses.

This basic philosophical distinction has strong public support. A 2008 Ministry of Justice study found public support for an approach that protects fundamental liberties – associated most closely in the public mind with liberty of the person, freedom of speech, freedom of conscience, freedom of worship, the right to a fair trial, personal privacy and freedom of movement. But it revealed popular concern about the current direction 'whereby individuals can selfishly exercise too much power against the system and find justification for antisocial behaviour in terms of their "rights". The report highlighted a common complaint that human rights 'burden [public service] providers and encourage unscrupulous individuals to seek unjustified compensation'. It found that many associate human rights with political correctness, lack of discipline amongst the younger generation and the compensation culture. Critically, whilst 84 per cent support a law to protect fundamental rights, 57 per cent believe that 'too many people take advantage of the Human Rights Act.' The inflation of rights beyond fundamental liberties has devalued their currency, tarnishing the credibility of human rights in general – at a time when preserving the British tradition of liberty has never been more important.

The second reason to curb the rights inflation is because it undermines the second pillar of our democratic architecture, namely the rule of law. The rapid expansion of human rights has created legal uncertainty and confusion for those on the frontline of public protection. For example, in 2004 Naomi Bryant was strangled and stabbed to death by Anthony Bryant, a dangerous criminal released on licence. The independent review pointed to lax supervision by probation officers, highlighting the corrupting influence of the HRA when designing licence conditions for dangerous criminals:

> This whole process is additionally complicated by the human rights considerations in each case which have grown in importance following a series of Court judgments. Prisoners are now legally represented at Parole Board hearings, often by counsel, who also have recourse to judicial review. It is a challenging task for people who are charged with managing offenders effectively to ensure that public protection considerations are not undermined by the human rights considerations.

Elsewhere, police have refused to make public the identity of convicted criminals – including fugitive killers – allowing fear of interfering with their privacy to trump the imperatives of law enforcement. Even the Serious Organised Crime Agency laments that it cannot publish the identities of fraudsters subject to Financial Reporting Orders, for fear of violating their newly-found privacy rights.

The third objection to the rights inflation is cost. The shift from negative to positive freedom is expensive. The expanded human rights are not just demanding that government interferes less with individuals (which generally, not always, is less expensive because it involves the state doing less). They often impose what human rights lawyers euphemistically call 'positive obligations' on the state to do things, often providing additional services. So while liberty-based rights are *protectors* – shielding the individual from the state – the new brands of human rights are increasingly *providers*, asking the state to do more not less.

Take the massive rise in prisoner claims against the prison service. The overall volume of litigation has skyrocketed since the HRA, with legal aid funding for prisoner claims rising from £1 million in 2001/2 to £19 million in 2007/8. In 2006, the Home Office paid over a million pounds to settle a series of claims by prisoners, following its efforts to get addicted offenders off their cycle of drug dependency. A number of prisoners claimed this was cruel, inhuman and degrading treatment – successfully demanding that the prison service supply their human right to methadone, a substitute dependency. I warned at the time that the government should have fought these claims in court, or there would be worse to come. Sure enough, a prisoner is now taking HMP High Down to court for withdrawing his tobacco privileges as a disciplinary sanction for misbehaviour – claiming a human right to cigarettes.

Astonishingly, as a result of the HRA, these claims are being brought under the same article of the European Convention that was designed to ban the kinds of torture and inhuman treatment inflicted by the Nazis. Not every such claim succeeds, but it costs the taxpayer millions just to defend them – not to mention the costs of funding them, as most prisoners rely on legal aid.

Other public services, including the NHS, face a similar explosion of legal claims, diverting vast sums away from providing healthcare. In May 2009, the NHS Litigation Authority lambasted the system as 'indefensibly expensive', as one estimate put the backlog of claims for compensation at £12 billion. The wider compensation culture has been fuelled by a range of factors – including the current no-win no-fee rules – but the HRA has also promoted unprecedented claims.

Some welcome the promotion of economic and social rights via the back door. Left-wing commentators, like Polly Toynbee, explicitly embrace this scorched earth strategy – arguing that such '"rights" to services will nail down enormous spending commitments, making it harder for any Conservative government to shrink the social state'. At least she is honest.

That leads to the fourth argument against the rights inflation: the democratic deficit. It is one thing for democrats on the left to favour the accumulation of public service entitlements as 'human rights', but it is fundamentally anti-democratic to support the creation of such rights by judges – at home or abroad – rather than by elected law-makers. Lord Hoffman highlights a Strasbourg case about night flights at Heathrow, legitimate legal claims by way of judicial review, but 'about as far from human rights as you could get'. Strasbourg overruled the delicate balance struck by the UK government between the economic interests of the country, and the concerns of local residents, ruling that the residents had human rights against noise and air pollution. For those of us who have lived under the Heathrow flight-path, this decision has a superficial attraction. But, if we expand human rights so broadly as to encompass a right to blue skies and quiet neighbourhoods, what don't we have a right to? And, when it comes to making the right decision in such finely balanced cases, do you want it decided by unelected European (or UK) judges, or elected British law makers whom you can hold to account at the ballot box?

Or, again as Lord Hoffman bemoans in the context of the growth of privacy rights at the expense of free speech:

> It cannot be right that the balance we in this country strike between freedom of the press and privacy should be decided by a Slovenian judge saying of a decision of the German Constitutional Court – 'I believe that the courts have to some extent and under American influence made a fetish of freedom of the press.'

The fifth reason to stem the rights inflation is cultural. As Roger Smith, Director of Justice, states, 'the [HRA] has led to a distinct change of legal culture'. In fact, the HRA is just one element of a much broader shift towards a claims culture, boosted by the current no-win no-fee arrangements, the growth of health and safety regulation that mollycoddles public servants and the wider public, compounded by steps via the new Equality Bill towards positive discrimination. The sense of personal grievance and entitlement in our society is now out of kilter, at the expense of the traditional British ethos of personal responsibility and civic duty. To take one concrete example, Article 14 of the European Convention bans discrimination against people on grounds of sex, race, colour, language, religion, political or other opinion, national or social origin, association with a national minority, property, birth or other status. This relatively uncontroversial ban on negative discrimination has morphed beyond recognition, partly as a result of the rights inflation and partly as a result of a related – albeit much broader – shift in attitudes. A job centre in Norfolk recently refused to display a job advert seeking a reliable and hard-working domestic cleaner. Why? Because it would discriminate against 'unreliable' applicants.

Discriminating via the back door

Britain should be aspiring towards a meritocratic society, but the Labour government – supported by the Equality and Human Rights

Commission – has headed in the opposite direction by promoting
'positive discrimination'. Under the new Equality Act, employers
interviewing more than one 'equal' candidate, can – and by implication should – decide on the basic of ethnicity, gender or some other
social category. I have never known a serious recruitment process
that has been unable to select candidates solely on merit – by testing
them in different ways, where the competition is strong. By making
gender, race, sexuality or other box-ticking social criteria the prism
through which such decisions can – and should – be made, the
Act introduces discriminatory attitudes via the back door. It is a
deeply symbolic Rubicon, a regressive step away from the liberal
ideal of a society where everyone is treated as an individual – not a
member of a social quota – and judged according to their character
and merit. What chance do we have of realising such a vision for
our society when it is acceptable for the head of the Equalities and
Human Rights Commission to say that there are too many 'white
middle-class lawyers' in Parliament – a statement that is explicitly
both racist and classist?

An agenda for change

Since 1997, the British tradition of liberty has been corroded from
opposite directions, an attack on our basic personal freedoms,
coupled with the contortion of human rights to pursue an expanding
welfare state. It has driven – and fed off – a much broader shift in
social attitudes, undermining individual liberty, personal responsibility and the ideal of a meritocratic society. This sea-change in
law, culture and attitudes will not be reversed overnight. However,
in 2010 under a new Lib-Con government, there is an opportunity
for reform.

After thirteen years of legislative hyperactivity, one measure of
great symbolic and practical significance would be a Repeal Bill
(explicitly included in the Lib-Con coalition agreement) to: dispense

with ID cards, row back some of the intrusive surveillance powers that have been abused, abolish many of the thousand state powers of forcible entry into our homes, revoke the ban on free speech around Parliament, end the prolonged retention of innocent people's DNA on the DNA database, review the arbitrary control order regime and bin many of the 3,000 new criminal offences dreamt up by Labour simply to score cheap political points.

It remains to be seen what survives of the Conservative manifesto commitment to replace the HRA with a British Bill of Rights. A Bill of Rights would enable us to strengthen our fundamental freedoms (including adding some new quintessentially British rights, such as the right to trial by jury), whilst prioritising those freedoms we have traditionally cherished most, like free speech. But it would also allow us to stem the rights inflation, by cutting the umbilical link to Strasbourg case law under the HRA – as the Lord Chief Justice recently called for – and promoting a home-grown human rights jurisprudence that respects the parameters of the European Convention, but builds on Britain's proud tradition of liberty in place of the continental approach to human rights. It could also reduce the scope for judicial legislation – a British Bill of Rights should be both pro-liberty and pro-democracy.

In addition to these two major macro-reforms, there are a range of micro-measures that would make a difference. Curbing the ability of lawyers hired on a no-win no-fee basis to recover excessive 'success fees' from losing defendants would dampen the growing claims culture. Scaling back health and safety legislation – and the role and remit of the Health and Safety Executive – would help rebalance legal and social attitudes towards individual risk and responsibility. We need to review the role of the Equality and Human Rights Commission – and re-focus its mandate on the elimination of discrimination, and away from social engineering.

We need to implement Britain's opt-out from the EU's Charter of Fundamental Rights, which at best represents unnecessary duplication of the European Convention, and at worst may be used by judges at the European Court of Justice in Luxembourg to promote a uniform continental model of human rights, alien to the British liberal tradition. There are other specific EU measures – like the European Arrest Warrant and EU data-sharing schemes – that need reform to protect the liberty and privacy of British citizens.

Above all, we need a renaissance in Britain's proud tradition of liberty, one that restores the other pillars of our democratic architecture – the rule of law, separation of powers and the democratic accountability of elected law-makers. We need a re-statement of the basic principle that risk and responsibility follow from such a renewed commitment to personal freedom. And we need to re-affirm our commitment to a society that judges every individual on merit and according to character – not colour or some other social quota.

Does the Human Rights Act really protect our freedoms?

Francis Hoar

The sad and untimely death of Lord Bingham, one of this country's finest jurists, calls for a reflection on the importance of the rule of law, about which he wrote so recently.[168] Most importantly, what lessons can we learn from the three decades in which Lord Bingham sat as a judge?

It is right to speak with pride of the legacy of Britain's common law system. Its principles are the foundation of legal systems throughout the world that protect the individual against the state. The common law experience shows the merit of laws derived not from the codification of abstract principles but through the resolution of real conflicts and disputes. Yet anyone who watched the BBC's brilliant *Garrow's Law* will have had an insight into how little protection was trial by jury in a world without a fair police force, thorough investigation and strict rules of evidence and disclosure. As we all know, the experiences of the Birmingham Six and Guildford Four demonstrated how inadequate protection against such abuses lived on into the late twentieth century.

The recent general election again brought to the fore debate about the effects of the Human Rights Act 1998 (HRA) and the European Convention on Human Rights (ECHR) it incorporated. As a criminal barrister, though, I would rather start with one of the finest pieces of legislation of the twentieth century, the Police and Criminal Evidence Act 1984. It is through this Act that suspects' interviews must be tape recorded, identification parades held and evidence obtained through oppression excluded. These parts of the criminal justice process may not appear particularly important to a layman, but they are critical. Fine principles are toothless without carefully drafted rules (whether from statute or case law) to ensure a process that appears fair isn't corrupted at critical stages, leading to injustice at best but at worst the imprisonment of the innocent for years, even decades.

This experience of the importance of the practical over the principle leads us to consider how far the HRA has really protected the fairness of the criminal process. Certainly the HRA has had a significant effect on public, criminal and family law. Not least of these was the landmark case of *A & Others* v. *the Home Secretary* (2004)[169] where Lord Bingham found that the provisions of the Anti-Terrorism, Crime and Security Act 2001 allowing the detention without trial of foreign terrorist suspects were incompatible with Article 5 of the ECHR. Elsewhere, the HRA has allowed lawyers to rely on articles of the ECHR in areas as widespread as planning applications (Article 8 – *Coster* v. *UK*[170]), housing law (Article 8 – right to private and family life; and Article 14 – prohibition against discrimination) and immigration law (most frequently Articles 2 – the right to life; 3 – protection against torture; and 8).

Yet we in common law countries know that our freedoms rest on older and surer foundations than the ECHR. The adversarial process, far from impeding the search for the truth, ensures that an individual presents his case to an impartial judge or jury, not an investigating magistrate whose role is impossible to disentangle from the state that prosecutes him. The jury system transfers from the state to a defendant's peers the decision about his guilt. And the many procedural protections built up by Parliament and the courts ensure, where the criminal process outside the courtroom has prevented the possibility of a fair trial, that the proceedings are stayed.

Indeed, the experience of the twelve years since the HRA passed into law is a troubling one, for it has seen the passing of perhaps the most illiberal body of legislation for two centuries. The DNA database expanded to all arrested, regardless of their guilt or the triviality of their alleged crime; hearsay evidence permitted as a matter of routine; bad character evidence routinely admitted; arrests permitted for any crime, even those that do not carry prison sentences; defendants facing accusations impossible to rebut through witness anonymity (see my writing elsewhere)[171]; and a marked increase in minimum sentences, hugely reducing judicial independence. Away from the strictly criminal sphere, the tabloid paranoia over paedophilia has led to a multi-headed hydra of overreaction through the Independent Safeguarding Authority (a report by Civitas[172] published in September argues that any family looking after other people's children faces vetting by the ISA); the Regulation of Investigatory Powers Act 2000 has allowed local councils to authorise 8,500 acts of covert surveillance in only two years (as an investigation by Big Brother Watch[173] uncovered in May); and, but for doughty campaigners such as Shami Chakrabarti and David Davis, we might have had 90-day detention permitted in the mother country of the common law.

This litany of authoritarianism reveals a worrying gap in the protection we have traditionally expected from Parliament as the guardian of our precious legacy of freedom. But it also raises an intriguing question. Why is it that such a sustained attack on freedom has been so exactly contemporaneous with the earliest years of the HRA? More particularly, is it actually the case that the HRA has allowed the last government to plead its respect for human rights knowing that the ECHR was ill-equipped to protect common law standards unique to Europe in the British Isles? If that is so, should we think again about the fundamental standards to which all (British) governments should be tied?

In answering these questions, it is important to consider not merely the limitations of the ECHR but the purpose for which it was instituted and the judicial context in which it has developed. It is right to say that the Convention played an important role in placing respect for human rights and due process at the heart of Europe's recovery from the ravages of war and, in many cases, decades of dictatorship – a role repeated after 1989 as former Warsaw Pact and USSR republics joined the Council of Europe. Yet the Convention's role, in providing a set of principles of due process and human rights, was never intended to do anything more than set down minimum standards of compliance throughout the Council of Europe. That this is a necessary conclusion is apparent not merely from the principle of the 'margin of appreciation' (the latitude given to member states in implementing judgments of the Court at Strasbourg) but also in view of its application both to common and civil law systems.

This is a critical point when it comes to the jurisprudence of the common law jurisdictions in Britain and Ireland. Principles such as habeas corpus, double jeopardy and jury trial have a greater or lesser application in some civil law jurisdictions but never the special status accorded them by the common law. (Readers will note that these three principles are not chosen at random – each of them has been eroded over the past thirteen years.) Thus, the protection afforded by the Convention, for example under Article 5, the right not to be detained without due process, is necessarily limited by the interpretation traditionally put upon such rights by the preponderance of countries in the Council of Europe. For example, while France restricts pre-charge detention to 72 hours, it allows pre-trial detention for up to four years,[174] a period inconceivable under English custody time limits that have developed from the common law tradition of habeas corpus.

Thus, the problem we have identified is not that the HRA has, in itself, been a negative step; rather, that the greater protection it affords against abuses of human rights and due process is insufficient. What is the solution? In my view, the answer is as obvious as it is overdue: a Bill of Rights drafted in Britain designed specifically to protect freedom and due process as we in common law countries understand it; one that doesn't so much override the Convention as complement it.

The arguments against this suggestion are either misinformed or flawed. It is suggested that those who argue for a Bill of Rights somehow wish to 'repeal' the HRA or derogate from the Convention. Anyone who appreciates the case for a Bill of Rights will understand that this is not so. Alternatively, it is suggested (or, perhaps, implied) that to implement a 'British' Bill of Rights is somehow limiting, a movement away from the concept of universal human rights. Those who buy into this fallacy perhaps fall into the trap of thinking that common law principles – which such a Bill would be designed especially to protect – had developed through a judiciary that focused on the rights of *Englishmen*, rather than the rights of *Man*; that Lord Mansfield considered that slavery was abhorrent only in England, not universally; or that jury trial was suited only to these islands. The absurdity of this proposition is laid most bare when one considers the spread of the common law throughout the world – even (most recently) in the United Arab Emirates, where a commercial court is formed of common law judges. Finally, they also ignore the example of Germany, where the constitution contains a Bill of Rights that is enforced in parallel with Germany's obligations under the ECHR.

One of the reasons why the idea of a Bill of Rights has long had so little support is due to an instinctive British aversion to a unified, entrenched constitution. This suspicion is well founded. It is through both Parliament and the judiciary that the common law has developed the protections of freedom which any Bill would be designed to safeguard. As Sir John Laws has argued,[175] this process has been gradual and largely led by the judiciary; there is certainly a risk that entrenching the protections we now recognise risks stifling the very process through which they were identified. Yet the events of the past two decades have surely taught us that this reaction is too glib and too trusting. At the same time, those who drafted and developed (through judicial interpretation) the HRA have done us a great service: introducing a form of entrenchment that provides a high level of protection against parliamentary attacks on human rights without damaging its sovereignty.

It does this in two ways. Firstly, the judiciary are required to interpret all legislation 'so far as it is possible' in order that it is compatible with the Convention. A particularly good example of this working to great effect can be seen in the case of *R* v. *A (No 2)* where the House of Lords effectively struck down an absolute statutory prohibition of complainants in rape trials being cross-examined on their sexual history[177] (a prohibition they found to contravene Article 6 – fair trial rights) by finding that the legislation 'must have' envisaged that such cross-examination could be permitted where it was 'in the interests of justice'.[178] Where such interpretation is impossible, on the other hand, the Act allows superior courts to make a 'Declaration of Incompatibility', which itself allows Parliament to put right any legislation so found by means of secondary legislation. The most notable example of this was the legislation following the case of *A & Others* v. *the Home Secretary* (cited above) abolishing detention without trial and establishing Control Orders.

What is particularly interesting about the last example is that the mechanism of the HRA, although it doesn't provide the judiciary with the power to strike down legislation, has a striking power to shame. In doing so, it gets the balance right. Were Parliament ever to refuse to repeal offending legislation, it could do so only in the knowledge that its decision had already been condemned by the parallel protectors of our freedoms, the independent judiciary.

So the problem – of growing disrespect and even contempt for fundamental common law freedoms – is clear. The mechanism by which the judiciary can be given a greater role in protecting them is already in force. What is needed is a period of reflection and consultation leading to a Bill of Rights we can really call our own. Such a process would indeed protect the rights of the most vulnerable; but it would also persuade the British people to value the freedoms developed thanks to the struggles of their ancestors, the wisdom of our institutions and of the men and women who have influenced them.

Against the Equality Act

Jason Smith

On 1 October the Equality Act 2010 became law. Its stated intention is to end discrimination in the workplace. The likely result is that it will poison relations between employers and their staff as well as hinder colleagues' and workmates' ability to get on together.

The Act encourages us all to see ourselves as victims in need of state intervention to police our working lives and relationships. This legislation and other recent developments should make us question what association there is between modern liberals and the true legacy of liberalism handed to us by Enlightenment thinkers. It is also significant that there has been little protest about this Act except from organisations such as Sp!ked and Big Brother Watch.

How did such a noble aspiration as equality become so sullied in illiberal regulation?

The legislation introduces the concept of 'discrimination by perception' and 'association' to more 'protected characteristics', which is particularly problematic. No discrimination needs to have taken place for a case to be made against a co-worker or employer. The 'victim' just has to perceive discrimination. The perceived offence does not even need to be against someone in the workplace – you can feel discriminated against because you know a Muslim and someone makes a joke about burqas. Or, as the Government Equalities Office and ACAS describe, discrimination by association in their guide to employers:

> June works as a project manager and is looking forward to a promised promotion. However, after she tells her boss that her mother,

who lives at home, has had a stroke, the promotion is withdrawn. This may be discrimination against June because of her association with a disabled person.

Or it may not be. The answer is in June's head. The point with this legislation is that the state has to decide whether June is discriminated against by association, based on her feelings about her manager's actions. Parliamentary Secretary of State Lynne Featherstone MP described the legislation when speaking to the Fawcett Society:

> Building a fairer society is at the heart of the coalition government's programme for change. We believe there are too many barriers to social mobility and equal opportunities in Britain today. For women we want to build a society that works with us and not against us – where women and men are afforded the same opportunities and choices to realise their full potential.

Fair enough, but is this what the Equality Act will do?

The Act brings together legislation governing unlawful discrimination, including the Equal Pay Act 1970, the Sex Discrimination Act 1975, the Race Relations Act 1976, the Disability Discrimination Act 1995, the Equality Act 2006, Employment Equality (Religion or Belief) Regulations 2003, Employment Equality (Sexual Orientation) Regulations 2003, Employment Equality (Age) Regulations 2006 and Equality Act (Sexual Orientation) Regulations 2007.

But the Equality Act is not simply a matter of bringing together discrimination legislation into one package. For a start, it contains a number of new pieces of legislation. The most notable of these is the concept of 'third-party harassment'.

While it was already an offence for an employer to pick on an employee on the basis of race or gender, an employer will now be liable for any employee 'harassment' too. This means that if someone at work feels that another person's comments 'violate their dignity' or create an 'intimidating, hostile, degrading, humiliating or offensive environment', they can sue their employer. All it takes is for one person to deem an interaction a 'violation of their dignity' and in comes the state to arbitrate.

The Act attempts to protect employees from offence, but what it does is undermine the ability of people to sort out issues between themselves. In fact, trying to sort out a problem between yourselves could itself be considered harassment. If someone is offended by something you have said – a joke for instance – explaining yourself to them could be seen as 'rubbing it in', multiplying the offence felt. Your intentions are not important; the psychological state of the offended person is primary.

This deeply illiberal Act encourages everyone to see their colleagues not as allies with a common interest, who can group together to fight redundancies for example, but as rivals, racists, sexual predators and sexists. The notion of discrimination has lost touch with any rationale. Instead, discrimination becomes a free-floating term to be applied to any relationship in which one party feels aggrieved. When feelings of victimhood are enough to sustain an accusation of discrimination, so people will self-censor and wilfully inhibit themselves – not because they actually really wanted to bully someone, but because they are worried that this is how their behaviour could be perceived. Far from enabling everyone to fulfil their potential, as Lynn Featherstone would have it, this legislation treats us all as children who have bad thoughts that must be policed.

Anyone who has worked in an office over the last ten to fifteen years will be aware that it has become increasingly necessary to mind what you say. There is always someone who might take offence easily. This legislation urges us to view all colleagues in this way. Furthermore, it sanctions state intervention as a means of sorting out everyday difficulties.

Banter between colleagues in the workplace is one of the things that makes many jobs worth having. Loyalty to colleagues can often make someone stay in a job they dislike. Tedious duties that form some part of most jobs are made sufferable by chit-chat and occasional ribbing from workmates. Yet it is these positive aspects of workplace relations that are being undermined.

In the past people had no problem coping in the workplace or with being offended.

A good friend of mine, who worked in a Midlands factory in the 1970s, still talks fondly of the practical jokes played on him, and the ones he played on his workmates, like the initiation ceremonies played on sixteen-year-old apprentices by the women in the factory – stripping them naked, tying them to a chair and covering them in sticky 'Barrier Cream' and tissue paper.

On one occasion, during a round of wage negotiations, someone put up a sign saying that the factory was to receive a visit from a Russian delegation that was coming to inspect parts being manufactured for the Soviet Air Force. Staff were 'advised' that they would need to learn the words of The Red Flag, and informed that song sheets should be obtained from the boss. The boss, already tense from the negotiations, was inundated by workers asking for words to the socialist anthem.

More everyday activities, like giving people 'the bumps' on his or her birthday, were concealed from the foreman by the person on the receiving end pretending they had fainted in the heat. 'Of course we could have got the sack for any of these antics', said my friend, 'but we covered up for each other'. 'Whatever you did to someone, they always got you back'.

I used the above examples in a article about the Equality Act recently. Almost immediately a comment was posted suggesting that the initiation ceremonies were child abuse and prosecutions could legitimately have been sought. Everyday activities from just forty years ago are already viewed through the gaze of illiberal liberalism.

The notion that we need to be protected from work colleagues is particularly bizarre.

It was only twenty-five years ago that over a hundred thousand miners fought pitched battles with the police over pit closures. The miners had a common interest. They banded together, often against the wishes of the union who supposedly represented them, and struggled toward goals they shared. Twenty-five years after a paramilitary police army occupied mining communities, arrested 10,000 miners, blocked motorways and did much else besides, the government wants to solve problems that arise between work colleagues. One wonders how this would have gone down in Yorkshire?

This legislation treats adults like children, incapable of managing their own relationships, let alone standing up for themselves. We are being encouraged to internalise a childlike mentality, as if we were in school. Unlike school, however, it is not a teacher managing the children's relationships, but the state, with all the punitive power that entails.

Insofar as it reinforces a sense of ourselves as helpless in the midst of social life, the Equality Act gives institutional form to some of the most retrograde social trends. On the one hand it further entrenches the state's intrusion in the private sphere, allowing it to mediate not just employer–employee relations but those between workmates. On the other hand, it legally enshrines members of civil society as potential victims in need of the state's outstretched hand.

This raises the question of what it means to be a liberal today.

When I first got involved in the Manifesto Club's campaign against 'state hyper-regulation' and around anti-terrorism legislation several years ago, before it was fashionable, there was a stony silence from liberal quarters over the erosion of our freedoms. The state now intervenes in many areas of life that would previously have been considered private. The Equality Act is part of a broader set of laws and practices that are shaping society in a direction which, while using liberal language, attacks the liberties on which our society is based.

In the name of liberalism we have had The Racial and Religious Hatred Act 2006, which removes people's powers to criticise, challenge or defend ideas. The Safeguarding Vulnerable Groups Act, which poisons the relationship between the generations. The Investigatory Powers Act 2000, which legally enshrined the state's right to monitor people's private electronic and material commu-nications. The Crime and Disorder Act, which enshrines hearsay as reason enough to take away someone's liberty. The Criminal Justice Act gave the judiciary the power to remove juries if they felt jury members had been intimidated or influenced by outsiders. Counter-terrorism legislation in 2000 set detention-without-charge powers at 48 hours plus a 7-day extension. In 2003, that was raised to 14 days, and under the 2006 Terrorism Act, it was raised again to 28 days.

What many consider to be the fundamental principles of our soci-ety – tolerance, a sense of justice, fair play – are being stigmatised, and in some instances, criminalised. These various pieces of legisla-tion are concerned with different aspects of our daily lives, but what brings them together is the degraded view of ordinary people that is the motivation behind them. They all assert the primacy of the state over individual rights and autonomy. The first legislation of this sort was the Macpherson report.

The landmark 1999 Macpherson report into the racist murder of Stephen Lawrence in 1993 introduced the concept of 'unwitting racism', and established that any incident could be legally defined as racist if it was seen as such by the victim 'or any other person'. The context or intended meaning of what was said or done were deemed irrelevant; all that mattered was that somebody somewhere felt racially offended or hurt, even if they were not involved.

Although I don't like the term, 'thought crime' springs to mind here. The Macpherson report introduced the concept of 'feeling a crime' rather than the more traditional committing, witnessing or being the victim of a crime. The thoughts and feelings of people unconnected with the offence were deemed relevant for prosecu-tion. The Racial and Religious Hatred Act, and the Equality Act, run with this notion. These three pieces of legislation share some overarching ideas – you and I cannot be trusted, we have bad thoughts, and we will do bad things to others and ourselves. We therefore need the authorities to step in and take charge, to mediate and bring order.

If people are seen in this way how is society to progress? How are we jointly, as a society, to put our heads together and come up with solutions to the problems we face? How are environmental concerns – feeding a growing population, creating economic growth and all the other issues and problems we need to resolve – to be tackled if we cannot handle a chance encounter at the office watercooler without needing to call in the authorities to check we haven't offended anyone?

It is worth considering the liberal tradition we are turning our backs on here.

> The natural liberty of man is to be free from any superior power on earth, and not to be under the will or legislative authority of man, but to have only the law of Nature for his rule. The liberty of man in society is to be under no other legislative power but that established by consent in the commonwealth, nor under the dominion of any will, or restraint of any law, but what that legislative shall enact according to the trust put in it. Freedom, then, is not what Sir Robert Filmer tells us: 'A liberty for everyone to do what he lists, to live as he pleases, and not to be tied by any laws'; but freedom of men under government is to have a standing rule to live by, common to every one of that society, and made by the legislative power erected in it. A liberty to follow my own will in all things where that rule prescribes not, not to be subject to the inconstant, uncertain, unknown, arbitrary will of another man, as freedom of nature is to be under no other restraint but the law of Nature[179]

The Enlightenment idea of liberty was bound up with government. Not to have government was to be 'inconstant, uncertain, unknown and arbitrary'. Government was not an imposition on man, though; rather it was an imposition on the law of nature. The power erected in the legislature is the power of 'every one of that society', as opposed to Sir Robert Filmer's defence of the divine right of kings to do what they please and be tied to no laws.

Government today is acting as if we are in 'a state of nature'. The Equality Act is inconstant, uncertain, unknown and arbitrary. It deals with perceptions, thoughts and policing ideas. Locke's argument from 300 years ago – not to be subject to the arbitrary will of another man – is being torn up. If legislation deals with perceptions and associations rather than actions, deeds and facts then we are very much subject to the arbitrary will, the imagination even, of other men.

Equality before the law – that is law applied to everyone in society and 'made by the legislative power erected in it' – is the basis for a universal system of justice. This is turned upside down by laws like the Equality Act. It is not law applied to everyone, but law applied to people with the wrong ideas; ideas that will offend; ideas supposedly at odds with equality. This used to be known as freedom of conscience. Today our conscience is an arena for policing because having the wrong ideas might lead someone to believe we have discriminated against them.

The choices we make about how to live our lives are a matter for our conscience because we are free, rational beings capable of using our intellect to justify our choices. If someone thinks we have the wrong ideas they can argue with us. They can try to change our minds. The Equality Act gets round this inconvenience by trying to impose morality. The problem with freedom of conscience is that people make the wrong choices, they hold 'unacceptable views'. Where thinkers in the liberal, Enlightenment tradition saw morality largely as a practical capacity of the reasoning individual, today's political class, estranged from any discernable public, suspect the individual of being incapable of reasoning.

The idea that equality can be imposed is another notion that Locke would have difficulty with. Equality as an aspiration arose from the depths of society. It was never a state-imposed objective, an ideal to be forcibly grafted on to a recalcitrant population. It was an articulation born of social struggle from the French to the Russian Revolutions, from the English Civil War to the Suffragettes. That this elite jargon of equality is now little more than a weapon to be wielded against people's freedom – to discriminate, to judge – others, shows just how wedded to the New Labour past the Lib-Cons are.

Supporters of this legislation should be careful. What gets defined as 'acceptable' and 'unacceptable' views changes over time. If you support the clampdown on views that you find unpalatable, then that is also to accept that your own views might reasonably be deemed beyond the pale by someone else at some other point in time. Unless we all have freedom of conscience then no one has it.

Since the 1990s the relationship between the state and the people has been reinterpreted.

As well as the new pieces of legislation listed above, a less regulatory but just as worrying intervention into our personal lives has been taking place. What we eat and drink and other – often intimate – aspects of our lives have become subject to state intervention.

There is no sphere, no matter how personal, in which government does not feel it knows best, and this impulse to nanny us is drawn not from sinister, authoritarian, behind-the-scenes machinations, but from the increasingly internalised belief that we as a people, as a civil society, do not know what is in our own interests. We cannot be trusted with our own freedom: we get drunk too often; we get fat; we say offensive things. Our judgement is considered to be awry. This is evident not just in the increasingly forensic obsession with the way in which we live our everyday lives but in the more traditional areas of concern for civil libertarians, from the erosion of trial by jury, the censorship of our speech, acts and laws like the Equality Act. In each we have ceded authority over our own lives to the state.

If the coalition government is really concerned with individual liberties and individual responsibility, as it claims to be when calling for things like a Big Society, then it would scrap the laws mentioned in this chapter. It would restore freedom of conscience and butt out of peoples' everyday lives to concentrate instead on what it was elected to do: develop a strategy for economic growth that will help the country prosper. People are perfectly capable of sorting out problems that arise in the workplace between themselves.

Eternal vigilance can only be part of the strategy

Mark Littlewood

The new coalition government pledges a renewal of civil liberties. There's no reason to disbelieve them at the outset – both the Conservatives and the Liberal Democrats opposed Labour's relentless assault on long-cherished freedoms, although not as consistently and vigorously as some libertarians would have liked. David Davis famously quit his frontbench role to force a by-election, initially in opposition to the proposal for 90 days' detention without trial, but he swiftly widened his campaign to encompass an entire *cri de cœur* at the loss of liberty sanctioned by the Labour government.

Nick Clegg's Freedom Bill, originally conceived when he was the Liberal Democrats' home affairs spokesman, will be unveiled in the autumn and promises a bonfire of red tape and nanny state rules and regulations. He has indicated that he is open to any and all suggestions from members of the public other than the specific – and rather bizarre – exceptions of the reintroduction of capital punishment and the lifting of the ban on smoking in public places.

Civil libertarians have some basis for optimism, but certainly no grounds for complacency. Firstly, neither the Conservative Party nor the Liberal Democrats have been wholly consistent in their defence of personal freedom in recent years.

Secondly, politicians of all stripes who develop a passion for liberty in opposition have shown an alarming tendency to abandon support for freedom when in government.

Thirdly, a toxic mixture of a tragic event, combined with extensive media coverage and an accompanying public appetite for answers and solutions, can threaten liberty at any moment. We don't yet know whether the coalition government can generally be relied upon to stand firm in the face of such pressures and resist the temptation to legislate as a form of public relations exercise.

Defenders of personal freedom therefore need to consider where the coalition can be encouraged in its avowed determination to re-establish and defend liberties which have been lost over the last decade, where the coalition needs to be talked out of any illiberal instincts or policy ideas, and what sort of strategy would be needed to deal with the unfortunate but inescapable reality that a whole range of unknowable and unforeseen horrific events will occur in Britain over the next five years, leading to calls for freedom to be curtailed.

The civil liberties credentials of the coalition parties

On the headline-grabbing and, it's fair to say, most substantial civil liberty issues of the last Parliament, both the Tories and the Lib Dems showed some impressively robust opposition to a range of Labour proposals.

Although more perhaps could have been done in the House of Lords to thwart the introduction of ID cards, the coalition has begun to tackle the seemingly unstoppable emergence of a database through the repeal of the identity cards legislation and the abandonment of ContactPoint, the children's database which was switched off in August 2010. However, much of the essential infrastructure of the database state remains in place and it's far from certain that the government has the determination to dismantle it properly.

Both the Conservatives and Lib Dems have less enthusiasm for, and faith in, anti-terrorism laws than the previous administration, but this did not prevent them pushing through the Academies Bill under a timetable supposedly reserved for anti-terror laws. Once again, those powers seen as unreasonable from the opposition benches suddenly have attractive practical benefits when sitting on the other side of the House of Commons.

Even in opposition, the coalition parties were not consistent defenders of freedom. And it's well worth pointing out where the Liberal Democrats – perhaps commonly seen as the more enthusiastic of the two governing parties in their support for civil liberties – were willing to adopt authoritarian positions, even without the extra temptations which come with office.

On fundamental liberties – such as freedom of speech and detention without trial – the Lib Dems have generally had a track record of being genuinely liberal. So, in February 2009, Chris Huhne, then handling the party's home affairs portfolio, both surprised and dismayed many in his own party by supporting the Home Office's decision to ban Geert Wilders, the leader of the Dutch Party of Freedom, from the United Kingdom. Wilders had been invited by two peers to show his short film, *Fitna*, a highly controversial condemnation of the inspiration for terrorism apparently found in the Koran. Wilders was eventually admitted to the UK later in 2009, having won his appeal against the ban.

It is also worth noting that the Lib Dems have a curious approach to a whole range of other freedoms. Very few Liberal Democrat MPs opposed the smoking ban, the party was highly sceptical about extending licensing hours, Nick Clegg is enthusiastic about enforcing a minimum price on the sale of alcohol and – perhaps most ludicrously of all – the party is insistent that airbrushed pictures of women in glossy magazines should be clearly labelled as such. Although at a national level, the party has sounded a sceptical note about the merits of CCTV, local Lib Dem activists have often been enthusiastic campaigners for its wider use. None of these policies can easily be reconciled with the label 'Liberal'.

The Conservatives, of course, have not always been enthusiasts for extending human freedom either. In office, they brought in a wide range of criminal justice measures that weakened the individual against the state, and it was Michael Howard, as Home Secretary, who advocated the introduction of national identity cards way back in 1996. It may well be that David Cameron's brand of Conservatism is considerably more sympathetic to civil liberties, but that proposition has yet to be properly tested.

The first substantial test of the new government's credentials came in the wake of two fatal shooting incidents. After Derrick Bird shot dead twelve people in Cumbria and Raoul Moat shot three people with a sawn-off shotgun in Northumberland, it was inevitable that there would be calls for a further tightening of firearms laws. After the Hungerford and Dunblane tragedies, gun laws were changed in the erroneous belief that this would help prevent similar occurrences in future. To the government's credit, a 'knee-jerk response' was resisted. David Cameron rightly pointed out that the UK already has some of the toughest gun laws in the Western world. However, the Home Affairs Select Committee will investigate these laws after the summer recess. The fear must be that the 'something must be done' tendency may yet prevail. And, of course, the Prime Minister himself couldn't resist criticising Facebook for refusing to take down a page commemorating Raoul Moat. Cameron's pronouncement had no legal force – and no actual effect – but again demonstrated the allure of calling for a restriction of liberty in the immediate aftermath of such gruesome events.

The overall conclusion must be that the coalition has some of the right instincts, but can't be wholly relied upon.

The intractable problem for supporters of freedom

It is worth remembering that the last Labour government came to office promising an extension of liberty and a series of limitations on state power. In its first term, it brought in both the Human Rights

Act and the Freedom of Information Act. However, it seemed to swiftly regret introducing either and latterly sought to row back from both.

The Human Rights Act, of course, has many critics even (perhaps especially) amongst those strongly committed to civil liberties. But, whatever its many flaws, it did represent a genuine attempt by Labour to curtail the powers of the state. The Freedom of Information Act has been used – often to devastating effect – by individual citizens and campaign groups to expose serious wrong-doing in the corridors of power. Labour's early good intentions were not to last, and from 11 September 2001 right the way through to its last days in office, the previous government seemed, at times, to be on a mission to reduce civil liberties across the board. A pessimist might well predict that the coalition government could fall into the same pattern of behaviour.

An intractable problem for civil libertarians has been that, in recent decades, the divide between those supporting and defending basic freedoms and those seeking greater powers for the state have not been along party political lines, but rather between opposition politicians, who have tended to speak out against draconian government proposals, and politicians on the government side who swiftly discover that legislating in response to tragedy can have a short-term positive public relations impact, even if the long-term effect in deterring future crimes is limited or possibly even counterproductive.

Approaches to look for and how to rebut them

There are some key telltale signs that pro-freedom campaigners should look for as possible indications that the coalition is moving away from its professed agenda of support for civil liberties.

The first is the use by government ministers of the 'balance' argument. This became a perennial refrain by Labour ministers in the last Parliament. Advocates of this argument make the assumption that there is a trade-off between freedom and security and if we want more of one we have to accept having less of the other. The challenge for government, they suggest, is to get the balance right between the two. They are always supremely vague about the criteria that should be applied in judging whether the balance is right and how they'd reach the conclusion that it's appropriate for us to have, say, 3 per cent less freedom in order to benefit from 3 per cent more security.

It's rare indeed for a politician to deploy the 'balance' argument and be on the side of extending freedom rather than increasing security. You don't often hear an MP arguing 'of course, if we adopt this proposal, it will probably lead to more children being sexually assaulted and even murdered. But on the upside, adults will be able to go about their day-to-day lives without having to answer to the state for their behaviour. In the balance between freedom and security, my judgement is that it's now desirable to reduce the security of children in modern Britain.'

Almost always, the argument is used to defend or justify further restrictions on liberty – in return for a supposed improvement in our own security, or that of others. If you try to press an advocate of this stance to list a range of plausible measures which, in their judgement, would improve security but would unreasonably diminish freedom, you get a very vague response or even a blank look.

It is vital for civil liberties campaigners to resist and reject the 'balance' argument altogether. In a public or political debate framed around an acceptance that freedom and security are part of a zero-sum game, security will always win. The plea that restrictions on freedom are disproportionate given the modest gains to security may be intellectually coherent in some instances, but is unlikely to win much support.

In some areas and at some times, it must be the case that there is a correlation between limiting freedom and improving security.

For example, scanning the luggage of passengers getting onto a flight does presumably help reduce the chances that the plane will be blown out of the air. But the trade-off between freedom and security is not a universal truth and, in most areas of our lives, we are now well beyond any reasonable expectation that still further restrictions on liberty can be expected to have any positive returns in improving security.

If coalition politicians begin to deploy the balance argument, supporters of civil liberties should attack the paradigm, not seek to argue for a more libertarian trade-off.

The second train of argument to look for and oppose is the clichéd, but widely deployed, 'nothing to fear if nothing to hide' mantra. Although these exact words are often spoken by presenters of or contributors to radio phone-ins, rather than politicians themselves, the latter are often comfortable in framing debates in this fashion. The essential argument is very straightforward – although proposal X has universal applicability, an individual could only have reason to oppose X if they have done something wrong or are planning to. Recent obvious examples include defending the introduction of national identity cards and applauding the mushrooming use of CCTV. Many members of the public seem attracted to the 'nothing to fear' line of argument – in large part as a means of publicly professing their clean record. 'Why would I mind carrying an ID card, I've done nothing wrong?' or 'I behave perfectly well and wholly legally in public, why should I have a problem with CCTV cameras lining the street?'

Again, civil libertarians need to attack the paradigm, not fall back on the lawyerly argument that a particular proposal is disproportionate.

I've yet to meet a single individual who clings on to the 'nothing to fear, nothing to hide' line of argument once exposed to even the slightest degree of cross-examination. Supporters of civil liberties need to frame a more compelling and aggressive defence of personal privacy. There is sometimes an initial, unspoken assumption that personal privacy is something that could only be substantially valued by terrorists, fraudsters and paedophiles. But, of course, nearly all citizens do place considerable store in their personal privacy when they stop to consider it. Very few would argue that we should abandon the secret ballot at elections because those who don't want their voting preference known must be seeking to hide something. Or that people's medical records should be freely available to anyone who wishes to look at them. Or that everyone's salary should be in the public domain – rather than usually being a private matter between employer and employee.

Too often in recent years, a defence of personal privacy has been wrapped up in the contorted legal definition in the Human Rights Act – or has revolved around the special cases of celebrities being able to protect their image rights. A much broader-based narrative, within a new policy framework, needs to be developed to link explicitly personal privacy with human dignity. This is ultimately the best, and possibly the only, way to combat the 'nothing to fear, nothing to hide' school of thought.

Play for time

Although often taken out of context, Jefferson's assertion that the price of freedom is eternal vigilance has seemed to be the guiding principle of civil libertarians' strategy in recent years.

But whilst vigilance is commendable, it is not enough to win the battle for personal freedom. Too often, the vigilance of civil liberties campaigners has succeeded in bringing authoritarian policies to public attention – but not in preventing or repealing them.

A key approach in years to come needs to be to play for time. Freedom is at its most vulnerable in the immediate aftermath of a shocking event such as 7/7 or Whitehaven. Once the coverage of the event itself draws to a close, the second leg of the media and political narrative is to ask what needs to be done to prevent a repetition. The size and scale of public anger, outrage and distress is often so great that, in this short window, virtually no idea is considered too outlandish. Very often the relatives and friends of those most affected by whatever event has occurred are – understandably – the most vocal in supporting draconian legislative responses.

In the wake of tragedies such as the Victoria Climbié case, the murder of Jamie Bulger, the disappearance of Madeleine McCann or the latest murderous act of al-Qaeda, civil libertarians are almost always on the back foot. Anyone who has sat in a TV studio next to the parent of a child who has been raped and murdered will know how seemingly impossible it is to frame a remotely attractive case for civil liberties.

Probably the most important thing that freedom campaigners can do is to play for time. Legislation and regulation should not be rushed through inspired by anger and distress. Very often, a careful look at the detailed circumstances of the tragedy – which can take many months – clearly shows that many of the draconian measures called for would have had zero impact on the case in question. Investigations and inquiries over a longer time frame are always preferable to the Home Secretary promising to 'do something' in an ill-thought-out press statement at the outset. Once such a pledge has been made, it is politically very difficult to retract it.

Supporters of freedom need to realise that the longer and more drawn-out the public discussion of possible legislative responses, the more likely it is that common sense and civil liberties will prevail.

The new government provides an opportunity to revive civil liberties in Britain, but there is no guarantee. To make the most of this opportunity, civil libertarians will need to reframe their arguments and hone their tactics. That is no easy task, but it is certainly a vital one.

The Department of 'No'

Toby Stevens

If the government is serious about its policy objectives of slashing administrative costs, bolstering the UK's cyber defences, moving away from proprietary software systems and putting data into the Cloud, and treating personal data with the respect it deserves, then it is time to reassess the role of information assurance and how it is delivered. There is a pressing need to reform the information assurance function so that we have proper security governance, and so that information assurance supports, not hinders, the government's policy objectives.

Public sector data leaks

With the announcement of a £650 million budget for cybersecurity, coupled with the axing of defence infrastructure that until recently would have been considered critical to the protection of Britain's national interests, Prime Minister David Cameron has delivered the unequivocal message that cybersecurity is a cornerstone of the UK's broader defence interests. UK defence companies will be switching their research budgets away from military hardware and into homeland security products, and information security companies around the world will doubtless be examining the UK security market, keen to get their share of the new government spend.

All this has to be a good thing for the central and local government authorities who have seen public confidence in their ability to protect information eroded by a seemingly endless string of high-profile data loss incidents. Ever since Chancellor Alastair Darling informed Parliament that HM Revenue & Customs had misplaced the details of child tax credit claimants, we have been bombarded with reports of files left on trains, memory sticks dropped in the street, emails accidentally sent to the wrong mailing lists, hard disc units lost and laptops stolen from cars. Despite senior managers time and again promising the Information Commissioner that 'lessons have been learned', the incidents keep on happening. Public authorities appear to be incapable of protecting information. What can possibly have gone so badly wrong with information assurance that our authorities are apparently unable to keep anything secret, at a time when the Prime Minister tells us that our cyber security has never been more important to the nation?

The Department of 'No'

The UK government's information assurance function is distributed across government through a number of agencies.[180] Perhaps the best known of these is CESG (formerly known as the 'Communications Electronic Security Group' of Government Communication Headquarters), the national technical authority for information assurance. Based in Cheltenham, and reporting to the Cabinet Office, CESG is tasked with delivering a range of products and services including threat monitoring, product assessment, adviser training and system testing.

The information assurance function is not exclusive to CESG. The Cabinet Office has a Security Policy Division (COSPD) which produces part of the Security Policy Framework (SPF) that replaced the Manual of Protective Security (the government's primary standards document for information assurance), and CESG produces the rest of the SPF. The National Cybersecurity Strategy also sits within Cabinet Office, but focuses more on protecting the broader Critical National Infrastructure (CNI) from major disasters, terrorist threats, foreign intelligence services and serious/organised crime than general systems security. The MoD uses equivalent standards and administration internally, which refer back to the products and services provided by the government's other security centres (all of which have a common root in standards that evolved into ISO/IEC27001:2005), but which operate completely separately. Other parts of the security governance function are fragmented across many committees and boards.

Significantly, this substantial infrastructure is focused mainly upon advisory services rather than actually implementing and managing systems security: that burden falls upon the Senior Information Risk Owner[181] (SIRO) in individual public authorities. This individual, who should ideally be from an information risk background, is the focus for information assurance delivery at a board level within their authority. In smaller bodies, the role of SIRO is often shared with other duties such as Chief Information Officer.

The Cabinet Office has recently established the Office of Cyber Security and Information Assurance (OCSIA),[182] which has yet to have an opportunity to reform the information assurance function, but publicly appears to be more focused upon the cyber defence agenda than the day-to-day mechanics of running information assurance.

With this advisory capability, one would imagine that the government's information assurance function would be robust and strong, drawing upon a wealth of shared expertise which is delivered in such a way that security enables and supports service delivery. Unfortunately, all too often the opposite is true.

Cost-effective information assurance? The Department says 'No'

Government lacks a focal point for information security: there is no 'Government Chief Information Security Officer' or 'Office for Government Information Assurance' – in other words, no one individual or organisation accepts accountability for the proper governance of data in the public sector.

The fragmented approach to information assurance has developed over many decades, and the cultural unwillingness for government bodies to accept responsibility for an issue as 'toxic' as information assurance has left the subject in the long grass as far as most CIOs are concerned. Even the proliferation of quangos under the last Labour government did not lead to the creation of a body that might deal with these critical issues, despite some of the highest-profile data loss incidents ever to impact the public sector occurring during their term of office.

Instead the various bodies tasked with information assurance focus upon their own jurisdictions and rarely cooperate successfully: the MoD does not discuss its security standards, although they are little different from those in use across the rest of government; CESG and COSPD will only release information to suitably cleared individuals, and rarely reference each other's work. Each department and agency has to pay to support its own security infrastructure rather than drawing upon the economies of scale that might be achieved by a central security team working for the common good of government. The information assurance environment is far from cost-effective.

Information risk management? The Department says 'No'

This lack of cooperation doesn't just mean that key activities are duplicated; it also means that without support from their managers, those tasked with protecting systems are afraid to take risks for fear of being blamed if an incident occurs.

The problem is that information assurance is not about absolute control, and any professional security manager will acknowledge that there is no such thing as 100 per cent risk avoidance. Instead, it is about assessing the information risks faced by the organisation, developing mitigating controls and actions, and ensuring that they are managed properly so that the risk levels are reduced to a point where they are proportionate and acceptable.

This means that incidents will always happen. This may be because security controls are judged to be disproportionately expensive (for example, spending many millions of pounds on security to protect assets worth only some thousands of pounds); because individuals failed to comply with the instructions given to them (for example, downloading unprotected files on to a memory stick to take home, then losing that memory stick); because the system is attacked by a capable and dedicated enemy (for example, an authorised user taking copies of MP's expense claims); or because of a 'zero day' exploit (for example, a hacker breaking into a system using a weakness that was previously unknown to the security officer).

Whatever the cause, security incidents will always occur, and the public sector culture is to look for someone to blame – remember how the HMRC incident was almost immediately blamed upon a 'junior clerical officer' before it was revealed that systemic failures were at the root of the problem? Security officers are rightly fearful of being blamed for incidents, and in the absence of someone who will act as an advocate for them when things go wrong, they are forced to fall back on the only safe path available to them, which is to say 'no' when the business wants to do anything which might carry an associated security risk. The likelihood of the current information assurance community being willing to support the government's cloud computing ambitions seems slim indeed.

As a result, most public servants view information assurance as an obstacle, not an asset. Because of poor leadership, excessive bureaucracy and a culture of unnecessary secrecy, public authorities are unable to obtain cost-effective information security controls. The current infrastructure will neither permit nor support the new commitment to respecting personal data, making government data available or protecting data that needs to be kept secret.

Secure systems? The Department says 'No'

Ironically, the culture of 'No' has not resulted in better security within the public sector. Project managers, afraid of having their plans thrown into disarray by uncooperative security professionals, simply avoid seeking security advice. Enterprising users who need to get their jobs done seek out risky ways to bypass security controls because the security departments won't allow them to get on with what they have to do. For example, it is common to find use of unauthorised online file sharing services to exchange information because the security department has shut down USB memory sticks and CD drives without providing an alternative. That's how accidents happen.

The problem has even deeper consequences outside of Westminster and Whitehall. Most important standards, guidelines and publications are protectively marked so that they are only available to individuals with appropriate levels of security clearance working on appropriately secured PCs. But local government bodies, for example, rarely conduct background checks on their staff beyond a basic criminal records check, so individuals tasked with securing local authority systems don't know how to secure them in line with government requirements because they are not cleared to see those requirements – and aren't allowed to hold copies because their PCs aren't sufficiently secure. Without the intervention of costly consultants who have the correct clearances and computers, this paradox can't be broken.

Those consultants are a very special breed indeed. Only the few hundred members of the CESG Listed Advisor Scheme (CLAS) are officially qualified to provide security advice across government. They hold the necessary clearances, and have access to CESG's source materials. What they do is not particularly 'special' compared with their private-sector colleagues, and because the pool of available talent is so small, and the barriers to entry are high (CESG only accepts a limited number of candidates once a year, and they need to pay a substantial fee for clearance, acceptance and training), public authorities have to draw from a relatively small – and therefore uncompetitive – pool of consultants for their information assurance advice.

CESG has for some years been attempting to move parts of the CLAS environment into the private sector, but this has yet to deliver any significant change in the way that systems are secured. The outcome of this 'closed shop' is that local authorities and 'arm's length' bodies very often fail to comply with government security standards simply because they don't know that those standards even exist, and if they do, they can't gain access to either the standards or cost-effective individuals who are able to assist them. We therefore have a public sector environment in which the prevailing culture and practices conspire against effective information assurance.

Privacy by Design? The Department says 'No'

Clearly a public sector that struggles with information assurance will also struggle to respect privacy: if personal data cannot be kept secret, then it cannot be kept private either. But public authorities' inability to manage personal data effectively runs much deeper than that, since CESG's formal policies until recently simply didn't get the idea of privacy. Formal risk assessment processes tried to assign protective markings according to the volumes of personal records rather than the sensitivity of the data: so, 999 personal records might be considered Not Protectively Marked, whilst 1,000 would be marked at the higher level of Restricted. Authorities could circumvent the more onerous controls by simply breaking databases down into smaller files of fewer than 1,000 individual records.

What's more, those risk assessment models are designed around an assumption that authorised users are always trustworthy – how else could designs such as the ill-fated ContactPoint, or the NHS

Summary Care Record, be allowed to exist where hundreds of thousands of users can access millions of individuals' sensitive private records? The risk assessment processes treat individuals as low-value assets whose privacy is significantly less valuable than, say, a minister's public reputation.

Private companies, and in particular those in the financial sector where the FSA has demonstrated an appetite to impose punitive fines for misuse of personal data, woke up long ago to the need to show greater respect for personal data. The public sector, where senior public servants are rarely held accountable, and the sternest sanction generally applied is a letter from the Information Commissioner's Office, has not kept up with the change. In their defence, CESG have made some positive revisions to their personal data handling rules in recent years, but much more needs to be done if the government is ever to meet individuals' expectations of privacy.

Open source software? The Department says 'No'

The new government's commitment to open source systems represents perhaps the greatest challenge that the information assurance community has faced in many years. The use of software that has been collectively developed, with publicly available source code, flies in the face of long-established security policies and practices, which have traditionally demanded that source code comes from an approved developer, is scrutinised for vulnerabilities, and is kept out of the public domain.

In general, software and hardware vendors are expected to have their products pre-tested for use in government systems (something which is not required in the private sector), and to pay up front for that testing. CESG has a number of services such as the CESG Claims Tested Mark (CCTM) and CESG Assisted Products Service (CAPS), which are used to test the security of products being sold to public sector organisations. When private companies sell to government, they can justify the expense of the testing process, since that will grant them access to a lucrative new market. But the same does not hold true for open source software: in the same way that drugs companies won't pay for clinical trials on products that they can't patent, vendors won't pay for the testing of public domain software when they cannot expect to charge for it at the end of the process. Furthermore, the test processes are notoriously long-winded and complicated, so even vendors of proprietary systems are reluctant to invest in them. Whilst not all products have to be subject to this test approach, failure to demonstrate test approval can count against them during procurement, and as a result public authorities are driven towards a small number of approved, tested, and often outdated technologies.

Once products have been selected, and designs are in place, the complicated process of accreditation begins. Security Officers – or more commonly CLAS consultants – conduct a tightly-proscribed risk assessment that is used to determine whether the system requires formal accreditation (a certificate to prove that a system is fit to handle a given level of data, and to interconnect with similarly secure systems), and potentially to prepare a Risk Management Accreditation Document Set (RMADS) that is used to define security controls. Accreditation of open source systems, where there are no vendors to make assertions about security levels, is very difficult indeed using current processes.

But accreditation isn't the end of the problem: like all software, open source software requires patching and upgrading to keep up with technology developments and newly-discovered security vulnerabilities. Without a vendor to pay for security-testing the patches and updates under the current regime, open source software will remain largely inaccessible for government.

In the private sector, where there is no obligation to verify the security claims of systems vendors, and organisations can select their own risk assessment approaches, these problems simply don't

exist. Independent testing schemes can be used to provide customers with greater assurance of security capabilities, but in general
market forces drive vendors towards delivering secure systems, since
a major failure will count against them in procurement processes.
Government's open source goals will remain hampered by information assurance until a new way of dealing with the security of open
source software can be developed.

The Department of 'Yes': Treating information assurance as a business enabler

The relative success of private-sector security practices, and the
fact that large corporations do not struggle to manage information
security in the way that government does, shows that it should be
perfectly possible to move to an environment in which information
assurance helps, rather than hinders, the delivery of public services.
In particular, we need to ensure that:

- information is available to all who legitimately require it, is
  appropriately protected, delivered and of assured integrity
  and accuracy, so that information can support the needs of
  government, industry and individuals;
- public confidence in the ability of public authorities to handle
  personal information is restored;
- public authorities can adopt open source systems and cloud
  technologies without security being a disproportionate
  burden;
- public authorities break away from the negative mentality of
  information assurance that blocks innovation, and instead
  move towards a new culture that is able to support, rather
  than hinder, the delivery of new technology policies.

The significant changes in government IT policy, the shake-up
of its delivery driven by the spending review, the government's
commitment to cybersecurity as a cornerstone of the UK's defence

strategy, and the establishment of the Office of Cybersecurity and Information Assurance (OCSIA) within the Cabinet Office collectively drive the need for reform. OCSIA may be the best hope for achieving reform, but will only succeed if there is a collective will in that office to do things differently. Ministers and senior civil servants are too quick to defer to GCHQ at Cheltenham on the assumption they are 'the experts', when evidence suggests they are behind the times and operating in a mainframe mindset in an internet age. They have become unaccountable arbiters of what does and does not happen, and what can and cannot be used. There is a clear need for leadership, to remove duplication of responsibilities, to improve availability of security standards and technologies, and to change the way that security is perceived across government. There is also a need for greater participation by local government and the private sector, whilst recognising that some aspects are better suited to remaining under government control.

A few simple actions would suffice to create the 'Department of "Yes"':

1. Appoint a pan-government Chief Information Security Officer as a new focal point for information assurance
Just as a large company would be expected to have a Chief Information Security Officer (CISO), the OCSIA should appoint a government CISO responsible for the proper implementation of information assurance across government. This role must not be one that is any way combined with the cyber defence agenda (which invariably becomes politicised and distracted from the day-to-day running of information assurance), but rather a 'hands on' leadership position that provides a figurehead for information assurance issues. Bringing in a CISO from industry, rather than public service, would ensure a break with past practices and a fresh approach to the task in hand.

2. Create a government CISO council
The government CISO should chair a new government CISO council within the OCSIA. This group, comprising CISOs and/or SIROs from all major parts of government, should act as the focal point for all information assurance issues, and hold responsibility for development and maintenance of security standards, accreditation, product certification and professional development across government. The CISO council should be engaged in policy development across central and local government to ensure compliance with national and international legal obligations. Where public sector security incidents occur, the CISO council should be involved in independent investigation and reporting.

3. Consolidate existing duplicate information assurance services
The government CISO should work with OCSIA across government to amalgamate existing policy and solutions branches, including CESG, COSPD and the relevant parts of MoD, into OCSIA. This, by implication, will require consolidation of duplicated services and roles. The newly-amalgamated security body should take responsibility for all aspects of establishing standards and procedures for the defence of public sector ICT infrastructure, and should develop and publish security standards for use in government and the private sector. The body should also operate 'how to' teams of experts who look for cost-effective solutions to security problems, and constantly improve the advice and controls available to government, drawing upon the best the private sector has to offer.

4. Ease the administrative security regime for lower-value data
The UK government operates a protective marking policy[183] for its data assets to ensure that they are used and secured in accordance with the value of those assets. Clearly some of that information – particularly when assigned a Top Secret or Secret marking –

requires very robust security controls. But the vast majority of data, particularly outside of Whitehall, sits at Restricted or even lower, and the nature of the data is not dissimilar to that which might be held by a private company such as a bank. Yet that information is subject to 'special' information assurance controls that are often significantly more onerous and administratively complicated than might be found in the private sector, despite those controls having their roots in the same standards.

If OCSIA were to relax the administrative processes for securing Restricted data, such that authorities may use any commercial services or products so long as they comply with the basic security policy requirements defined in the Security Policy Framework and supporting materials, then the market would be opened up for any commercial product or service vendor to compete in the public sector. Rules will need to remain in place to ensure that data is correctly marked, and not 'upgraded' to higher protective marking levels than appropriate. Implemented correctly, this change would not result in chaos or insecurity, but instead allow greater competition to bring down the cost of delivery, and free up local authorities to get on with securing their information without the burden of complying with security frameworks that are intended to deal with data at much higher levels of security. CLAS consultants could shift their focus to systems operating at the higher protective marking levels.

5. Sort out the existing mess of unaccredited Whitehall systems

The imperative that information assurance reform does not apply solely to new systems: there is little value in securing new ICT infrastructure if it has to interface with older systems with unproven levels of security. The government's own report into data losses (the Hannigan report[184]) identified approximately 2,300 government systems that have not been subject to any form of assurance certification (known as accreditation) but made no demands that those legacy systems should be secured. Significantly, recent changes to the Security Policy Framework introduced a new marking level of Protect which was, in part, intended to ease the burden of accreditation, but anecdotal evidence suggests that it has the opposite effect, and is instead seen as a new unfunded administrative burden. This needs to be addressed as a matter of urgency: those systems must either be secured or scrapped.

Equally importantly, senior civil servants still have the power to override the need for accreditation if they so choose: in other words, to disregard security requirements if these are too expensive or likely to take too long. This exemption must also be dropped: if system security is too expensive, then the system itself is too expensive, and other more affordable ways must be found to deliver the same outcomes.

6. Voluntarily accredit open source software where appropriate

If the current approach to accreditation remains in place, then government must take responsibility for accrediting testing and maintaining the security of open source software. There is no reason why OCSIA, or even a private company, could not provide and maintain its own secure builds of the likes of Linux, OpenOffice or OpenSQL for use in government. Builds and patches would be checked and tested by a central team without the need for a vendor to sponsor the work, thus making the software available across government, and saving costs on software licensing and duplicated testing.

7. Develop the information assurance profession

If the government is to obtain access to the best possible security expertise, then the profession needs major reform. OCSIA should take responsibility for development of the information assurance profession, working in close partnership with relevant information security professional bodies. This will include:

- defining a career structure for information assurance in the public sector;
- developing information assurance professional development and training syllabuses for delivery by commercial organisations;
- providing examination and certification of government security professionals, with an emphasis on facilitating simple and affordable cross-qualification from the private sector, so as to expand the pool of professionals available to government;
- governing the certification and management of inspectors and accreditors;
- maintaining a pool of expert instructors and project managers to coach and where necessary manage particularly large, innovative or sensitive public-sector projects.

CESG has already taken steps down this route by moving aspects of the professional qualifications across to the Institute of Information Security Professionals (IISP). If it were to go a little further and insist that all government information assurance professionals must become IISP members who maintain Continuing Professional Development (CPD) training, and could be struck off for malpractice, unprofessional conduct or incompetence, then there would be a case to argue for abandoning the overhead of CLAS altogether.

More for less from the Department of 'Yes'

In the world of the Department of 'Yes,' information assurance will be a service enabler. Public authorities will have the confidence to adopt innovative new technology schemes, knowing that they will be supported in doing so by their information assurance teams. They will be look to their information assurance groups for support at the earliest stages in projects, rather than trying to hide from them. They will understand that on the rare occasions that their security advisers say 'no', there is a good reason for them to do so.

If we want an information assurance function that really supports public authorities, and that can deliver more for less, then these changes are cheap and easily done. We simply have to ask OCSIA to reform the information assurance function, give that office the power to do so, and support it when it encounters inevitable resistance from within the security establishment. All it takes is the will to say 'Yes.'

Body scanners

Alex Deane

The introduction of body scanners at international airports followed the case of Nigerian Umar Farouk Abdulmutallab, who tried to blow up a flight to Detroit on which he was a passenger. He had flown from Yemen via Lagos and Holland's Schipol Airport. I shall talk about them at a little more length than other issues here as there is simply no real public debate about them at present, and there should be. There are real questions about whether the scanners work. Furthermore, they're not needed, they invade privacy and they're potentially unsafe. In evidence before the Canadian parliamentary group investigating scanners, Rafi Sela, a leading Israeli security expert, derided them as 'useless'. His experience is acquired in a country which really knows something about security, and has no plan to introduce scanners. The scanners seem unable to penetrate beneath skin. So hiding material in body cavities or in implants conceals them.

What if they are only a tiny bit effective? We are constantly told 'if it makes us a little safer, it's worth it' … 'if it saves one life, stops one crime…' What a specious argument that is. It would 'save one child' to ban flying, or the motor car, or introduce a night curfew, but we don't, because it would be disproportionate and we have to get on with normal life, even if we incur a higher element of risk in doing so. We don't encourage people to take wild risks with cars, but we don't make liberty-reducing and disproportionate laws, either. We should react to the threat of terrorism in just the same way. And scanners that don't work create a sense of security which is entirely false.

Even if they could be made to work, scanners would be disproportionate and unnecessary. President Obama has said that Abdulmutallab was able to board the Detroit flight because of systemic failure by the security services with the information they already had. Rather than ensuring that those authorities competently use what they've already got, both the USA and the UK are giving more power and new tools to the same organisations whose systematic incompetence caused the problem in the first place.

We're told this technology 'might have helped' – to be accurate, if true, that would have to be 'might have helped if it had been installed *in Lagos*'. Which I think underscores the weirdness of the routine to which we now subject passengers going through Heathrow et al.

Let's remember the tools already available to the services entrusted with significant powers and big budgets in order to protect us. First, and most importantly, intelligence – ranging from the research and knowledge and expertise of the security services to the common-sense and experience of border guards. Secondly, infra-red scanners which don't show your body parts. Thirdly, sniffer dogs. Fourthly, standard metal detectors. Fifthly, swabs to detect explosive material particles. We're hardly without protections already. All of these devices are cheap, they work, they're available now and they don't violate privacy. Scanners are expensive, often don't work, are not available in large quantities for months and they violate privacy.

And they're expensive, at £80,000 to £100,000 each. With an airport like Heathrow, with five terminals, one appreciates that that's a lot of scanners. The cost will be passed on to fliers (along with the sizeable delays they cause at the terminal). It is because of the cost issue that the head of Interpol has said that expenditure on scanners is not a good use of law enforcement resources. But why put good money into something practical when there's a more fashionable toy to be played with, which might make your government look decisive? It's a classic example of the desire to be seen to be doing something.

If you've seen images from the scanners (and Google is filling up with them), you will know that they leave little to the imagination. For people with prosthetic body parts, with medical conditions, for those who are just plain modest, this is hard to contemplate. People in all categories have been in touch with us. Many who say that they are unconcerned by scanners vis-à-vis themselves find it difficult to contemplate scans of their partners or (particularly) their children. Some passengers won't be upset by the scanners. Others will. Those who do object should not have to choose between their dignity and their flight. Unlike the Canadian or US authorities, the British government allows no exemptions for passengers selected for scans – they permit no alternative for people with moral objections, or for children, or for pregnant women.

We're assured that mature, responsible, sensitive, trained professionals will operate the scanners. Such assurances should come with health warnings. One Heathrow 'professional', John Laker, received just such training before working the scanners, but nevertheless took a picture of a colleague who entered the machine by mistake, telling her he loved 'her massive t*ts'. In Florida, Rolando Negrin went 'postal' and beat his colleagues who had professionally, maturely and responsibly mocked the size of his genitalia, revealed by the scanners. This is how they treat one another: what do they do to the rest of us?

We have been given assurances that the images generated from scans will immediately be destroyed (first we were told that they could not store images at all, a claim disproven by documents obtained by the US Electronic Privacy Information Centre). Given that the machines have the capacity to retain images, one wonders how that non-retention policy is to be enforced, and how controllers can in the long term be stopped from simply taking pictures of the screen they're watching with their mobile telephones.

Furthermore, the British government's record on data security and data loss is appalling. In 2006 HMRC lost the personal records of 25 million individuals, including their dates of birth, addresses, bank accounts and national insurance numbers when they lost the authority's entire data relating to child benefit payments. In January 2008, a laptop computer containing the personal details of 600,000 people was lost by the MoD. It was one of 658 lost laptops.

The Equalities and Human Rights Commission has stated that scanners are potentially illegal on privacy grounds. For the same reason, the European Commission has questioned their necessity. There are alternatives. The British company ThruVision has created terahertz scanners (a milder form of infra-red) which create images which demonstrate objects of concern on a body outline without being graphic; no genitals are shown. I can see no proper reason to use the graphic version instead. Indeed, laws against child pornography and indecent imagery are arguably breached by the scanners; that the government didn't even bother legislating to ensure that this point was covered speaks volumes about the attitude it had/has towards the rule of law.

It is true that the level of radiation to which one is exposed in scans is small. However, there's a reason the doctor stands behind a screen when you're X-rayed; even small doses, particularly when relatively frequent (as they might be for regular fliers) can be harmful, especially to some parts of the body (like the genitals). The levels estimated are compared to radiation incurred whilst flying – but this isn't radiation absorbed instead of flying, it's as well as flying. Some short-haul pilots and cabin crew will be exposed to scans six or eight times a day.

The Inter-Agency Committee on Radiation Safety includes the European Commission, International Atomic Energy Agency, Nuclear Energy Agency and the World Health Organization. The Committee has written a report that stating that:

1) Air passengers should be made aware of the health risks of airport body screenings;

2) Governments must explain any decision to expose the public to higher levels of cancer-causing radiation; and

3) Pregnant women and children should not be subject to scanning.

By failing to publicise the health risks, by failing to explain the danger, and worst of all by making scanning compulsory for all, the British government is failing to do all of these things and is potentially jeopardising the health of vulnerable people. For two vulnerable groups, our government has made it compulsory to do that which the best available evidence says should not be done. The ThruVision alternative doesn't come with radiation risks, either.

When the IRA was active, it posed a more real threat to the people of the United Kingdom than al-Qaeda and co. – and regularly delivered on that threat. We didn't allow the IRA to change our way of life to anything like the degree we now permit these terrorists to change our liberties and freedoms. They hate us because we are free. We should think about infringing our freedoms carefully in the face of their threat. I mean, what sort of free society does the government think it's protecting with these scanners? When we have to expose ourselves to a man at the airport in order to fly, perhaps the terrorists have won.

Libel & liberty: the case for reform of our defamation laws

Michael Harris

When US academic Rachel Ehrenfeld wrote *Funding Evil* she was unconcerned about English libel law. Although she accused Saudi billionaire Khalid bin Mahfouz of channelling money to al-Qaeda, a serious accusation, her book wasn't to be published in the UK. Furthermore, it was highly questionable whether bin Mahfouz had a reputation to defend at all. In 1992, he paid $225 million to escape criminal charges over the collapse of the notoriously corrupt Bank of Credit and Commerce International. A report by senators John Kerry and Hank Brown said the CIA knew that the BCCI was a 'fundamentally corrupt criminal enterprise'. At the heart of this criminal enterprise: Khalid bin Mahfouz, its Chief Operating Officer. Ehrenfeld thought she was safe to exercise her First Amendment right to free expression. Yet across the Atlantic, in the High Court in London, Justice Eady decided that a foreign citizen, who was Chief Operating Officer of a bank the CIA called a 'criminal enterprise', had a reputation to protect against a book not even published in the UK. When Ehrenfeld refused to fight the case in London, Eady awarded Mahfouz and his two sons £10,000 in damages each.[185]

English law is rarely offensive to other civilised nations. Many global businesses use English law to guarantee their liberty to trade without unfair restrictions. There is a notable exception: English libel law. Our libel laws are so archaic and restrictive to free expression that on 10 August 2010, President Barack Obama signed into US law the Speech Act protecting American citizens from foreign, namely English, libel suits. To say this marks a historic low in Britain's standing as a bastion of free expression is not hyperbole. For decades now, London has been nicknamed a 'town called Sue' by foreign lawyers incredulous that our High Court would hear suits for defamation by foreign plaintiffs like bin Mahfouz with little or no reputation in the United Kingdom. And whilst 'libel tourism' (and US legislation to protect its citizens from it) may seem to be the most egregious manifestation of the iniquities of our libel laws, the principal danger lies in its acute effect on free expression here at home.

Libel tourism is only one element: English libel law is rotten to the core. The defences available to defendants are unclear, there are few alternatives to a full trial (which can only be held at the High Court), the costs of defending yourself against a libel action are highly prohibitive and massive multinational corporations are free to sue individuals. Due to these factors, the UN Human Rights Committee, the Culture, Media and Sport Select Committee and a specially convened Ministry of Justice Working Group have all found that English libel law has a detrimental effect on free expression and scientific enquiry.

According to Oxford University, the average cost of a libel trial in England and Wales is 140 times the European equivalent.[186] 'Rip-off Britain' is certainly at its most extreme when comparing our legal costs against similarly wealthy Western democracies. Of the 154 libel proceedings in 2008 identified in the Justice Jackson Review (of 259 taken to the High Court), the most expensive libel action cost £3,243,980 and the average cost for the twenty most expensive trials was £753,676.95. It's not hard to see how these incredible costs add up: libel lawyers from firms Carter-Ruck and Schillings charge in the region of £400 per hour. Perversely, when Lord Woolf reviewed libel costs in 1994, libel lawyers privately admitted their fees were so high even they couldn't afford to defend themselves against a libel action. Hardeep Singh, a writer facing a three-year libel action against a foreign claimant, could face a £1 million bill if he loses his case. He told our campaign: 'I have friends who work as airport baggage handlers, when I explained to them I spent the same amount on a barrister for a day as they earn in a year, they realised why free speech is imperilled by our libel laws.'

These costs do not aid those whose reputation is impugned. Damages will often be dwarfed by legal costs. In the recent case of *Martyn Jones MP* v. *Associated Newspapers Limited*, the MP won £5,000 in damages, yet his costs were £387,000. Associated Newspapers was found to have caused £5,000 damage to Mr Jones's reputation but had a final bill of in excess of £392,000 with its own legal costs above and beyond this.

Part of the problem has been the introduction of Conditional Fee Agreements (CFAs), or 'no-win, no-fee' agreements which allow claimants to sue with little or no upfront cost to themselves (the risk taken on by the lawyers), but upon winning the lawyers double their fees (called a 'success fee' which is supposed to reflect the 'risk') and they are charged to the losing party. The success fee which is usually 100 per cent (i.e. to double the loser's costs) is set on the calculated basis that lawyers will win half of cases and lose the other half. There is a consensus that for claimant lawyers the 'risk' certainly does not match the success fee of 100 per cent. Of the previously mentioned 154 cases in the Jackson Review, not a single case was won by the defendant.

On top of the doubling of the most expensive libel costs in Europe (if not the world), libel insurance that can be taken out after the event (ATE) can also be recovered against the losing party. This routinely adds £65,000–£100,000 to the cost of a libel case.

With costs so high, and losing catastrophic, a significant amount of material is withdrawn before publication. Editors lean heavily on the advice of their lawyers, who more often than not have no expertise in the discipline they are advising on. The advice is nearly always to play safe. Dr Fiona Godlee, editor-in-chief of the leading medical journal the BMJ, told us that on legal advice she has had to pull scholarly articles on subjects in the public interest. As one example, the journal *Archives of Disease in Childhood* turned down a series of case reports illustrating clinical signs suggestive of child abuse. The editor was keen to publish, but the legal advice was that there was a small possibility that cases may be identifiable and thus run a risk of libel action. The paper was later published in an American journal.

Even when work that questions corporate interests makes it into print, this work can quickly disappear. In 2007, two Swedish professors of linguistics published in the *International Journal of Speech Language and the Law* an article questioning the scientific evidence that lie detectors based on voice analysis are effective. Nemesysco, the Israeli manufacturer of the device named by the authors, threatened legal action against the publisher of the journal. It withdrew the article entirely, leaving only the abstract online. Unsurprisingly, the legal action was pursued through the English courts. Professor Lacerda, one of the authors, is scathing about our laws: 'what I was expecting was debate, a productive academic fight. The company would say: "No, you are wrong because of this". This is the way science progresses. But that is not what we got, and that was a surprise.'[187]

Professor Lacerda is not just concerned about the effect of English libel laws on our home scientific community (important as this is), but science internationally, with the 'huge chill' on research exacerbated by the resource imbalance between scientists and companies.

This is clearly a matter of public interest. Twenty-five councils across the UK have used public money to pay for the system to try to detect people lying in phone calls. The Department for Work and Pensions spent £1.5 million on the software. Yet the academic research that questions whether this is throwing public money at a system which, in the words of the professors, is 'at the astrology end of the validity spectrum', has been pulped thanks to English libel law.[88]

Writing in the public interest is unprotected

Index on Censorship's award-winning magazine has been placed in the invidious position of having to censor articles to avoid libel actions that the magazine simply couldn't afford to fight. An extract from a book about the abduction and torture of a journalist, which was freely available in Mexico, had to be censored to reduce the risk of libel action. What Mexicans could read could not be read in the UK.

As part of our campaign we surveyed NGOs anonymously on how libel affected their daily activities. Most were anxious about revealing previous threats and actions unless guaranteed anonymity.

One NGO told us 'we have a reputation for robust research-led publications and campaigning positions and so our methods fit quite well with the concept of "responsible journalism" but the uncertainty of the defence means that we have to be circumspect about the issues we cover.' When a charity does press ahead and take on vested interests, it is resource intensive. Another NGO told our campaign that they felt they had to pre-emptively meet the requirements for a Reynolds defence for a recent report on the looting of state assets in Cambodia, in case of a libel action. The total cost in staff time, legal advice and the delivery of letters to sources and subjects overseas was £17,000. This is a cost beyond the expensive insurance that NGOs will take out to protect themselves from libel actions.

We were also told that a further issue that restricts the ability of NGOs to run a successful Reynolds defence is if investigations are carried out in dangerous places, where local populations cannot freely express knowledge of corruption without fear of facing reprisals: 'in these situations, information from such vulnerable individuals means they cannot be relied upon to take the stand in the event of a court case due to risks to their lives and livelihoods.'

It's hardly a fundamentalist free speech position to argue that Professor Lacarda's work or that of the above NGOs ought to be protected by a strong public interest defence. Yet, the Reynolds defence is a deeply uncertain defence to mount, and the ruling in the Court of Appeal on 13 July 2010, *Flood* v. *Times Newspapers Limited*, against the newspaper proves how hard this defence is to use.

The Reynolds defence comes from the *Reynolds* v. *Times Newspapers Ltd* 1999 case. The *Sunday Times*' article accused Albert Reynolds, the former Taoiseach, of misleading Parliament. Mr Reynolds sued for defamation. The newspaper would have found it extremely hard, if not impossible, to run with the traditional defences of justification or fair comment, given the factual nature of the article. So it argued the allegations were published in the public interest, after the paper took care to check its facts. Beyond the defence of justification, the *Sunday Times* argued that regardless of whether the allegations were proven true or not, with due care taken to fact-check the basis of their report, as a newspaper it ought to have been able to report them and be legally protected by 'qualified privilege'. For if newspapers could only print proven facts a lot of information in the public interest would never see the light of day.

When the case went to the House of Lords, the Law Lords ruled this defence (the Reynolds defence) was a valid one. From this judgment came ten criteria which, it seemed, a successful Reynolds defence would need to meet.

Lawyers Niri Shanmuganathan and Lorna Caddy from Taylor Wessing LLP note: 'however, it should not be forgotten that the House of Lords' judgment in that case described the substantial lengths that the journalist went to in attempting to verify his story prior to publication. The success of the defence should be seen in that context.'[189]

This wasn't a cast-iron public interest defence to protect free expression, but a defence that could be used, with significant effort and at significant cost.

It wasn't until the Jameel judgement that it became implicit that the Reynolds defence also extended beyond journalism, and covered NGOs, scientists, writers and bloggers. Jameel also made it clear that the ten points of the Reynolds defence were not a checklist that needed to be ticked off, but to be considered.

Yet, even with the Jameel judgement many libel lawyers considered this public interest defence still too uncertain.

This led Lord Lester to place a workable defence at the heart of his Private Member's Defamation Bill (covered in detail later):

> The 'Reynolds defence' has not been of great practical value. Human rights campaigners, doctors at conferences and those exchanging views in online chat rooms, when threatened with libel action, have not been able to show that they did an investigative report beforehand, as required, and nor should they have to. We need a simpler statutory public interest defence, which clearly applies to everyone and covers opinion as well as fact.[190]

The Duke of Brunswick rule

> *Unless he may be solicitous to proceed, as upon a rather profitable speculation, in his attacks upon the liberty of journalism, we would suggest to the ex-Duke of Brunswick the propriety of withdrawing into his own natural and sinister obscurity... he will find it little short of an impossibility to vilify still more his already sufficiently vilified reputation.*[191]

The notoriously fat Duke of Brunswick was particularly litigious, and a scourge of the free press. Incredibly, now over 160 years later, one of the Duke's many libel cases lives with our law today in the Duke of Brunswick rule. The judgement was made before the invention of the lightbulb, telephone, let alone internet, yet still affects online publication.

The *Weekly Dispatch* wrote a story about the Duke in 1832 to which he took offence. He ordered his manservant to travel from London to Paris to obtain a copy of the journal in order to claim he had been defamed. Ordinarily at this time, there was a six-year statute of limitations. Yet, the court ordered that by producing the new copy of the *Weekly Dispatch* from France, and also by procuring a copy from its London publishers, the libel had been re-published. It probably helped that the Duke was high European aristocracy.

The judgment became known as the multiple publication rule. It means every single publication, and any re-publication of a libel, can give cause for a libel suit. So thanks to an 1849 libel case, a single hit on a website today is actionable in court. If the claimant can prove internet visits in the UK (in the case of *Mardas* v. *New York Times Co & International Herald Tribune SAS* there were 27 hits of the *IHT* article online, and a derisory four hits for the *New York Times*),[192] and that they have a reputation here, the High Court will take the trial.

As leading media lawyer Mark Stephens argues: 'because of the international nature of the internet, it is proving simple for claimants to demonstrate that an actionable tort has occurred, no matter how far England is from the location of the original publication.'[193]

In 2002, the Law Commission tried to bring an end to the archaic Duke of Brunswick rule, arguing that there ought to be only a single act of publication (the first publication of an article) and one place to bring an action, where the article was originally published.[194] To the last government's shame, nothing was done until 2009 when the Ministry of Justice published a consultation document. It proposed a single publication rule, a ten-year maximum limitation period and a qualified privilege defence to publishers of online archives after the expiration of the limited period. A start, but not bold enough. The English PEN/Index on Censorship report called for the abolition of the Duke of Brunswick rule, proposing a single act of publication rule, actionable only within a year of publication.

The Libel Reform Campaign

As with many great campaigns in the history of British liberty, part of the Libel Reform Campaign had its genesis in a pub. In the unlikely setting of a JD Wetherspoons on Holborn, lawyer David Allen Green held a packed and 'thirsty' meeting to discuss Simon Singh's ongoing case and its implications. Singh's case, of a lone science writer battling a well-resourced association over what he assumed to be comment, hit a vein with 'skeptics' already concerned over a wave of irrationalism and sensationalism that seemed to be infecting public debate. The science charity Sense About Science took the head of steam generated by anger at Singh's case to build a public campaign. Concurrently, English PEN, the writers' charity, and Index on Censorship, the free speech charity, were developing proposals for reform of our libel laws after the UN Human Rights Committee's damning report of July 2008. At the launch of their report, 'Free Speech Is Not For Sale', the organisations grouped together to form the Libel Reform Campaign.

The 'Free Speech Is Not For Sale' report makes ten clear recommendations to protect free speech:

1. In libel, the defendant is guilty until proven innocent

Recommendation: Require the claimant to demonstrate damage and falsity

2. English libel law is more about making money than saving a reputation

Recommendation: Cap damages at £10,000

3. The definition of 'publication' defies common sense

Recommendation: Abolish the Duke of Brunswick rule and introduce a single publication rule

4. London has become an international libel tribunal

Recommendation: No case should be heard in this jurisdiction unless at least 10 per cent of copies of the relevant publication have been circulated here

5. There are few viable alternatives to a full trial

Recommendation: Establish a libel tribunal as a low-cost forum for hearings

6. There is no robust public interest defence in libel law

Recommendation: Strengthen the public interest defence

7. Comment is not free

Recommendation: Expand the definition of fair comment

8. The potential cost of defending a libel action is prohibitive

Recommendation: Cap base costs and make success fees and 'after the event' (ATE) insurance premiums non-recoverable

9. The law does not reflect the arrival of the internet

Recommendation: Exempt interactive online services and interactive chat from liability

10. Not everything deserves a reputation

Recommendation: Exempt large and medium-sized corporate bodies and associations from libel law unless they can prove malicious falsehood.

The report by Jo Glanville and Jonathan Heawood generated the first significant debate on our defamation laws in a generation. With a slick internet operation (if we say so ourselves), the campaign mobilised over 50,000 people across the country to email their MPs to back a parliamentary Early Day Motion (EDM 423) calling for a Libel Reform Bill. Even after their battering at the hands of the press over the expenses scandal that hung heavy over the last Parliament, over half of all eligible MPs signed the motion.

The UK Parliament's Culture, Media and Sport Select Committee of MPs released its 'Press standards, privacy and libel' report on 24 February this year. It marked a clear shift of opinion amongst MPs that something ought to be done, and we welcomed it as 'a great starting point to ensure an unprecedented overhaul of our libel laws'. Amongst its recommendations, the Committee accepted our concerns over 'libel tourism', and argued for 'additional hurdles' to be placed before jurisdiction is accepted in our courts. A politically brave stand on this issue was taken, stating: 'the reputation of the UK is being damaged by overly flexible jurisdiction rules'.[195]

The Committee also took a robust stance towards corporations suing individuals, recommending in these cases that 'it would be fairer to reverse the general burden of proof'. It further recommended that there should be a new category of tort, entitled 'corporate defamation', which would require a corporation to prove actual damage to its business.

The MPs also backed our campaign's calls for a stronger and more accessible public interest defence and also accepted that the 'fears of the medical and science community are well-founded', and proposed the government 'take account of these concerns in a review of the country's libel laws, in particular the issue of fair comment in academic peer-reviewed publications.'[196]

With law firms charging £400 an hour 'base rate', the Committee strongly advocated that there should be 'maximum hourly rates that can be [possibly] recovered from the losing party in defamation proceeding', it added that ATE premiums ought to be 'wholly irrecoverable' to reduce costs in many libel cases by £65,000–£100,000. As an incentive to minimise costs, the MPs suggested that success fees in CFAs recoverable from the losing party should be limited to 10 per cent of costs with the excess negotiable between solicitor and client.[197]

Just before the end of the parliamentary session, Justice Secretary Jack Straw decided to act on the recommendation in our report on CFAs, echoed similarly by the MPs' report. He used a statutory instrument (a mini-Bill often used to change single lines of existing legislation) to cut CFA success fees to 10 per cent. As an instructive lesson into how vested interests may scupper future reform, the statutory instrument (SI) was blocked at every turn. Firstly, the disgraced ex-Speaker of the House of Commons Michael Martin tabled a 'motion of regret' (an arcane way of attempting to slow the passage of a SI) in the Lords. He didn't kill it off entirely, but he needn't have bothered. At what was supposed to be a strictly whipped Bill Committee on 30 March, a group of MPs turned up simply to vote down the SI. One Ministry of Justice insider said it was 'almost unheard of' that a SI would be voted down with MPs voting against their party's whip. One Labour politician told friendly MPs the SI was 'Paul Dacre's Bill' (the editor of the conservative *Daily Mail*). Straw's SI was certainly rushed through (and some of its critics had merit to their arguments),[198] but the unprecedented opposition it faced gave us cause for concern.

Against this background there was cause for optimism. The accumulative impact of the MPs' Committee report, the debate originating from the 'Free Speech Is Not For Sale' report, and our high-profile campaign led all three of Britain's main political parties to make a commitment to libel reform in their general election manifestos. When no party secured a working majority, our campaign found itself in the unusual (but not unwelcome) position of having both political parties in the new coalition government committed to libel reform as part of their election platform.

In the months running up to the election, Lord Anthony Lester QC, the architect of the Human Rights Act, had been assiduously working on his Defamation Private Member's Bill. I imagine at this time Anthony probably considered our aim for all three parties to make a manifesto commitment a naive pipe dream. After the coalition formed, with both the Conservatives and Liberal Democrats pledging reform, he tabled his Bill in the House of Lords.

Lord Lester's Bill did not include all the reforms we advocated. It was, however, the first opportunity for significant reform of our defamation laws in a century, and devised by a peer with a pretty exceptional track record of getting Bills through the often tortuous parliamentary process.

The reforms in Lord Lester's Bill aimed to address the lack of a robust public interest defence; the use of the multiple publication rule; confusion over the scope of privilege when reporting on parliamentary debate; confusion over the 'fair comment' defence; the inappropriate use of defamation law by corporate bodies; and the incoherence of the law's approach to online publication.

During the second reading debate of the Bill, Lord McNally, the Justice Minister, announced that his department would be taking forward Lord Lester's work through a government Bill it would draft by the spring of 2011. Lord Lester was astounded, saying to a packed House of Lords: 'I wonder whether I am alive at all or whether I am in heaven'.

The government have a lot of work to do – and our campaign will continue to lobby hard to ensure one of our most essential liberties, that of free expression, is protected. Walter Bagehot remarked that 'even the incomplete, erroneous, rapid opinion of the free English people is invaluable'. It's a sad state of affairs when our laws are used to suppress free speech in nations we would consider less free than our own. Stopping libel tourism is essential so that never again can our High Court be used by a near-failed Icelandic bank to silence a Danish newspaper. There is no justifiable reason that the cost of a libel case here is 140 times the comparable European average, or that, in 2010, scientific articles are pulped because there is no reliable public interest defence. Free speech is not for sale: over 50,000 people are now active on this issue. The high-minded liberalism of both the Conservative party and Liberal Democrat party in opposition must now be translated into action. Or our international reputation as a safe haven for liberal and democratic values will be muddied further.

Privacy under the coalition

Simon Davies

After a long decade which witnessed the devastation of privacy in the UK, there is a sense of cautious optimism about the prospects for the new coalition government. Both the Conservatives and the Liberal Democrats have agreed a commitment to a range of important reforms which could help roll back the tide of intrusive measures which have made Britain the most surveillance-intense country in the democratic world.

The shift in direction has come not a moment too soon. Since the late 1990s surveillance has been a core component of almost all private and public IT systems. The laws providing protection have been ravaged, and the limitations applied by judges have been routinely snubbed. Surveillance of our personal information, our activities and our lifestyle became a target that reaped rich rewards for developers.

This surveillance disease reached into every fibre of government, even stretching into its international relations. Surveillance became a state requirement. The dialogue and the vocabulary of those in power had no capacity to include respect for rights. Instead, the dialogue centred on how law can be circumvented to ensure maximum information collection and maximum intrusion. In the hothouse of 10 Downing Street and Whitehall, those who spoke of privacy rights were quickly isolated.

One of the most notable examples of this malaise was the audacious clause 152 power in the Coroners and Justice Bill that would have allowed for wholesale data-sharing across the public and private sector without the consent of the individuals concerned.

If that amendment had been enacted it would have given ministers the power, through secondary legislation, to effectively nullify the protections contained within the Data Protection Act, and indeed the very purpose of the DPA.

In effect, these powers would permit a minister to allow any person (including a company or government department) to share information about any person (e.g. name, address, date of birth, ethnicity, credit history, medical records, DNA and genetic information, tenancy records, social work records etc), if to do so serves the government's policy objectives.

Clause 152 would have permitted an almost limitless range of data-sharing opportunities both within government and between commercial organisations, including, but not limited, to:

- Provision without patient consent of NHS files to medical research organisations;
- Massive expansion of the national DNA database, including for purposes other than the detection of crime;
- Bulk provision of NHS and other medical files to the insurance industry;
- Disclosure of police intelligence data to private investigators and investigation departments of companies;
- Bulk transfer of personal financial data to HMRC and other government departments;
- Disclosure of all vehicle insurance data from insurance companies to DVLA;
- Routine sharing of information from government departments to the intelligence and security service;
- Transfer of UK police data to foreign police agencies in Europe and elsewhere;
- Disclosure of police records to social services and children's data systems, and vice versa;

- Access by Criminal Records Bureau to police intelligence data, and an Information Sharing Order could also permit employers to share CRB check data;
- Sharing of data between council tax records and national databases including the electoral roll, and between national databases and councils for collecting council tax;
- Bulk disclosure of hotel registration data to police and HMRC;
- In the context of anti-prostitution policy, STD clinic data to be shared with the government.

It says a lot about the strength of the privacy issue that this fundamental power was withdrawn after a two-week campaign by privacy activists and the opposition. In the dying days of the Labour administration, privacy was just being recognised as a crucial right that could not easily be compromised. Sadly, the realisation came too late for the government. Even up to the last minute, ministers were still defending an ID scheme that has lost all support.

At some levels the mood music has most definitely changed. Even a year ago the right to privacy was barely tolerated in conversation between ministers and officials. Now a new administration has come to power, in part on a platform of rights protection rather than surveillance. Many of the key figures in government have been long-standing supporters of privacy.

Understandably, anyone who cared about freedoms and rights took a brief moment to feel delighted about this remarkable outcome. It was a tribute not just to the integrity of many parliamentary candidates, but also to the privacy and rights advocates who down the years have fought to change the hearts and minds of the political parties.

However, enthusiastic as advocates were with the prospect of repealing identity cards, scrapping onerous databases, deleting DNA profiles of the innocent, restraining the fingerprinting of children, regulating visual surveillance, restricting communications surveillance and the prospect of political reform, we were guided by an understanding that the price of freedom is eternal vigilance. When people become satisfied and complacent, the opportunities for intrusion are magnified.

The 'brief moment' of celebration was over almost before it began. A commitment to rein in the NHS database insanity was abandoned less than two weeks after the government took office. It was a sign that the civil servants were still to a large extent in control of IT implementation.

Added to this concern is the reality that the 'database' mania is a state of mind as much as an economic driver. When governments think about change and reform, they think in terms of database development. It's a retardation of the organisational mind that blocks out more rational and human-centred alternatives.

Over the coming couple of years we must be ready to undertake the difficult task of galvanising and consolidating the political commitments that have been made. It is one thing for a government to repeal the most repugnant initiatives of its predecessors, and quite another to show sensitivity and restraint when future opportunities become available for new surveillance measures. Put simply, it is easy to condemn what has gone before, but it is infinitely harder for any government to resist the temptation to introduce new and even more intrusive initiatives.

Rather than relaxing in the sunshine of Britain's new era of liberty and freedom, it is crucial that people intensify their efforts to drive the privacy message deep into the DNA of government. Anything short of that Herculean effort will result in a complacent society and an indolent Parliament. The outcome would be disastrous.

This is not the moment in history to relax. This is the moment to press regulators to be more aggressive, for Parliament to be more proactive, for civil society to be more confidently assertive and for the public to demand the restoration of its rights. Those who claim to be our guardians must lift their game. We must also continue to keep the debate alive, informed and rich to ensure that the public continues to be aware of its rights and that it can seek redress through the courts and regulators.

Having said all this, the political outcome in Britain should send a message to governments around the world. Privacy matters. Rights matter. Government can be seduced by officials and industry into believing that the electorate wants surveillance, but the UK political outcome tells a different story. Ultimately people believe in the right to privacy and they will be prepared to defend that right at the ballot box.

The Case for a British Bill of Rights

Martin Howe QC

Paradoxically, the decade since the introduction of the Human Rights Act in 1998 has been marked by the accelerated erosion of civil liberties on many fronts. The creation and expansion of a series of giant state databases, the proposed introduction of identity cards, a series of assaults on the right to trial by jury, and extended pre-charge detention and control orders on terrorist suspects all took place under the supposedly benign regime of the Human Rights Act.

The formation this year of the Conservative–Liberal Democrat coalition has transformed the political landscape as regards the protection of civil liberties. Neither of these parties shares (at least not to anything like the same degree) the instinctive love of big government and general desire to control everyone and everything which seemed to beset New Labour. There is definitely a change of climate. A large part of the New Labour thicket is being cut back with the prompt scrapping of identity cards and of the intrusive national database which was being created supposedly to improve child protection, although there is disappointment in the government's apparent decision to go ahead with the dangerous and costly programme of centralising NHS medical records on a giant national database.

However a cynic would argue that the first flush of enthusiasm for civil liberties on the part of politicians who are fresh from opposition will fade as they become increasingly entrained into the government machine. And without being cynical, being in government does impose very serious responsibilities to get things right. The whole area of how to deal with terrorist suspects involves extremely difficult judgements about how to protect civil liberties at the same time as protecting the public from terrorist attacks, and getting these judgements wrong could have real and disastrous consequences.

This means that the new government needs a principled and effective framework for safeguarding civil liberties. A Bill of Rights for the United Kingdom could be a key part of that framework.

Relationship to the European Convention

The principles enshrined in the European Convention on Human Rights rightly enjoy near-universal support. A British Bill of Rights would continue to protect those principles.

The supporters of the Human Rights Act claim that this can only be achieved by the particular mechanism used in that Act. That mechanism is the direct incorporation of the text of the Convention into United Kingdom domestic law. According to this over-simplistic and fallacious view of the world, a British Bill of Rights would either say the same thing as the Convention, in which case it is unnecessary; or say something different, in which case it is pernicious.

But nothing could be further from the case. A British Bill of Rights can achieve a number of very important things. First, greater clarity and precision in the law. The Convention was drafted as an international diplomatic text to be observed by states. It was not drafted in the form of a statute suitable for daily application in our domestic courts or daily observance by our public authorities. Many of its key articles are broadly and vaguely worded and leave much room for interpretation and indeed misinterpretation. This is a particular problem because under the Human Rights Act the provisions of the Convention have to be applied day-to-day, on the ground. Supporters of the Act in its present form cannot disclaim, for example, the actions of police who wrongly advise shopkeepers that they cannot put up 'wanted' pictures of shoplifters because it would infringe their human rights.

A law must be tested by how it operates in practice – not in a theoretical make-believe world where everyone is perfect and has the skills of a top-class human rights lawyer able to interpret and apply the Convention to day-to-day situations without any difficulty.

A Bill of Rights could define more clearly than the words of the articles themselves the scope of the rights enshrined in the Convention and the proper limitations of those rights. It would dovetail those rights into our legal system and our laws. By making the law clearer and more specific, it would enhance the effective protection of our rights in circumstances where they deserve to be protected and make it more obvious where specious and unjustified claims are being put forward.

Protecting additional rights

Secondly, a British Bill of Rights can provide specific protection for rights and liberties which are not covered at all by the European Convention, or which are inadequately covered. For example, it can protect the right to trial by jury in serious criminal cases from further erosion for reasons of administrative convenience. Jury trial obviously cannot be a feature of a Convention which includes many countries who have no tradition of using juries in their criminal legal systems. However the right to jury trial is featured in the US Constitution and in the bills of rights of other common law countries, including New Zealand and Canada.

The European Convention was drafted sixty years ago. Since then, new technology has led to new dangers against which the citizen today needs to have specific protection. There has been a huge and unparalleled growth in the 'Database State'. This can be tempered by giving citizens specific rights over the way in which their personal information is gathered, stored, shared and disseminated by the organs of the state.

The present position is that the state's activities of gathering and using data about citizens are governed under the Convention only by the general words of Article 8, which states that 'Everyone has the right to respect for his private and family life, his home and his correspondence'. The vagueness of this Article meant that our own highest court, the House of Lords (now replaced by the Supreme Court) decided that the UK's vast and indiscriminately gathered criminal DNA database was compatible with Article 8 of the Convention; whilst the European Court of Human Rights at Strasbourg reached the opposite conclusion.

This is an area where a set of principles attuned to the modern IT-driven age is needed to ensure appropriate protection of civil liberties and also to define the circumstances in which the state's use of data is legitimate and proper. These principles can be inserted into a British Bill of Rights. The courts should no longer be left alone in the uncharted sea of the interpretation of Article 8 of the Convention.

Correcting imbalances under the present system

Thirdly, a British Bill of Rights can correct some of the imbalances between different rights which have grown up under the Human Rights Act – acting within the margin of appreciation which is permitted to states under the Convention. One unintended consequence of the Act has been the creation by the courts of a full scale law of privacy, under the guise of giving effect to the right to respect for private and family life under Article 8 of the Convention.

This judge-made law of privacy in many ways is a model of what a privacy law should not be. It is vague, unclear and discretionary. The press is hampered by not knowing what it can and cannot do. In practice this law is available mainly for the benefit of rich and powerful people. It may be used for the suppression of inconvenient and embarrassing truths of public interest as much as for the protection of genuinely private matters.

Article 10 of the Convention on 'freedom of expression' is much weaker in the protection it provides to the media than, for example, the First Amendment to the US Constitution. A British Bill of Rights gives the opportunity to strengthen the freedom of the press in this country and to give the media clear rights to report matters in the public interest.

Re-connecting with our historic civil liberties

Fourth, a British Bill of Rights would re-connect our citizens and our courts with our own deeply embedded historical traditions of the protection of liberty. The liberties now set out in the European Convention are not a foreign import into this country from Europe. The fundamental right to a fair trial stems under our law from Magna Carta, and the independence of our judiciary from the Act of Settlement; Article 6 of the Convention, which speaks of fair trials before an independent and impartial tribunal, came a lot later. Our right to liberty of the person stems from the Habeas Corpus Act which long predated Article 5 of the Convention.

The perception that the rights conferred by the Convention are a foreign import from Europe has coloured much of the debate on the Human Rights Act and has accounted for some of the media and public hostility towards it.

In interpreting and applying our own Bill of Rights, our courts would be able to draw more extensively on our own historic common law principles and on the case law of other common law countries. This would reverse the present trend under which the courts are increasingly confined to looking at cases under the European Convention itself. This actually leads to the erosion of our historic liberties because the Convention merely provides a minimum standard to be applied across all European countries and in important respects its protections fall below the standards previously recognised in our own law.

A more positive contribution to the interpretation of the Convention

Fifth, the Bill of Rights would give our courts greater freedom and confidence, where appropriate, to challenge some of the more questionable jurisprudence of the Court of Human Rights in Strasbourg. In his address last year to the Judicial Studies Board, Lord Hoffmann powerfully criticised some of the rulings of that Court and its general approach. But our higher courts have on the whole been unduly craven in their approach to Strasbourg case law, acting almost as if Strasbourg is a harmonising court by whose rulings they are bound, like the EU Court of Justice at Luxembourg.

Re-engaging Parliament with civil liberties

Sixthly and lastly, and probably most importantly, a Bill of Rights for the United Kingdom would re-engage our legislators directly with the process of safeguarding the rights and liberties which it protects. Like it or not, the Human Rights Act is unloved by the British public and is viewed by politicians as an instrument which seeks to impose external restraints on the freedom of action of Parliament.

This is reflected in some of the important legislation passed under the last government, in which Parliament effectively 'farmed out' its own responsibility for protecting civil liberties. For example, the Prevention of Terrorism Act 2005 (which introduced control orders) contained a general provision requiring that the powers under the Act be exercised so that so-called 'non-derogating' orders must be compatible with the right to liberty under Article 5 of the Convention. This effectively left it to the courts rather than Parliament to define the boundaries of the powers which Parliament had conferred in the Act.

The Bill of Rights of 1689 (and in Scotland the parallel Claim of Right) were instruments by which Parliament imposed its will on the executive in order to protect and enhance our liberties. The new Bill of Rights for the United Kingdom should be seen in a similar light and as serving a similar purpose. It would provide *guidance* for Parliament itself in the laws it passes, and would be protected against unintentional or casual repeal but not against a conscious and deliberate parliamentary decision to depart from it.

A huge volume of laws under our present system are created by statutory instruments which emerge from the Whitehall machine and are not scrutinised effectively, or in many cases at all, by Parliament itself. The Bill of Rights would prevent the passing of incompatible statutory instruments, or executive actions which conflict with its provisions; and if laws are found unintentionally to be contrary to its terms then Parliament itself would be intimately involved in addressing the problem – unlike the Human Rights Act where a quickie corrective statutory instrument bypasses Parliament.

In conclusion, a new Bill of Rights for the United Kingdom can strengthen the protection of our vital liberties; reduce the scope for absurd and inappropriate claims; speed up our courts; reduce muddle and confusion on the part of public authorities, police and others who have to apply it; reduce friction between politicians and the judiciary; and return lawmaking to our elected representatives in Parliament rather than the courts.

European privacy in the internet age

Luca Bolognini, Stefano Mele, Pietro Paganini

The European Privacy Association and the Italian Institute for Privacy were founded to confront some of the most fundamental challenges over the next few decades in our so-called Information Society, namely data protection and security, in light of European experience and values. If Europe is able to cultivate the opportunity for development offered by innovation and by new web applications, while at the same time protecting the privacy, freedom and security of its own citizen consumers, it will create trust and confidence that will permit the market to grow rapidly and harmoniously. Furthermore, Europe will be in a position to offer best practice solutions to the rest of the world.

Among fundamental rights, the 'right to privacy' has been known for centuries but has assumed a new and crucial significance in the Information Society or internet era, as it is increasingly endangered by the progress of technologies and by increasing governmental encroachment. We believe in an open society, able to protect this right and defend it from the various threats it faces. However, we also believe that privacy must be interpreted in light of other important rights, duties, and freedoms, such as the right to operate in a free market and the right to private property. Privacy is often seen as a threat by market operators; we believe that in many cases it can become a stunning opportunity.

We will discuss some of the most relevant e-privacy issues that are challenging individuals' daily lives. As science is the attempt to solve complex problems, the aim of our work is to provide a comprehensive analysis of some of the situations occurring online where privacy becomes an issue. Such analysis requires a new methodological approach, as the methods employed so far are no longer sufficient. This article is not about methodology or the epistemology of privacy, but it will try to use a new approach. A new methodology is, in fact, the primary step if we want to fully comprehend contemporary privacy and meet its challenges.

We do not intend to provide any final solution to e-privacy issues. This is such a new issue – solving it will require a long time and a great deal of effort. Furthermore we believe that the goal of science is to provide newer and newer angles of analysis and responses to the evolving problem of privacy. In this article we shall point out a series of very simple but very contingent situations that demonstrate (i) how users' privacy is under threat; (ii) how users could protect it; and (iii) the role of the online operators. We will briefly try to follow users from the very moment they log on to the internet, by a computer or a mobile device, to the upload of data, whether text, music, pictures or videos. It is an important moment in human history; it is when a user finally stops being a passive spectator and becomes an interactive participant in the online community.

Finally, we will investigate whether (i) we will soon celebrate the death of privacy as some online operators argue in their funereal visions of the future (driven by closed-minded business strategies); (ii) we will welcome the return of a digital communism as some operators have shown the way; or (iii) we will succeed in making privacy a solid individual right and an amazing opportunity.

A new multidisciplinary approach to privacy

In a contemporary, fast-growing, global ICT-oriented environment, privacy cannot be investigated under the old paradigm that limited the protection of our personal lives to jurisprudence and the study of law. Furthermore, with the advent of new technologies and the rapid increase in globalisation processes, it would be unthinkable and scientifically inaccurate to face the problem of personal information with a legal instrument alone. Case law provides the references, the backbone that supports the skeleton, but it is no longer sufficient on its own. Privacy has evolved in perfect symbiosis with social transformations. As with scientific revolutions, the current phase has resulted in a series of new problems and the chance to look at these problems from different perspectives. The pervasive nature of technology and the current integration of the various scientific doctrines allows us to examine the different disciplines with real interest, including computer engineering and genetics, economics and management, sociology and psychology, new media and everything that contemporary society uses to collect, manage and quantify personal information.

Privacy in the age of interactivity: user generated content

Until the end of the last century and the very first years the 2000s, only specialised individuals and companies were able to produce, share and retrieve data over the internet. As in the previous fifty years, dominated by television, users were only able to undergo information like simple spectators. Users were uniquely consumers, passive spectators.

In recent years, with the massive decrease in the cost of production and the development of new software and hardware, the role of users has dramatically and progressively changed. Such a radical transformation has been so powerful that our online behaviour and attitudes have profoundly changed. Users are no longer spectators; they are producers, interactive players. First file sharing platforms and then social networks such as YouTube and Facebook have allowed ordinary users, with no software or hardware expertise, to release on to the internet millions of videos, pictures, and terabytes of text. These bytes of information are very often related to their personal details, describing and identifying their customs, personality, habits, intimate thoughts or wishes – who they are or wish to be. In many cases the information is not just about them, but involves their family and friends, or even people they do not even know. What we know as the Web 2.0 is also known as the User Generated Content (UGC) internet.

It is an amazing victory for liberty, for freedom of speech and expression, for emancipation. It is a certain victory for human progress. Such a stunning achievement, however, bears some risks for privacy. These risks need to be balanced if we want such an achievement to remain a victory and not turn into a defeat. In fact, once all these terabytes of information are uploaded in the network of networks, they can become a dangerous tool that violates privacy. Thus, as argued above, liberty is not the sole right to speak freely without any impediment; it is the balance between such a fundamental freedom and the right to be left alone and to protect any private or personal information.

The role of web hosts and Internet Service Providers

To analyse the legal problems that can arise from the connection between UGC and privacy in-depth, we must first consider the role assigned to the subject/operator (Google, Flickr, YouTube etc) that this type of content offers.

Therefore, 'Access Provider' means the 'subject who allows the user to connect to the computer network'.[199] The task of the 'Access Provider' is more or less to verify the identity of the user who requests the service, obtaining his personal information and, later, sending the request to the authority so that it can open the relative web space. At the same time, however, 'Service Provider' normally means the 'subject who, once access to the network is granted, allows the user to perform determined operations, like use email, share and catalogue information, send it to determined subjects, etc'.[200] Further, the 'Content Provider' is the 'operator that provides all kinds of information and works to the public (magazines, photographs, books, databases, e-versions of newspapers and periodicals etc), uploading them to the memory of computer servers and connecting them to the computers on the network'.[201] Finally, the 'Hosting Provider' is the operator who hosts the content uploaded by the users, user generated content (UGC) on its servers or on websites, often managed independently by third parties. The UGC material must be considered to be in the former category. In this case, we must observe the European Directive on E-Commerce,[202] which explicitly states that, in providing a service that involves storing the information provided by a third subject (hosting), the provider is not responsible for that information so long as he is not actually aware of the fact that the activity or information is illegal and, in terms of requests for compensation for damages, is not aware of the facts or circumstances that make the activity or information illegal or, as soon as he is aware of these facts, takes immediate action to take down the information or take away access to it.[203] Subsequently, it is obvious that there is no general obligation for the provider to provide oversight nor is he obliged to look for illegal activity.[204] There is merely the general obligation to inform the public authorities of activities or information deemed to be illegal as well as to report information that allows for the author to be identified at the request of the legal authorities.

Culpa in vigilando

The *provider* 'responsibility system', while ensuring the lack of a general oversight obligation, states that the provider is bound by an obligation to report any illegal act to the judicial authorities and to provide all helpful information in its possession. The literal tone of the regulation, which is particularly generic and abstract in this case, leaves room for interpretation aimed at including the possible existence of a *guilt by negligence* – similar to the well known and severe editorial liability in all cases where the provider has not suitably controlled the data recorded. The part of the doctrine favourable to a similar theoretical reconstruction argues that:

> by equating a website host to an editor, we can theorise the application of a regulation for crimes committed in publications and thus attribute to the *provider* the obligation to verify the legitimacy of all the material published on its server, including that set by third parties. From this point of view, the *provider* would be jointly liable for the illegal actions of third parties based on *guilt by negligence* which consists in not fulfilling the obligations to check the material located on its server.[205]

In essence, however, as correctly interpreted in several rulings,[206] it must be underlined that, affirming the provider's liability due to a lack of control, in a sector where it is physically impossible to conduct in-depth controls of all the data packets sent online (*deep packet inspection*),[207] this would be the same as introducing a new and unacceptable theory of objective liability – regardless of guilt – in clear objection to the general laws set forth in our legislation[208] that is the basis of the civil liability of the injuring party.[209] In fact, if it confirms not only the rejection of objective liability, to the detriment of the company on the one hand but the aggravated subjective liability models on the other, the current law translates into making the provider's liability subject to the provider knowing about the illegal activity or information or, simply, to the existence of the activity or information.[210] The accepted rule is the prevailing one: the *provider* will be liable for the illegal activity of the user of his services if he is fully aware of their illegal nature. The provider is therefore, on the basis of subjective liability, culpable if the service vendor, aware of the presence of suspicious material on his site, does not verify whether it is illegal and, at the same time, does not remove it; wrongful when he is aware of the user's illegal behaviour and, once again, does not intervene.[211]

Providers' responsibility

The legal liability of the provider in the event of a violation of privacy must necessarily fall on the subject who places the material on the site, releasing the *hosting provider* (Facebook, YouTube, etc) and deflecting any accusation of liability in all cases where the provider can show that it was not aware of the illegal activity or information conducted on its systems and, in terms of requests for compensation for damages, where it was not aware of the facts or circumstances that would make the illegal activity or information clear. Subsequently, with notice from the competent authorities, the information deemed illegal must be removed quickly and the user responsible for it must be denied access to avoid repeating the crime and any direct involvement.

The single weak point is the one set forth by the Privacy Code regarding a lack of information or incomplete information provided to the user right before the content is uploaded. This could invoke the culpability of the *hosting provider* for not having taken all measures, including purely informative ones, to avoid the user acting illegally. It is therefore of fundamental importance to provide terms and conditions for use of the site that are clear and strict, as well as to establish the specific policies for users in order to mitigate the risk of publishing information that could harm third party rights or, in general, material that has clearly illegal content. In particular, the following is necessary:

- the user who wants to upload digital data verifies that he has the right to distribute the content prior to uploading it;
- the website host publishes clear and detailed guidelines on what is and what is not considered 'acceptable' content on the system, specifying that the operator will delete inappropriate content;

- the provider ensures that users can report illegal or offensive contents, specifying the cases where the operator may remove them directly;
- the provider considers the application of age verification procedures, given that the terms and conditions of use cannot be legally binding for minors unless they are able to understand the nature of their contents;
- the provider offers a specific privacy policy in order to inform users about the obligation to report data on the systems that could impact investigations and legal proceedings.

The users' perspective

From the point of view of the user who provides or 'suffers' from the digital contents, the situation is certainly not rosy or easy to solve. The platforms that are based on user generated content have made a significant impact on accessibility to personal data for a large part of the world's population, making the publication and sharing of information not only immediate but the classic distinction between providers (content authors) and users/consumers (content users) weak.

In terms of privacy, therefore, the most important challenge is this peculiarity that arises from the success of these platforms, where the majority of personal data distributed is provided voluntarily by the users. The 'traditional' legislative provisions on privacy focus on defining rules that protect citizens from the unfair or disproportionate processing of their personal data by public subjects or individuals. There are very few regulations that govern the publication of personal data at the direct initiative of users, there never having been an argument on this matter, at least before the advent of the social network services and Web 2.0. The legislation on data protection and privacy has always looked favourably and with certain 'superficiality' on personal data processing from public sources.

The risks – particularly the high ones – for user privacy that can currently be identified can be divided into the following main categories:

No right to be forgotten. The data published is not actually deleted and almost always continues to reside on the 'original' servers – even if the person involved deleted them – or on third party subjects that involve, for example, archiving or searching for information online (like search engines with their 'copy cache' feature). It is also a given that several service providers based on user generated content later refuse to fulfil direct deletion requests for simple data or entire user profiles.

No transparency about information-sharing methods. This means, in some specific cases like social networks, that the data in the user profiles (photos, videos, notes, message boards etc), often classified as confidential and sensitive data, is shared without restriction by the person who generated it.

No transparency about the direct methods to use information. Many of the sites that base their services on user-generated content actually share it with users, reusing the data collected for direct marketing purposes. In the 'quicksand' of the land of UGC and Web 2.0 services, users behave differently from normal: in fact, they use their real names, are in contact with their real friends, publish their real email addresses, share their real opinions, actual preferences and real news. This is absolutely 'new', based on what we learned from the profiling done by search engines that, apart from the chronology of the requests and sole navigation, in comparison with social networks know very little about their users. Registering, cross-referencing and profiling this huge amount of data from navigation, which for the first time is not anonymous, is a serious blow to people's online privacy.

Identity theft. The widespread availability of more or less complete user data often leads to its abuse by unauthorised third parties.

Unsecure infrastructures or data theft. The security of the system where users keep often confidential and sensitive data is actually an essential element in protecting information and privacy. It is certainly true that UGC providers now focus more attention on measures aimed at strengthening the security of their systems and, subsequently, personal data, but there is still a lot left to do. At the same time, it is highly probable that new system security problems will arise in the future, notwithstanding the low probability of the objective of total safety ever being reached, particularly considering the complexity of the software applications at any level of internet services.

Protecting users' right to be 'let alone'. The concept of single sign-on with a unique online personal ID is increasingly used (as well as offline with electronic cards). The subject has one private profile with his/her own credentials, allowing him/her to do anything both on and offline. This system would make things much easier for citizens/users/consumers without a doubt because every time s/he purchased merchandise or services, paid a utility bill or membership fee, accessed confidential areas, registered, made a reservation, asked a question, answered a question or voted, s/he could use the same ID with minimum effort, maximum efficiency and with a certain, rapid authentication. The many codes that we have today (who among us doesn't have at least five or six passwords without even counting credit card, bank account and telephone numbers?) could become a tomorrow with one important electronic certificate, recognised everywhere, for both commercial, administrative and tax purposes.

The client-user certainly wins out, feels 'understood and cared for' by welcome and helpful contents and commercial offers in line with his own preferences and taste. Nevertheless, his privacy is in danger and that is a high price to pay. By analysing the 'tracks' of the interested party, we could figure out almost every detail of his private identity, including sensitive or intimate elements that must reasonably remain secret. The problem, before being legal, is first and foremost ethical: is it right that someone – even if this doesn't hurt the subject in any way – knows potentially delicate information while the person involved remains in the dark? This is the second factor to consider: how much is shared and when do you need consent to process personal data?

The legal question today must focus on the methods through which the user is made aware. Is an information note and its acceptance enough, signed when the party registers, or does the interested party need to be 'updated' in real time about which data, indicators and profiles are being looked at each step of the way and about each search query or visit to the site, with the possibility of withholding consent from those processing? The majority of European and American consumer associations are asking for just that.

The second question, which is based on the exponential explosion of electronic information, is the probable oligopoly (not in an economic sense but in a legal sense!) of the data holders and controllers, giving rise to hyper data controllers and hyper data processors (due to mergers). Progressively fewer players will control almost all the information on things and people: a Big Brother with unimaginable potential.

If an administrative single sign-on system can be used, this would focus on a single subject's ability to process (and know) the life of people not only as consumers but also as political and fiscal citizens. These questions are asked to help protect the reputation of safety measures used to store data: data that – being more overlapping and, in theory, almost infinite in terms of combinations and the subsequent knowledge obtained from that – becomes continually more sensitive and dangerous. From matching three or four neutral pieces of information, we can reasonably estimate the preferences and tastes of a person: the effects of a 'news leak' or improper processing by a hyper-controller who can mix all this information could be devastating.

The death of privacy and the rise of digital communism

Our analysis clearly demonstrates that privacy is profoundly changing, so much that it requires a new approach. As much as the disappearance of privacy is the desire of some, in the opinion of the authors, privacy is not dead; it is actually a relatively new right. As individuals, we will always seek our privacy, the confidentiality of our own ideas and identities. This is not a fault; quite the contrary, it is an act of freedom. These are fundamental subjective rights, which are part of our 'belonging to a community', and the digital revolution will not erase them – at least we hope. Laws and regulations serve to defend this right.

A final consideration from an economic and social perspective: which conception of 'community' seems to move internet content providers and social networks? It would seem to be the idea of total openness of information and the transparency of personal lives: the idea that information must be as 'free', 'diffuse' and 'public' as possible. There does not appear to be an underlying ideology. The interest of content providers and search engines in total openness is obviously connected to the fact that the more information circulates freely online, and the more users use this information, the more material there will be to advertise to users. Essentially, advertising volume will increase. Obviously, there's nothing wrong with defending one's own interests; just be unambiguous, rather than masquerade behind evangelical tones or great noble principles.

The (economic, social, legal) choice of total openness is unconvincing and worrisome, however. Why? It allows the totalitarian ideal of communism that history has closed its door on back in through the window. Digitally, we mean. Like in a hippy commune, privacy rights would be cancelled and people would be 'socially naked'. Like every good totalitarian environment, this could also have the single super-capitalist who knows everything and decides everything and manages on behalf of everyone (in the classic models, this would be the state, but in the digital model it could be the dominant operator). Like every communist society, it would impoverish the world because, by taking away the 'ownership' and 'privacy' of people's things (their ideas, in the digital world), it would destroy their value.

Conclusion

Alex Deane

The recent Yemeni bomb plot could not have come at a worse time. Just as the government - already showing deeply worrying signs of bureaucratic capture and authoritarian reactions to headlines - comes to decide on the next steps to be taken in counter-terrorism, a plot like this is discovered.

In reaction to it, serious commentators effectively advocate the abandonment of the government's commitment to a freedom agenda, saying that 'this campaign for civil liberties is a gift for al-Qaeda'. They would have us resume business as usual, as things were in the Blair/Brown years.

But to do so would be to lose all sense of proportion. It seems almost forgotten by the scareocrats that the attack was actually foiled, that incidents like this are relatively uncommon, that nobody was injured; moreover, much more importantly, it is entirely overlooked by the authoritarian lobby that our forebears withstood appalling actual harm without caving into such pressures. Members of Margaret Thatcher's cabinet were pulled from the rubble of the Grand Hotel, in an attack in which five people died, but her Brighton conference went on and liberties were not curtailed. Likewise, in the course of the 'Troubles', the IRA killed thousands. And yet, faced in the present day by this small band of ineffectual thugs, the knee-jerkers would have our Home Secretary abandon the path of freedom upon which she and her party pledged to embark when offering themselves as candidates at the ballot box a mere few months ago.

Let's be plain about what's at stake. Detention without trial for a month. Random stop and search, under which the police can demand your papers, bullying the law-abiding and demonstrating who's in charge, interfering with your basic freedom of movement, freedom of association, freedom of speech. Control orders, anathema to any democratic society, under which the freedom of the individual can be curtailed – in principle in perpetuity – without him knowing the details or even nature of the charge against him. When you cannot know the nature of the accusation or the name of your accuser, it is of course impossible to rebut the allegation concerned. Certainly, it doesn't affect you at present – after all, first they came for the 45 people who have been subject to such orders to date. But who's next? And when the charge never has to be justified to any objective standard, don't be fooled – it could happen to anyone. It could happen to you. Let us hope that if that were to happen, others would not turn away from you as d'Ancona and co. turn away from those whose liberty is thus curtailed now. Then there's the ridiculous end of privacy and freedom and dignity that is the circus at modern airports. All these things matter enormously.

Values held only in good times are without worth. Indeed, they can be positively harmful, providing a false sense of freedom in a society in fact all too willing to resort to knee-jerk curtailment of rights at the first sign of trouble. Freedom is not free. It will cost us something to defend, yes – but it would cost us something far more vital, were it to be abrogated. It will involve risk - but it is the lot of democracies to fight with one hand tied behind our backs, to put aside some tools even though they might help.

It is a very slippery slope when you start abrogating freedoms, and the retention of them – even when the going gets tough – is what makes us different from the terrorists we face.

Across the contributions to this book, whatever the disciplines of the contributors and subjects about which they write, I believe that there is a common theme – a lament about the extent to which everyday life is being hemmed in, watched and controlled.

To reinforce that theme, let me offer a final example which has not yet been touched upon. The authorities in this country watch over us in ways unimaginable to our forebears. That might sound alarmist, but it isn't; Big Brother Watch research showed that local council bureaucrats carried out 8,500 covert surveillance operations on their own residents in the course of two years, for such heinous offences as fly-tipping (including outside a charity shop – that is, leaving donations), trimming a hedge and breaking the smoking ban. At best, such operations targeted benefit fraudsters – at worst, they were used for many 'offences' for which one cannot even be arrested. Taxi touting may be wrong, but should it be the subject of secret snooping? Our bureaucrats love nothing more than heading out, kitted with telephoto lenses and movement logs, spying on people suspected of lying about the school catchment area in which they live, or monitoring dog walkers to catch their animal in the act of fouling.

Such operations aren't carried out by MI5 or the police, and they're not targeting the serious criminals and terrorists one might think merit covert surveillance. This is the man from the council on steroids, the bureaucrat who thinks he's James Bond. Faced with authorities that feel such surveillance is proportionate and reasonable, it's plain that the state is unashamedly more intrusive than ever. From the gravest end of things, in which detention without trial and control orders are justified by the ever-present bogeyman of terrorism, to the ubiquitous surveillance of the most trivial aspects of everyday life, we live in an environment in which our masters are inexorably more authoritarian. In his piece, Brian Monteith asks, 'Is the Bully State on the Run?' Doughty defender of freedom and good friend that Brian is, I know that he won't mind me suggesting that he has inadvertently offered a submission for John Rentoul's running column, 'Questions to which the answer is "no".

The Big Brother Watch Mission Statement says that we look to expose the sly, slow seizure of control by the state – of power, of information and of our lives – and we advocate the return of our liberties and freedoms. I wish we lived in a society in which an organisation with such a mission statement was surplus to requirements. The contributions to this book display the fact that such a wish yet remains very far from fulfilled.

Notes

1 Unless otherwise stated, facts and figures in this section are drawn from the National Fraud Initiative 2008/09: National report, Audit Commission, May 2010 ('National Report' in what follows): http://www.audit-commission.gov.uk/ SiteCollectionDocuments/Downloads/10_0084_NationalFraudInitative_Report_ WEB2.pdf

2 Very specific, see: http://www.audit-commission.gov.uk/nfi/instructions/ dataspecifications/pages/default.aspx

3 National Report, p. 14.

4 http://www.audit-commission.gov.uk/nfi/newparticipants/pages/default.aspx

5 See NO2ID's briefing on the Serious Crime Bill as it then was for more discussion: http://www.no2id.net/IDSchemes/ NO2IDSeriousCrimeBillBriefingFEB2007.pdf

6 Though perhaps we should worry about that, given the zeal of the Commission. India has for some years had an association for living people who are officially dead. See 'Plight of the Living Dead', Time ASIA, 19 July 1999: http://www.time.com/ time/asia/asia/magazine/1999/990719/souls1.html

7 'Protecting the Public Purse: local government fighting fraud', Audit Commission, September, 2009 (p. 7): http://www.audit-commission.gov.uk/ SiteCollectionDocuments/AuditCommissionReports/NationalStudies/20090915pro tectingthepublicpursea4summary.pdf

8 National Report, pp. 12–20

9 National Report, p. 20

10 http://www.ukba.homeoffice.gov.uk/travellingtotheuk/beforetravel/ advanceinfopassengers/

11 SI No. 5 2008, The Immigration and Police (Passenger, Crew and Service Information) Order 2008. http://www.opsi.gov.uk/si/si2008/uksi_20080005_en_1

12 'Securing the UK Border', Home Office, March 2007. Now lost in government web archives, but available from David Moss, to whom I am grateful for pointing it out: http://dematerialisedid.com/pdfs/Securing_the_UK_Border_final.pdf

13 'Spy centre will track you on holiday', Sunday Times 8 February 2009: http:// www.timesonline.co.uk/tol/travel/news/article5683677.ece

14 '2.1bn to funding to strengthen UK's eBorders', PublicTechnologyNet 2 August 2007: http://www.publictechnology.net/content/10665

15 Home Affairs Committee Twelfth Report, Session 2009–10: http://www. publications.parliament.uk/pa/cm200910/cmselect/cmhaff/406/40602.htm

16 Michael Cross, 'The illegal e-Borders disaster', *The Guardian*, 18 December 2009: http://www.guardian.co.uk/commentisfree/libertycentral/2009/dec/18/illegal-eborders-disaster-it-profession

17 Home Affairs Committee, ibid., Written Evidence item 12

18 'Partial Regulatory Impact Assessment: Data capture and sharing powers for the Border Agencies', Home Office, undated [2005]: http://www.privacyinternational.org/issues/terrorism/library/ukebordersria.pdf

19 See Home Office press release, 'Government Ramps Up Passenger Screening', 11 March 2010 at, e.g. http://trustedborders.com/nbtc.shtml

20 'Database State', Foundation for Information Policy Research for Joseph Rowntree Reform Trust, 2009: http://www.jrrt.org.uk/uploads/Database%20State.pdf identifies and assesses some 46 major UK government databases, all of which involve some degree of data-sharing. (Some of those I would call 'hives' rather than databases, since they are clusters of related projects involving multiple databases and agencies.) It is not an exhaustive list.

21 'HM Government Information sharing vision statement' DCA 47/06, September 2006: http://www.foi.gov.uk/sharing/information-sharing.pdf
At the same time we have, for example, the FAQ here, addressed to the civil service: http://www.foi.gov.uk/sharing/faqs.htm

22 'Privacy and Data-sharing: the way forward for public services', Cabinet Office (Prime Minister's Innovation Unit), April 2002: http://www.cabinetoffice.gov.uk/media/cabinetoffice/strategy/assets/piu%20data.pdf for example the FAQ here, addressed to the civil service: http://www.foi.gov.uk/sharing/faqs.htm

23 http://www.dcsf.gov.uk/everychildmatters/strategy/deliveringservices1/contactpoint/contactpoint

24 Archived at: http://webarchive.nationalarchives.gov.uk/+/http://www.cabinetoffice.gov.uk/cio/transformational_government/strategy.aspx
See also: http://webarchive.nationalarchives.gov.uk/+/http://www.hm-treasury.gov.uk/d/pbr_csr07_service.pdf

25 'Child benefit data loss: timeline of scandal', *Daily Telegraph*, 25 June 2008: http://www.telegraph.co.uk/news/majornews/2191680/Child-benefit-data-loss-timeline-of-scandal.html

26 http://www.justice.gov.uk/reviews/datasharing-intro.htm

27 More detail at: 'Government Information Sharing Review – "Read the small print", says NO2ID', NO2ID, 25 November 2008: http://www.no2id.net/news/pressRelease/release.php?name=Read_the_small_print

28 http://www.justice.gov.uk/docs/NO2ID-Data-Sharing-Response.pdf

29 'A Surveillance Society?' (Fifth Report of Session 2007–08): http://www.publications.parliament.uk/pa/cm200708/cmselect/cmhaff/58/5802.htm

30 E.g. 'Online or in-line: the future of information and technology in public services', 2020 Public Services Trust, Building Block 4: http://clients.squareeye.com/uploads/2020/documents/online_or_inline.pdf

31 http://edmi.parliament.uk/edmi/EDMDetails.aspx?EDMID=41138&SESSION=905

32 Identity Documents Bill, introduced to the House of Commons on 26 May 2010 [Bill 1]

33 Cabinet Office Ref: 401238/0510, 'The Coalition: Our Programme for Government', May 2010

34 In 2007/08 there were 210,670 disposals in total for young offenders, of which almost 90,000 (43%) were reprimands and final warnings. (House of Commons Library Research Paper, 'Youth crime and punishment in England and Wales', SN/SG/5277)

35 'Between January 2004 and 1 April 2006, the police used the power to disperse unruly groups in more than 1,000 designated areas.' (Hansard, 30 April 2007, Col. 1231)

36 Home Office, 'Police Powers and Procedures, England and Wales 2008/9', April 2010, Table 2.01; Ministry of Justice, 2009, 'Statistics on Race and the Criminal Justice System' 2007/08

37 'Report On The Operation In 2008 of the Terrorism Act 2000 And Of Part 1 Of The Terrorism Act 2006', By Lord Carlile Of Berriew QC, June 2009

38 Surveillance Studies Network, 2006, 'A Report on the Surveillance Society', reported by BBC News Online: http://news.bbc.co.uk/1/shared/bsp/hi/pdfs/02_11_06_surveillance.pdf

39 Big Brother Watch Report, 'Big Brother Is Watching', 18 December 2009

40 Hansard, 17 June 2009, 494 c396-8W; Hansard, 1 July 2009, 495 c275-7W

41 NPIA, 'National DNA Database Annual Report' 2007–09, 2010

42 Human Genetics Commission, 'Nothing to hide, Northing to fear?', November 2009

43 NPIA, 'National DNA Database Annual Report' 2007–09, 2010

44 Home Affairs Select Committee, 'Second Report: Young Black People and the Criminal Justice System' HC181-1, 2007

45 European Court of Human Rights, *S and Marper* v. *The United Kingdom* Judgment (Applications nos. 30562/04 and 30566/04), Strasbourg 4 December 2008

46 Youth Justice Board/MORI Youth Survey 2008: 'Young People in Mainstream Education'

47 House of Commons Library, 2010, 'Social Indicators', Research Paper 10/02

48 Home Office, 'Crime in England and Wales 2008–9', 22 October 2009, Revised Table 2.04; Home Office, 'Crime in England and Wales 2008/09', 16 July 2009, p.57

49 Surveillance Studies Network, 2006, 'A Report on the Surveillance Society' reported by BBC News Online: http://news.bbc.co.uk/1/shared/bsp/hi/pdfs/02_11_06_surveillance.pdf; the *Daily Telegraph*, 'Number of crimes caught on CCTV falls by 70 per cent', Metropolitan Police admits, 5 January 2010

50 Department for Children, Schools and Families, Statistical First Release: 'Permanent and Fixed Period Exclusions from Schools and Exclusion Appeals in England, 2007/08,, 30 July 2009

51 ibid

52 ibid

53 Reform, 'The Lawful Society', September 2008

54 Snook, Harry: Crossing the Threshold – 266 Ways the State Can Enter Your Home (Centre for Policy Studies, 2007)

55 See, for example, 'Stand-off that Saved the Cow on Defra's Death Row'; *Daily Mail*, 21 January 2007.

56 http://news.bbc.co.uk/news/vote2001/hi/english/main_issues/sections/facts/newsid_1134000/1134970.stm

57 http://www.telegraph.co.uk/news/newstopics/politics/6485966/Labour-made-mistakes-over-immigration-Alan-Johnson-admits.html

58 http://www.legislation.gov.uk/ukpga/2001/24/contents

59 http://news.bbc.co.uk/2/hi/uk_news/4100481.stm

60 http://news.bbc.co.uk/1/hi/uk/4100481.stm

61 http://www.statutelaw.gov.uk/content.aspx?activeTextDocId=1414108

62 http://critical-reaction.co.uk/2775/13-10-2010-the-coalition-and-civil-liberties

63 http://www.guardian.co.uk/guantanamo/story/0,,1712066,00.html

64 http://it.tmcnet.com/topics/it/articles/59729-ibm-signs-7-year-national-
biometric-identity-service.htm

65 http://www-03.ibm.com/press/uk/en/pressrelease/27972.wss

66 http://eur-lex.europa.eu/LexUriServ/LexUriServ.do?uri=OJ:L:2008:115:0001:00
07:EN:PDF

67 http://news.bbc.co.uk/1/hi/7450627.stm

68 http://www.ukba.homeoffice.gov.uk/travellingtotheuk/beforetravel/
advanceinfopassengers/

69 http://www.legislation.gov.uk/uksi/2008/5/contents/made

70 http://www.legislation.gov.uk/uksi/2008/5/schedule/2/made

71 Judah, Tim, *Kosovo: War and Revenge* (New Haven and London: Yale University
Press, 2000)

72 http://www.icar.org.uk/download.php?id=588

73 http://www.guardian.co.uk/uk/2010/may/14/
immigration-asylum-children-detention-centres

74 http://www.publications.parliament.uk/pa/jt200506/jtselect/
jtrights/245/24507.htm

75 http://www.guardian.co.uk/uk/2009/oct/20/
trafficking-numbers-women-exaggerated

76 http://treaties.un.org/Pages/ViewDetails.
aspx?src=TREATY&mtdsg_no=XVIII-12-a&chapter=18&lang=en

77 http://www.thegovmonitor.com/world_news/europe/the-coalition-
government-and-a-uk-immigration-cap-32154.html

78 http://hansard.millbanksystems.com/lords/1998/feb/12/
crime-and-disorder-bill-hl#S5LV0585P0_19980212_HOL_127

79 It had been an offence under the 1986 Public Order Act to stir up racial hatred,
but that part of the Act was not frequently used.

80 Historic Hansard, 12 Feb 1998.

81 Edward Royle, 'Gott, John William (1866–1922)', *Oxford Dictionary of National
Biography, Oxford University Press*, 2004; doi:10.1093/ref:odnb/47693.

82 http://www.liverpoolecho.co.uk/liverpool-news/local-news/2010/04/24/
militant-atheist-harry-taylor-hit-with-asbo-for-offensive-images-in-john-lennon-
airport-100252-26307049/; http://www.independent.co.uk/news/uk/crime/
atheist-given-asbo-for-leaflets-mocking-jesus-1952985.html

83 Jon Davies, 'A New Inquisition: religious persecution in Britain today', London:
Civitas, 2010.

84 Hate Crime: Cross-Government Action Plan, 2009, p. 17.

85 House of Commons Library, SN/HA/4983, 26 May 2010.

86 House of Commons Library, SN/HA/4983, p. 6.

87 House of Commons Library, SN/HA/4983, pp. 7-8.

88 *Brutus* v. *Cozens* [1973], a House of Lords decision reported at AC 854, 867.

89 http://www.bailii.org/ew/cases/EWHC/Admin/2004/69.html

90 House of Commons Library, SN/HA/4983, p. 9.

91 'Hate Crime: Cross-Government Action Plan', 2009, p. 10.

92 http://www.cps.gov.uk/publications/prosecution/rrpbcrpol.html#a13

93 'Hate Crime: Cross-Government Action Plan', 2009, p. 9, footnote 8.

94 http://www.cps.gov.uk/westmidlands/about/

95 CPS, Hate Crime Report 2008-09, pp. 2-3.

96 ibid, p. 10.

97 Crime in England and Wales, 2008-09, pp. 124-126.

98 http://www.bailii.org/ew/cases/EWHC/Admin/2004/69.html

99 http://www.timesonline.co.uk/tol/news/world/ireland/article6797620.ece

100 ACPO, Hate Crime Manual, 2002, p. 2.

101 ibid, p. 7.

102 ibid, p. 11. Bold in original.

103 ibid, p. 9.

104 ibid, p. 8.

105 ibid, p. 59.

106 ibid, p. 40. Bold in original.

107 ibid, p. 40.

108 ibid, p. 16.

109 Dennis, N., 'Racist Murder and Pressure Group Politics': http://www.civitas.org.uk/pdf/cs05.pdf

110 http://www.telegraph.co.uk/news/uknews/crime/7656837/Teenage-white-supremacist-convicted-of-terror-charges.html

111 http://www.independent.co.uk/news/uk/crime/neonazis-convicted-of-race-hate-charges-2009533.html; http://www.telegraph.co.uk/news/uknews/crime/7821034/Neo-Nazis-urged-eradication-of-all-ethnic-minorities-on-Aryan-Strike-Force-website.html

112 'Managing Monsters: Six Myths of our Time', Marina Warner, *The Reith Lectures*, Vintage, 1994

113 'Bridging the Gap', Social Exclusion Unit, HMSO, 1999

114 'Children at risk green paper', press release, Cabinet Office, 30 October 2002

115 19th Report, Joint Select Committee on Human Rights (JCHR), 8 September 2004

116 'The Common Assessment Framework for Children and Young People: a guide for practitioners', Children's Workforce Development Council 2009: http://www.dcsf.gov.uk/everychildmatters/_download/?id=1290

117 'Information Sharing Guidance for Practitioners and Managers', HM Government, 2008: http://www.teachernet.gov.uk/_doc/13023/isgpm.pdf

118 'The law and children's consent to sharing personal data', Action on Rights for Children, 2009: http://www.archrights.org.uk/index.php?option=com_phocadownload&view=category&id=2&Itemid=23

119 'Reversing the rise of the surveillance state', Conservative Party, September 2009 http://www.conservatives.com/News/News_stories/2009/09/~/media/Files/Policy%20Documents/Surveillance%20State.ashx

120 'Onset referral and assessment framework', Youth Justice Board, 2003

121 'Asset (B108)', Youth Justice Board, 2000

122 'Youth Justice: The Scaled Approach (D99)', Youth Justice Board, 2008

123 'Risky people or risky societies? Rethinking interventions for young adults in transition', Garside, 2009: http://www.crimeandjustice.org.uk/t2arisk.html

124 Leaton-Gray, Sandra, quoted on 'Leave Them Kids Alone' website: http://www.leavethemkidsalone.com/expert.htm#fact_00

125 'Anger over York schools that fingerprint their five-year-olds', York Press, 8 January 2007

126 Schoolchildren "prefer junk food"', BBC News 14/07/05 http://news.bbc.co.uk/1/hi/education/4683697.stm

127 'School puts CCTV in toilets to stop bullies', Manchester Evening News, 7 February 2007

128 'I spy with my little eye: the use of CCTV in schools and the impact on privacy', Emmeline Taylor, 2010: http://onlinelibrary.wiley.com/doi/10.1111/j.1467-954X.2010.01930.x/abstract

129 'Dirt and bullies lead children to avoid school toilets, a survey finds', BBC, 14 October 2010 http://www.bbc.co.uk/news/health-11539933

130 'The IP opportunity: school building projects', Info4Security, 17/04/08: http://www.info4security.com/story.asp?storyCode=4118427&sectioncode=9

131 'Schools 'break law' to spy on pupils', Guardian, 15 March 2010 http://www.guardian.co.uk/education/2010/mar/15/schools-break-law-to-spy

132 Jørgensen, Vibeke, 'The Apple of the Eye: Parents' Use of Webcams in a Danish Day Nursery', Surveillance & Society, CCTV Special (eds. Norris, McCahill and Wood), 2(2/3) 2004, pp. 446–463

133 'Teens 'hanging around' seen as antisocial behaviour', Children and Young People Now, 25th June 2010

134
'Respect and Responsibility – Taking a Stand Against Anti-Social Behaviour', Home Office, 2003 http://www.archive2.official-documents.co.uk/document/cm57/5778/5778.pdf

135 'Teenager-repellent 'mosquito' must be banned, says Europe', Guardian,20th June 2010 http://www.guardian.co.uk/society/2010/jun/20/teenager-repellent-mosquito-banned-europe

136 'Store drops anti-yob device in autism row', The Observer, 4th May 2008 http://www.guardian.co.uk/business/2008/may/04/supermarkets.retail1

137 http://rogerhelmermep.wordpress.com/2010/05/29/the-derby-two-the-agony-continues/

138 http://www.bigbrotherwatch.org.uk/home/2010/07/the-european-investigation-order-foreign-police-looking-at-you-without-judicial-oversight.html

139 http://www.tfa.net/tfa_blog/2010/01/european-public-prosecutor.html

140 http://www.eurogendfor.org/

141 http://www.statewatch.org/news/2006/jan/03eu-gendarmarie.htm

142 http://nds.coi.gov.uk/content/Detail.aspx?ReleaseID=415452&NewsAreaID=2

143 http://stakeholders.ofcom.org.uk/consultations/copyright-infringement/

144 http://www.informationisbeautiful.net/2010/how-much-do-music-artists-earn-online/

145 http://www.bbc.co.uk/blogs/bbcInternet/2010/10/net_neutrality_and_the_bbc.html

146 http://europa.eu/legislation_summaries/internal_market/single_market_services/l24108h_en.htm

147 See Commission website, 'EU budget at a glance – Next year': http://ec.europa.eu/budget/budget_detail/next_year_en.htm

148 The Judicial Studies Board Lecture 2010, Inner Temple, 17 March 2010: http://
www.judiciary.gov.uk/docs/speeches/lcj-jsb-lecture-2010.pdf

149 House of Lords European Union Select Committee, 'Behind closed doors: the
meeting of the G6 Interior Ministers at Heiligendamm', 19 July 2006, p. 5: http://
www.publications.parliament.uk/pa/ld200506/ldselect/ldeucom/221/22102.htm

150 There are certain exceptions. See European Commission's Justice and Home
Affairs website for details: http://ec.europa.eu/justice_home/fsj/criminal/
extradition/fsj_criminal_extradition_en.htm

151 House of Commons research paper 02/79, 'The Extradition Bill: Bill 2 of
2002-03', 6 December 2002: http://www.parliament.uk/documents/commons/lib/
research/rp2002/rp02-079.pdf

152 Open Europe, 'EU strengthens trials in absentia', September 2008: http://www.
openeurope.org.uk/research/tia.pdf

153 BBC, 'Battle looms over EU arrest warrant', 13 December 2001; http://news.bbc.
co.uk/1/hi/uk_politics/1708571.stm

154 Cited in Liberty, 'Liberty's Second Reading Briefing on the Policing and Crime
Bill in the House of Lords – Part 6, Extradition', May 2009, p. 12: http://www.
liberty-human-rights.org.uk/pdfs/policy-09/policing-and-crime-2nd-reading-
lords-on-extradition.pdf

155 *The Independent*, 'Briton arrested over 1996 murder of French filmmaker', 25
April 2010: http://www.independent.co.uk/news/world/europe/briton-arrested-
over-1996-murder-of-french-filmmaker-1953592.html

156 *The Telegraph*, 10 August 2009: http://www.telegraph.co.uk/news/newstopics/
politics/lawandorder/6001357/A-request-to-snoop-on-public-every-60-seconds.
html

157 Report of the Interception of Communications Commissioner for 2008,
July 2009, p. 7: http://www.official-documents.gov.uk/document/hc0809/
hc09/0901/0901.pdf

158 Hansard, 24 March 2009, Column 627: http://www.publications.parliament.
uk/pa/ld200809/ldhansrd/text/90324-0011.htm

159 *The Independent*, 'Big Brother database threatens to "break the back of
freedom"' 21 October 2008: http://www.independent.co.uk/news/uk/politics/big-
brother-database-threatens-to-break-the-back-of-freedom-967673.html

160 *The Telegraph*, 'National database dropped but all our communications will
still be monitored', 28 April 2009: http://www.telegraph.co.uk/news/newstopics/
politics/5230459/National-database-dropped-but-all-our-communications-will-
still-be-monitored.html

161 EUobserver, 'EU court to deliver judgment on data retention', 9 February 2009:
http://euobserver.com/9/27573

162 Speech at the College of Europe, Brussels, 4 March 2009: http://www.sweden.
gov.se/sb/d/10959/a/122436

163 BBC, 'European Swift bank data ban angers US', 11 February 2010; http://news.
bbc.co.uk/1/hi/world/europe/8510471.stm

164 See European Parliament: http://www.europarl.europa.eu/parliament/
archive/elections2009/en/turnout_en.html

165 It should be noted that a future government could apply to opt back in to
legislation on a case-by-case basis, although once the UK is opted in this cannot be
reversed and the ECJ would have jurisdiction on these matters in the UK.

166   The Conservative Party Manifesto 2010, p. 114: http://media.conservatives.
s3.amazonaws.com/manifesto/cpmanifesto2010_lowres.pdf

167   The Liberal Democrat Manifesto 2010, p66: http://network.libdems.org.uk/
manifesto2010/libdem_manifesto_2010.pdf

168   *The Rule of Law* by Tom Bingham, Allen Lane, 2010

169   [2004] EWCL 56

170   [2001] 33 EHRR 20

171   'There is no Justice in Anonymity', Counsel magazine, August 2008; cited in
the House of Commons research paper on the Coroners' and Justice Bill, 22.2.2009
(at pp 38/39) (http://www.parliament.uk/documents/commons/lib/research/
rp2009/rp09-006.pdf)

172   'Licensed to Hug' (second edition) by Frank Furedi and Jennie Bristow, Civitas,
27.9.2010

173   'The Grim RIPA', Big Brother Watch, 23 May 2010: http://www.
bigbrotherwatch.org.uk/TheGrimRIPA.pdf

174   'Counter Terrorism Legislation and Practice: a Survey of Selected Countries',
Foreign and Commonwealth Office, 2005

175   'Law and Democracy', Public Law, 1995

176   [2002] 1 AC 45

177   S 41 of the Youth Justice and Criminal Evidence Act 1999

178   I am indebted for this example and much more generally, to Anthony Speaight
QC's excellent apologia for a Bill of Rights: 'Human Rights Act: Legal Pathways',
Society of Conservative Lawyers, 2007: http://www.conservativelawyers.com/
Anthony%20Speaight%20paper.pdf

179   John Locke, *Two Treatises of Government* Chapter IV 'Of Slavery' para 21

180   Note that all information provided is in the public domain

181   http://www.cabinetoffice.gov.uk/media/45149/mandatory-roles.pdf

182   http://www.cabinetoffice.gov.uk/intelligence-security-resilience/national-
security/cyber-information-security.aspx

183   http://www.cabinetoffice.gov.uk/media/cabinetoffice/corp/assets/foi/
classifications.pdf

184   http://www.cesg.gov.uk/products_services/iatp/documents/data_handling_
review.pdf

185   Nick Cohen, 'Libel tourists will love the tales of Lord Hoffmann', *The Observer*,
7 February 2010

186   Oxford University, 'A Comparative Study of Costs in Defamation
Proceedings Across Europe', http://pcmlp.socleg.ox.ac.uk/research/project/
comparative-study-costs-defamation-proceedings-across-europe

187   Zoë Corbyn, 'Research intelligence: Words of warning', *Times Higher
Education*, 25 March 2010.

188   Charles Arthur, 'The truth is on the line', *The Guardian*, 12 March 2010.

189   http://www.taylorwessing.com/topical-issues/details/reporting-criminal-
investigations-just-got-trickier-flood-v-times-newspapers-ltd-2010-07-15.html

190   Anthony Lester, 'Libel must be rebalanced in the scales of justice', *The Times*,
24 May 2010.

191   'Reports of cases argued and ruled at nisi prius: in the courts of Queen's
Bench, Common Pleas, & Exchequer: together with cases tried on the circuits, and
in the Central Criminal Court from Hilary term, 6 Vict, Great Britain, Court of
Exchequer'; S. Sweet, 1852 [Oxford].

192   Report of the Libel Working Group, Ministy of Justice, 23 March 2010: (http://www.justice.gov.uk/publications/docs/libel-working-group-report.pdf)

193   Mark Stephens, *The Guardian*: Comment Is Free, 24 September 2009 (http://www.guardian.co.uk/commentisfree/libertycentral/2009/sep/24/multiple-publication-libel-tourists)

194   Law Commission, Defamation and the internet, Scoping Study, 2002

195   Paragraph 178, House of Commons Culture, Media and Sport select committee, "Press standards, privacy and libel', 24 February 2010; http://www.publications.parliament.uk/pa/cm200910/cmselect/cmcumeds/362/36202.htm

196   Paragraph 142, ibid.

197   Paragraphs 262, 306, 307, ibid.

198   Tom Watson MP, Liberal Conspiracy, 31 March 2010: http://liberalconspiracy.org/2010/03/31/why-i-opposed-libel-costs-reform-yesterday/

199   Court of Bologna, ruling no. 3331 of 14 June 2001 in AltaLex, http://www.altalex.com/index.php?idnot=1167

200   Court of Bologna, ruling no. 3331 of 14 June 2001, *cit.*

201   Court of Bologna, ruling no. 3331 of 14 June 2001, *cit.*

202   Directive 2000/31/CE

203   Article 14 of Directive 2000/31/CE

204   Article 15 of Directive 2000/31/CE

205   Cerasani, 'Notes on the Joint Liability of the Provider for Violating Distinctive Signs on the Internet', in Archivio Ceradi, Luiss: http://www.archivioceradi.luiss.it/

206   The first was the one from the Court of Catania, ruling no. 2286 of 29 June 2004.

207   Among other things, in our legislation, the principle of nothing more can be done applies. In this regard, Antolisei writes, 'The obligation to prohibit the event is not unlimited: it ends when the controlled action cannot be carried out since the principle of nothing more can be done applies in our law' in Antolisei, Criminal Law Manual – General Part, Milan, 2008.

208   Specifically Article 2043 of the Italian Civil Code.

209   See the Court of Monza, independent district of Desio, 'Doctor Glass' case, ruling of 14 May 2001, where it was stated that: 'even if we wished to hide the provider's liability under the label of guilt by negligence, this liability would actually be an atypical legislatively objective liability since we cannot in any way imagine concrete means through which the provider could provide this oversight, considering that monitoring must be constant: in fact, it is known that each site can be modified at any time with a simple operation that can be done "remotely," 24 hours a day, 7 days a week.'

In the same vein, the ruling of 4 July 1998 of the Court of Rome (*Banca del Salento v. Pantheon s.r.l.*) published on InterLex, which claimed that a website is not similar to a journalistic publication and dismissed the appeal that asked for an emergency injunction to remove an allegedly defamatory message from a newsgroup since it was not moderated and the provider not having the powers of control.

210   Court of Catania, ruling no. 2286 of 29 June 2004, *cit.*

211   Court of Catania, ruling no. 2286 of 29 June 2004, *cit.*

5 DAYS TO POWER

THE JOURNEY TO COALITION BRITAIN

With unique access to key figures involved from all three political parties Rob Wilson MP tells the story of the coalition talks in a manner and depth in which it has not been told before. In *5 Days to Power* Rob Wilson talks to those involved from all three parties to shed further light on the negotiations that led to the historic coalition government.

5 Days To Power gives the first full account of the negotiations that led to the political earthquake of a Conservative and Liberal Democrat coalition government.

304pp paperback, £9.99

Available from all good bookshops or order from
www.bitebackpublishing.com

BROWN AT 10

ANTHONY SELDON & GUY LODGE

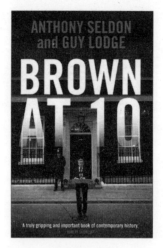

'A truly gripping and important book of contemporary history'
Robert Skidelsky

Gordon Brown's three years in power were among the most turbulent in Downing Street's post-war history. *Brown at 10* tells the compelling story of his hubris and downfall, and with it, the final demise of the New Labour project. Containing an extraordinary breadth of previously unpublished material, *Brown at 10* is a frank, penetrating portrait of a remarkable era. Using unrivalled access to many of those at the centre of Brown's government, and original material gleaned from hundreds of hours of interviews with many of its leading lights, *Brown at 10* looks with greater depth and detail into the signal events and circumstances of Brown's premiership.

'Seldon and Lodge's book is the product of deep historic research and sheds fresh light on both Gordon Brown and his extraordinarily problematic premiership. It is the definitive history and will be read for years to come' Dennis Kavanagh

528pp hardback, £20
Available from all good bookshops or order from
www.bitebackpublishing.com